By Thomas Gallagher

———————

To my son, Michael
with love, affection, and respect

———————

Contents

Contents

Prologue

FOR most of my adult life, I have been interested in Ireland and the Irish conflict with England. My father emigrated from Ballaghaderreen, County Roscommon, Ireland, in 1903, at the age of fifteen. He crossed the Irish Sea to Liverpool and made his way to London, where a friendly Englishman advised him to switch his given names from Patrick Joseph to Joseph Patrick, "Joe" being far less liable to abuse than "Paddy," the centuries-old British byword for everything ridiculous about Ireland. "Joe" Gallagher became a singing waiter in a popular pub in London, where he was treated with the kindness and respect that a young man alone in the world remembers all his life.

When "Joseph P." moved on to the United States, married a young lady born there, and raised a family of ten children, my brothers, sisters, and I never heard a word spoken against England. A natural result of this was that the Gallagher children did not know what to make of the anti-British remarks made over and over again by other Irish children in the Amsterdam Avenue neighborhood on the upper West Side of Manhattan where we lived. It was almost as if some essential part of Irish heritage had been denied us. This, of course, only made me curious as I grew older. What lay behind this antagonism? How did it become so deeply rooted that even among the American Irish it had turned to hatred?

Most of the balanced historical views pointed to the great famine of 1846–47, often referred to as the watershed years in Irish history. The more I investigated the generally available works on the subject, the more aware I became that the great famine was not a separate or isolated part of Irish history but, rather, the nadir of that history, so stark and devastating in its effects, so crucial in what it said about the country's relationship with England, that it was to shape not only the future of Ireland but the attitudes of the Irish all over the world on into the twentieth century—indeed, right up to the present moment. And yet, to my amazement, this famine experience in terms of the Irish peasant had been treated superficially or at a remarkable remove. It was clear that the individual peasant was in fact the victim. But the victim of what? Who spoke for this victim?

With this book in mind, I undertook in-depth research, probing all available archives in the United States, England, and Ireland. I naturally could not exclude politics from an event so catastrophic to an entire nation, but I decided, given the past emphasis on all the overriding debates, rationales, and expediencies, to keep that aspect of the story to a minimum while giving as much space as possible to what happened in the daily life of the Irish farmer, what influences affected his family, his institutions, his beliefs, his very existence. The deeper I probed, the more shocked I became. The evidence, though plentiful, was scattered in dusty places, and it went all the way back to the reign of Queen Elizabeth I, in the latter half of the sixteenth century, when civil wars and local rebellions in protest against religious oppression and the appropriation of land erupted throughout Ireland.

In the next century, Oliver Cromwell led an expedition to Ireland to quell once and for all this ever-growing discontent of the Irish Catholic population. Following his triumphant return to England, a new kind of Protestant colonization of Ireland began. Much of the newly confiscated land became the property of settlers from Scotland and England, who then leased small parcels of it to those who had previously occupied it. The latter, the indigenous Irish, thus joined the country's burgeoning tenant-farmer population, and despite predictions and expectations to the contrary, they continued to cling to their Roman Catholic faith.

But even with its two separate and distinct societies, Ireland had its own Parliament in Dublin, which, however packed it might have been with Anglo-Irish landlords, developed a pro-Ireland stance if for no other reason than self-interest. The Irish peasant had no voice in this Parliament, but he did receive a noblesse-oblige kind of representation from landlords genuinely interested in his welfare. And if he still spoke Gaelic, he was often defended in eloquent English by great Protestant writers like Jonathan Swift.

Then came the American Revolution and the great success it achieved in freeing the thirteen colonies of British rule. Little more than a decade later, the French Revolution sent even greater shock waves throughout the world. The aspiration for freedom from oppression everywhere in Europe became linked to that aspiration in Ireland. This led in 1796 to an ambitious attempt by fifteen thousand French troops, in concert with Irish rebels, to free Ireland of British rule. Had this incursion succeeded, it would have drastically changed Irish history from that day to this, but extremely bad weather destroyed many of the sailing ships carrying the French troops from Brest.

A few years later, in 1800, the British Parliament in Westminster, ever fearful of a free Ireland allied to Europe and the risk of invasion such an alliance would create, offered Ireland what at first glance seemed a most generous offer—nothing less than union with England. The Irish Parliament in Dublin would be disbanded and its members made part of the English

Parliament in Westminster. A most important suggestion was included in this proposal: namely, Catholic emancipation in Ireland would soon follow that country's union with England.

The Union of 1800 became law and went into effect in 1801. Members of the Irish Parliament in Dublin became members of the English Parliament in Westminster, where they constituted an almost powerless minority—about 15 percent of the Westminster seats, whereas on a population basis they were entitled to more than 30 percent, there being in 1800 about five million people living in Ireland compared with eleven million in all of England, Scotland, and Wales. Nor was the promise of Catholic emancipation, whereby Catholics would be permitted to sit in Parliament and hold elective office in Ireland, kept.

I confess now that I should not have been as surprised as I was at the dominant role religion played in the centuries of turmoil, conflict, and suffering that preceded the point in Irish history where this book begins. My surprise was no doubt due in part to the fact that, being neither Roman Catholic nor Protestant, I started this project with no preconceptions and no idea what my research was going to make me say. The horrors described and the ameliorations attempted are not the products of my imagination. They are all corroborated—in most cases by Englishmen of the type who were just as kind to my father when he crossed the Irish Sea as they were to me during my research for this book.

And so I determined to bring the evidence into glaring light as best I could. I would speak for the victim, comment on his behalf, and describe the suffering he endured. I would try to avoid the role of propagandist and cling to the record. Let the eyewitness reports and corroborated facts and figures speak for themselves, and if they amount to an indictment, so be it. In light of what my research uncovered, I could do no less.

What I present may bring the present conflict no closer to a sane, peaceful solution. But if the intense hatred that exists is to be confronted and dissipated, it had better be understood. This book is therefore focused on what happened during a momentous event, perhaps the dividing line when centuries of hostility turned into undying hatred, when an accident of nature influenced the course of history in three nations—Ireland, England, and the United States. If the past is prologue, we would do well to heed it.

I

The Doomed Country

Chapter One

No vegetable . . . ever effected the same amount
of influence upon the physical, moral, social, and
political condition of a country, as the potato
exercised over Ireland.

—Tables of Death, 1851

IRELAND in 1846 offered the same splendid sight from
Ballycastle in the north to Skibbereen in the south. Every field
and garden where seed had been sown teemed with the dark-
green leaves and purple blossoms of a thriving and abundant
potato crop. The year before had been a near disaster; a disease had attacked the growing plants without warning and
destroyed almost half of them. The people had suffered, but
most had been saved by their long apprenticeship to scarcity
and want, by salvaging what they could and making that do.

Now more land than ever, almost two million acres, had
been seeded, and the familiar leaf-laden stalks, shooting up
from the edible underground tubers known the world over
as Irish potatoes, looked healthy and erect in even the miserable patches of land sown by squatters. Altogether, the crop
was valued at sixteen million to thirty million pounds, and
everyone from the wealthiest landowner to the lowest farm
laborer was thanking God for the abundance that would soon
be theirs. The family pig would be fattened, the landlord
paid his rent, and the children fed as they deserved to be.[1]

1. Notes are on pages 297–312.

On June 3, on a few contiguous farms in County Cork, the disease appeared again but caused little damage and did not seem to spread, even in that localized area. In July, the weather variations were extreme even for Ireland, where, as one Irish farmer in Roscommon put it, "The sun here is not a steady thing. Sure, it will blind you, but only long enough for the rain to hit you."[2] Mild, dry mornings were followed by heavy afternoon rains, thunder, and lightning. The temperature in some areas dropped thirty degrees in the middle of an afternoon, and clouds tumbled down the mountainsides like soft, silent avalanches of snow, their whitish vapors twisting and rolling in flurries into the valleys, where they seemed to smother all that was growing. Not a bird was to be seen or heard during these visitations, and this heightened the peculiar silence, the bleak, depressing twilights, that came with them. The birds did not return until the wind lifted and cleared these pockets of fog from the ground, and then there remained on the potato stalks a light frost like a powdering of snow.

Near the end of July, the disease appeared again, this time not only in Cork but in several places. And as the report got abroad that the blight had struck again, so did the stench confirming the report. It was a sulfurous, sewerlike smell carried by the wind from the rotting plants in the first-struck places. Farmers who had gone to bed imbued with the image of their lush potato gardens were awakened by this awful smell and by the dogs howling their disapproval of it. They could see nothing in the dark; they could only smell the rot. But in the dawn's first light they found brown spots on the leaves, some of which were already withering and turning black. Here and there the stalks were themselves discolored with what looked like spreading sores—cankers where the tissue of the plant had already died. But all around these dead spots the stalks appeared to be still living, and this gave the farmers, so desperately in need of this year's crop, a wild, crazy kind of hope that they could stem the spread of the disease by cutting it away. They called their wives, their sons and daughters, to come and look, come and help!

The ground in most places was so sodden from rain and dampness that the water splashed from their feet as they ran from one stricken plant to another. Fumbling through the putrid mess, dislodging stones, reaching and testing, they found that every discolored stalk broke like rotten wood where the canker had eaten through it. Meanwhile, more and more of the seemingly untouched leaves of other plants were beginning to wither and turn black, while the stalks supporting those leaves became spotted. It was almost as if their attempts to stem the disease had accelerated its spread, as if they were in a race against the thousands of localized deaths that were taking place in the tissue of all the plants around them.

In one last effort to save the potatoes, if not the plants, they ripped up the stalks to prevent the "gangrene" from descending down the stem into the potatoes in the ground. They thought the potatoes would be safe if left in the ground, unattached to the withering, dying stalks, but when they dug down into the ground with their hands to check, they came up with a blackened mass of corruption—slimy pockets of potatoes that broke into mush under the slightest pressure.

The fungus did not reach the potatoes via the stem and stolon, but came directly from the soil. The farmers did not know this, but those who immediately ripped up what potatoes were left and laid them out to dry were luckier. Some potatoes, but not many, were saved in this way.

"Only a handful of potatoes were left," said one eyewitness, "and they were so small that it took twelve of them to weigh four-and-a-half ounces, the weight of an average, edible tuber. But even these poor remnants were of little value, being soft and watery."[3]

Unlike the previous year, when large areas in both the north and south were unaffected, the blight this time spread to every area in so short a time that a kind of wailing lament rose throughout the country wherever neighbors gathered. Those with tin cans of holy water flicked it into their faces, wet their fingers and made the sign of the cross, prayed and genuflected as though before an altar. Keeners at a wake could not have sent up more varieties of anguish and despair than did these Irish families at the sight of their entire year's food supply being destroyed. And by putting their worst fears in print, the daily and weekly press only added to the gloom: "Where no disease was apparent a few days ago, all now is black." "The failure this year is universal; for miles a person may proceed in any direction, without perceiving an exception to the awful destruction." "The disease appears to be of the most malignant character; the leaves and stalks appear tainted as if with a corroding mildew, or as if vitriol or some caustic material had been thrown upon them." "Fearful progress of the disease in Cork, Mayo, and Sligo; the stench from the fields was intolerable: the odour from decaying flesh could not be more offensive." From Fermoy, County Cork, one writer said "that within the last three days the blight has committed dreadful ravages, and is now so decided that we can no longer flatter ourselves with even the chance of escape; it is north, south, east, and west of us."[4]

In another part of Ireland, Father Mathew, the beloved abstinence leader who was responsible for so many Irishmen taking the pledge, was an eyewitness to the havoc: "On the 27th of last month [July] I passed from Cork to Dublin, and this doomed plant bloomed in all the luxuriance of an abundant harvest. Returning on the 3rd instant [August] I beheld with sorrow one wide waste of putrefying vegetation. In many places the wretched people were seated on the fences of their decaying gardens, wringing their hands and wailing bitterly the destruction that had left them foodless."[5]

Some enraged, heartbroken farmers looked up from their fields as if trying to find an explanation for the rot in the clouds scudding low over the iron-dark hills. The putrid smell, some claimed, had been carried by the clouds, for it was when they descended and became fog that the stench, which reminded one man of "the bilge water of a ship,"[6] permeated everything. Perhaps the disease itself had been carried that way, from one rotting field to another. Why else did everything turn to slime so soon after the whitish vapors tumbled down the mountain-sides onto the fields and gardens?

Neither scientist nor farmer knew what caused the blight, nor why this year it was so widespread and devastating. The deadly fungus, known today as *Phytophthora infestans*, had actually come from America, conveyed by ship. No one knew that then, and it would have made no difference then to the Irish, whose very lives depended on this one crop over any other grown in the country for the previous half-century.

"God have mercy on us. There will be nothing for us but to lie down and die."[7]

"If the English desert us now, God in His glory they'll never see."

"The English, is it? Depend on yourself and don't mind the English. From the English we'll get plenty of legislation, but little food."

"I swear by the broken heart my mother died of, the hand of God is in this. It's a curse that has fallen on the land."[8]

All their lives, they had wisely not tried to see far into a future over which they had so little control. Knowing only a precarious existence from the time they were born, they had seen to their month-to-month wants and were not greatly troubled by a disaster too remote in time for them to perceive or do anything about. Now, without warning, the disaster had come; next month was not what mattered, nor was next week. With their only food turning into slime before their very eyes, they were worried about today and especially tomorrow, when what little was left over from yesterday would be gone.

"It's over there in America I'd be now, only for the pig the landlord took from me for his rent," said one embittered man whose eyes had been turned to the New World ever since the previous year's blight. "The passage money was in that pig, but it's the landlord always has the bailiff on his side." He looked out over his rotting garden of potatoes, which all his life had been "a torment and a heartbreak" to him. "Give it up I would, surrindher it as a bad bargain, wash my hands o' it, if I could.

If I could! May God reward the man who can come up with the answer. For it's here I was, and here I am, with no pig to sell, no potatoes to eat, and no passage money out of the putrid mess. God save me. How am I to get through life at all?"[9]

One small farmer who had been unable to salvage a single potato, whose cupboard was absolutely empty except for two pounds of oats, tried to cheer his children through the first day of the many pinched, dismal days that lay ahead by adding one of his six chickens to the pot. Even this killing of a fowl, commonplace enough in normal times, absorbed every member of the family waiting to share it. Watching the bird spasmodically shake its wings as its lifeblood drained from its quivering body into a pot was like saying grace in silence and with absolute sincerity.

No one living in Ireland at the time who saw the rotting fields and caught their stench, who saw and heard the people wailing, had to be told that for the majority of its population all the great and simple purposes of existence were soon to be forgotten in the oncoming struggle with death. A famine unprecedented in the history of the Western world, a chapter in human misery to harrow the human heart, was about to start, ánd even the little children could see its quick, sure approach in the nakedly fearful eyes and faces of their parents. A terrible sense of danger and dread descended on the land like the thick fog that covered the countryside on the fatal night, the fog that people in Ireland still speak of as the "potato fog."

Chapter Two

> In a very short time there was nothing but
> stillness, a mournful silence in the villages, in
> the cottages grim poverty and emaciated
> faces. . . . The tinkers . . . fled to the cities, the
> musicians . . . disappeared and . . . never
> returned. Many of the residents too made their
> escape at once, finding employment or early
> graves elsewhere. . . . There were no more
> friendly meetings at the neighbors' houses in the
> afternoons, no gatherings on the hillsides on
> Sundays, no song, no merry laugh of the
> maidens. Not only were the human beings silent
> and lonely, but the brute creation also, for not
> even the bark of a dog, or the crowing of a
> cock was to be heard. . . .
>
> —Hugh Dorian, "Donegal 60 Years Ago"

WITHIN days, streams of poor people came begging their way through the different parishes. They stopped at the doors of small farmers with "the grass of two cows," whose yield was small but who tried to give a little food to every hungry group. If the farmer's wife expressed fear at the prospect of their own food running out, the son or daughter, seeing the beggars so sorely put to it to live, would say something like "Ah, mother, you will be at Peter's door yourself yet and you would not want to be turned away."[1] Sometimes, when a wanderer with a few potatoes of his own stopped by, he was permitted by the farmer to boil them in the same pot with the family's potatoes, which were separated from his by a few leaves of green cabbage or a bunch of nettles. For among the lower classes in Ireland there was always a tendency to look favorably on any stranger who laid aside all pretensions and accommodated himself to the situation.

"Praties and dab at the stool," they called it. When the potatoes were cooked, the pot was hooked off the fire, drained, and set on a stool with the salt and mustard in the middle of the floor. The whole family and the one or two wanderers would gather round and each would dip his or her potatoes in salt, or mustard if the farmer had raised the seed for the purpose. If the family had buttermilk to go with the potatoes, the stranger, treated with civility, respect, even affection, would be given an equal share; if there was nothing but potatoes and salt, that was it.[2]

Though many farmers with a varied crop of produce hastened the sale of the potatoes they were able to salvage, the scarcity was such that the price of even these suspect potatoes rose to famine levels: from two shillings a hundredweight, then to seven shillings, and finally to an unheard-of twelve shillings. The poor, unable to pay the famine price, became turnip eaters; they even devoured mangel-wurzel, a large, coarse, reddish-orange beet grown as fodder for cattle. The fields where these two crops grew, fields considered almost worthless in normal times, soon became coveted by families whose potato patches had been destroyed.[3]

On moonless nights the outer rims of the mangel-wurzel fields were raided by men using the care and stealth of grave-robbers. Shunning the use of spades for fear the scraping sound of metal would give them away, they dug by hand down under the stalks, pulled out the tuberous roots, and left the stalks standing so that the theft would go unnoticed until the stalks withered. Even old potatoes from the previous year's harvest were unsafe. These were usually stored in locked barns, but any thief hungry or desperate enough would "spear" them, one by one, with a long pointed rod that he slipped through the thatched roof of the barn.[4]

In Tipperary a farmer named Tom Purcell, whose name is still honored, was able to save most of his potato crop. "He was an extensive farmer who carried on quarrying for lime-burning during most of the year," explained a neighbor of his named Patrick Lyons. "All the starving people of the county flocked to Purcell's quarry, where they were regaled with potatoes, roasted at the Lime-kiln from the raw, about the best way of cooking a potato. This man Purcell, a dog fancier, shot his dogs to save food for the poor."[5]

In districts where farmers considered their potato crop a total loss and allowed the poor to pick through the putrid mess for anything they could find, the partly rotten potatoes were scraped and reduced to pulp, and this was made into "boxty." The pulp was placed in a cloth, squeezed as dry as possible, then flattened into cakes and baked on tongs over the red coals or placed on the warm hearthstone. When one side was baked, the cake was turned, until all or almost all of the liquid evaporated and the cake became as hard and dry as a cookie.

Oatmeal cakes, consisting of oatmeal and milk or oatmeal and water, were made by placing a leaf of cabbage on coals of fire, the oatmeal cake resting in the center of the leaf. Then another cabbage leaf was placed on top and coals were laid over this. The juice of the cabbage leaf penetrated the cake and made it more palatable. "Cabbage was grown especially for this purpose," an old woman recorded in a handwritten memoir, "and there is a story told of a charitable lady who lived in Killala who had a large plot of cabbage. People came from far and near for leaves and at last there came two poor old women and the charitable lady found that all the cabbage was gone. She was very disappointed and told the women to come again next day. On looking out her window, the following morning, she was amazed to see a full plot of cabbage with heads as plentiful as possible, and each as large as a two-stone pot."[6]

Other farmers with larger holdings were forced either to kill their cattle one by one or to extract blood from them at regular intervals to sustain their families. Since cattle and horses died from unskilled or excessive bleeding, the choice of the bloodletter was often a matter of life and death for both animal and owner. In most cases, the animals of a whole district were taken to the same location (still known in certain parts of Ireland as "the hollow of the blood" or "the moor of the blood") and bled by the same man, whose reputation as a bleeder of animals was based strictly on performance. Usually a farmer himself, he took a maximum of a quart of blood from each fully grown animal, a pint from each young one, and was paid a commission of roughly 10 percent in blood, which he either consumed or bartered for other kinds of food.

The procedure, though simple, was watched with the kind of avid, consuming interest that only the starving can give to the sight of food being produced before their very eyes. The bloodletter would cut a vein in the neck of the fettered animal and control the flow of blood by exerting pressure against the vein with his fingers. When the blood reached a certain level in a bucket held in place to catch it, he would stop the flow by slipping a pin through the skin across the incision in the vein and tying it securely in place with a few hairs cut from the animal's tail.[7]

Using jars, bowls, or buckets, the owners of the bled animals would carry the blood home and add it as a fortifier to various other foods. Some made "relish cakes" with it by mixing it with mushrooms and cabbage and making patties to be baked until dry by the peat fire. Others boiled it with milk, oats, herbs, meal, or vegetables or simply salted and fried it as is. The Irish farmer, aware that animals became weak after being bled and often died when bled too much or too often, considered blood the very essence of the animal's flesh, a concentrated food that would get them through the famine.

Those without cattle to bleed or to kill and eat began following every plough in the hope of "meeting" a stray potato; they rooted in the ground for chickweed, sorrel, pignuts, or the roots of dandelion or fern, which they crushed and added to meal to make bread. If they had no meal, they roasted, crushed, and ate them as is, with plenty of water, to satisfy their hunger long enough to get through the day and into the next. Children searched the woods for watercress and mushrooms, the bogs and mountains for berries. Families ate the leaves and barks of certain trees, and the fruits of holly, beech, crab apple, and laurel trees.

Along the coast, seabirds and their eggs, shellfish, sand eels, periwinkles, limpets, and all varieties of seaweed were greedily devoured, often with fatal results. Even the dulse, or salt leaf, as the Irish called it, safe as an occasional condiment but dangerous when eaten often, was used as the sole support of life. The coastal people, who in ordinary times bartered edible seaweeds for potatoes or cabbage, knew that dulse eaten often was dangerous and that certain shellfish must be boiled and not eaten raw, especially after a long hunger. Most of the starving multitudes did not know the danger, and those who did often allowed their hunger rather than their knowledge to guide them. The skeletons of these victims were found many years later beside huge piles of shells, in caves along the coast, or in fields turned up by the plough.[8]

Inland, once-comfortable farmers ashamed of having nothing to eat but turnips began closing their doors at meal-time. Starving cottiers too far gone to feel or show shame gathered in the turnip fields at harvest time and made a contest of picking up the turnip cuttings left by the harvester. Fierce were the scrambles among boys for these turnip bits, which were jealously guarded once secured. But let another boy, too small to have gathered up a few himself, put out an empty hand to an older boy, and the latter would immediately give half his share to the little tyke. It was the same everywhere: a boy or man willing to fight for what he thought was his to get and keep was more than willing to divvy once he won the fight.

The poorest families roasted the turnip cuttings slice by slice on the tongs over turf fires, the children often burning their fingers and tongues in their eagerness to get something into their stomachs. Those lucky or bold enough to catch a fish or shoot a hare, a rabbit, or wild fowl would boil it in the same water with the turnip cuttings and, if they had any, some oatmeal, which they used as a thickener to bind and blend all the ingredients together.

"Anybody's house you come to, talk is all of misery and starvation," said one man living in Ireland at the time. "There is no fun at all among them now. . . . Their natural vivacity and lightheartedness has been starved out of them."[9]

An Irish landlord's daughter put it this way:

In good years the beggars shared the farmers' potatoes and warmed themselves at his blazing turf fires. They built huts surreptitiously in the villages in which they roosted at night, some getting occasional work, others starting on a daily round of the countryside with cheerful certainty in search of food.

There are many differences between the English and the Irish, and one of the most marked is the difference in their attitude toward beggars. The English regard beggars as being, if not exactly criminals, then close to the criminal class. The Irish, on the contrary, regard their relief as a sacred duty. That kindly sympathy enabled these poor outcasts to exist, but now all was changed, the wolf was at the farmer's door, there was absolutely nothing to give away.[10]

Still, the people continued to hope; they had survived bad years before, and they refused to believe that the potato was forever doomed in the soil of Ireland, the one country in Europe where seven out of eight people were almost completely dependent on it. Farmers with modest supplies of unaffected produce, such as turnips, cabbages, and oats, comforted one another with fatalistic Gaelic sayings like "The luck that is not on us today may be on us tomorrow" or "There is no disaster from which one person does not escape." Others tried to resist the panic they felt engulfing them by making optimistic remarks that they knew to be based on false hopes: "Sure, this land is full of barley, wheat and oats. The English have only to distribute it."[11]

The ebullient wit and sense of humor of the Irish also prevailed for a time, blunting the edge of sorrow and making more tolerable the country's misfortunes. There was the story, for example, of the man who was going to be hanged in Galway: "His wife went to see him the night before, and all she said was 'Where will I sow the flax this year?' He was vexed at that and he said, 'Is that all you are come to say to me?' Says the Wife, 'Is it that you are in a sulk because you are going to be hanged in the morning?' That was all she said."[12]

Even the well-to-do, assailed everywhere by beggars who came forward with their hands out, interspersing prayers with compliments until refused, then turning away with cynical grins and face-saving jokes, found it impossible at times not to be amused. "One little six-pence, your honor," cried the leader of a dozen other boys to a young gentleman passing through Kilkenny. "It's but a half-penny apiece for the poor crathers." The young gentleman turned to the boys, whose rags hung on by a miracle, and said that he had nothing less than half crowns. "May your honour never have less," cried a second boy, his wit jumping. "I dare say," said the gentleman, "you would take the coat off my back." "And if your honour gave it with good will, maybe we would," cried another.[13]

In the same way, when some destitute cottier was found lying dead of starvation by the roadside, with pieces of grass or leaves in his mouth and his face stained with the juice of plants he had been chewing to satisfy his hunger, the first inclination among the living was to separate his fate from theirs. "Jim Boylan had no further to go," they'd say, or, "There is nothing but that which is laid out for a person." To the dead man's son or daughter, a friend might say, "What is there seems worse to a man than his death? And yet he does not know, but it may be the height of his good luck."[14]

In time the landlords and large farmers became jaded by the scenes of misery; they turned from the horror and retrenched in self-protection. Mostly it was the stranger, someone new in Ireland, a stray traveler still capable of shock and response, by whom the starving were given food to eat. This impromptu help, temporary and haphazardly given, was often by its nature the cause of the most distressing mob scenes among the destitute.

At the height of the famine, the Reverend S. Godolphin Osbourne, a minister long familiar with Ireland's distress, witnessed one such scene while on a tour of the country with an English friend as wealthy as he was generous. In Limerick, a city divided into an English and an Irish town, they were passing through the Irish town when they were both almost overwhelmed by the dirt, disorder, and decay. Every street was dilapidated, dark, hideous, filled with a ragged swarm of humanity. Stark eyes stared out all the dirty windows, frail children paddled up and down the broken steps around their soiled and unkempt mothers, whose careworn and frightened looks told of their continual worry over how to feed them. It made no difference where the minister and his friend went; every sight reminded them of the fearful desolation that was progressing around them. It was as if not just this Irish town but every one in every city in Ireland were undergoing an unspeakable calamity from which there would be no recovery.

The men, pale and gaunt, their eyes wild and hollow, and their gait feeble, tottered about as though barely able to support the threadbare garments hanging from their bodies. The garments themselves, coarse frieze coats as decrepit as their owners, gave the appearance of having been worn without interruption in the street and at home, in bed and at work, from the day they were purchased. Nor was there the slightest sign that any attempt had been made to replace a button or mend a frayed pocket or lapel. Where sewn-in patches should have been, bare elbows poked through the threads that scarcely held the whole together. In some cases the coats were so worn that they looked more like a net hanging from the shoulders than a tailored cloth covering the body; the edges of some lapels were so raveled that they formed a fringe, and often a man whose sleeves had fallen off appeared to be wearing a fragmented cape rather than a coat.

"Beggars, beggars . . . wretched streets . . . the extremity of raggedness," wrote Thomas Carlyle after his Irish journey during this period. "The whole country figures in my mind like a ragged coat, one huge gabardine, not patched, or patchable any longer."[15]

Perhaps worst of all was the grotesquely comic way these coats were cut. For though coarse enough to scratch the skin, and squalid enough to be germ-ridden, they were fashioned after the French swallow-tailed dress coat, with its high collar, the breast open in front, the cutaway over the hips, and last and most ludicrous, the tapered skirts behind. These drooping skirts, which almost touched the ground, were usually the first casualties during the protracted life span of the garment itself; they were pulled and tied into a knot around Paddy's waist to keep them out of mischief while he was at work; they were stepped on by the children while Paddy was lying down to rest at home; their edges were singed by the peat fire while he was reaching for another spud. At last, the unnecessary but beloved impediment, doomed from the start, became a mere fragment hanging by threads that were mysteriously never reinforced, until it fell to the ground, forlorn and unretrieved.

Short knee breeches, stockings, and shoes were to be worn with this full-dress coat, and on Sundays before the famine, some of the more successful tenant farmers could be seen going to Mass in the complete outfit: the frieze coat with the four buttons behind and the six in front, the clean breeches and stockings, the shined shoes, and, last but not least, the tall hat, a rough, somewhat squatter replica of the stately beaver or silk hat worn by the British and French.

In Limerick's Irish town, many men were still wearing the remains of these stovepipe hats. Years of being soaked with rain, of drying again after being fashioned into new shapes by Paddy's pulls, twists, pinches, and slaps, made them a sight that in all the world could be seen only in Ireland. Some hats were worn with half a brim, or with the high part caved in to within inches of the brim, or with their tops gone and the stiff black brushes of their owners' hair exposed to the sun and rain.

In a London theater, the audience would have found the scene laughable for being so far-fetched, overdone, beyond the reach of reality. An English beggar would not have lifted off the ground the clothes these people were wearing—a wardrobe for scarecrows. But this was the Irish town in Limerick, and these wasted forms, festering with fever and pinched with hunger, represented real people.

Suddenly Osbourne's companion rushed to a bread shop and bought loaf after loaf of bread to feed the poor in the streets. This created such commotion among the shocked and overwhelmed wretches that he and the reverend were forced by the pressure of the crowd back into the shop. In almost any other country, such an electrifying event would have resulted in the shop's being broken into and emptied of its remaining bread. But even in the midst of famine and the absence of police, the shop was neither entered nor damaged.

Meanwhile, from the rear of the shop, the reverend and his companion were able to see, themselves unseen, some of the given bread consumed. "There was no deceit in the way it was devoured," Osbourne said. "More voracious reality, it would be hardly possible to conceive; to see the fleshless arms grasping one part of a loaf, whilst the fingers—bone handled forks—dug into the other, to supply the mouth—such mouths too! with an eagerness, as if the bread were stolen, the thief starving, and the steps of the owner heard; was a picture, I think neither of us will easily forget."

Later, when they tried to escape, the whole crowd set off in full chase after them. The taste of fresh bread had inflamed the spirit of some; the report that it had been given away sent others in hot pursuit. The reverend and his companion were soon surrounded by the hungry pack, from which came the cries so familiar now in Ireland: the subtle supplication of the professional mendicant, the passionate cry of the ragged and really destitute, and finally the whining entreaty of the naked children, whose lean bodies suffered starvation sooner. The quickly acquired volubility of Irish beggary, created and sharpened by a hunger national in scope and now excited by the rare chance of appeasing it, gave vociferous voice to all those in chase of the reverend and his friend.

"No two luckless human beings were ever so hunted," Osbourne said. "No ravening wolves ever gave more open expression of their object—food. A little coaxing—my friend's; a little violence—my own; a little distribution of copper coin from both of us, at last rid us of the inconvenient, but natural result of an Englishman, with money in his pocket, and a baker's shop near, wishing in Ireland to feed some starving people."[16]

Chapter Three

Have we not seen, at pleasure's lordly call,
The smiling long frequented village fall?
While, scourg'd by famine from the smiling land
The mournful peasant leads his humble band;
And while he sinks, without one arm to save,
The country blooms—a garden and a grave . . .

Ill fares the land, to hast'ning ills a prey,
Where wealth accumulates, and men decay . . .

—Oliver Goldsmith,
The Deserted Village

THE almost immediate starvation and distress that followed the failure of the potato crop in 1846 could have happened only in Ireland, a country forced by its union with Britain to depend for its subsistence on this single crop. For although three-quarters of Ireland's cultivable land was in "corn"—a general term that included such grains as wheat, oats, and barley—almost all of it was shipped to England. The cattle and sheep grazed in Ireland, and the pigs fed, were likewise not eaten in Ireland but sent to Britain for consumption by either the British people or those maintaining her colonies.

The Irish farmers, cottiers, and farm laborers, roughly six million of the country's population of eight million, were forced to subsist on produce grown on the remaining quarter of the land, and no crop other than the potato could have borne this burden of feeding so many people at the expense of so little arable land. The Irishman's greedy consumption of it was therefore no mere accident, for it was the only food allowed him by the gentry, who maintained the status quo by perpetuating his hopeless degradation. Wheat would have taken three times the acreage to feed the same number of people, but since the potato plant's waste also fed the pigs and chickens of Ireland, it would be more accurate to say that for every person who might have been maintained on wheat, three persons, a pig, and some chickens were maintained on the potato. Even the kind of potato grown had to be considered, for some multiply faster than others. The Irish, with the limited amount of land left over for their potato crop, were forced to choose the worst kind of potato—the lumper—the least agreeable to the taste but by far the most fertile.

Unfortunately, the cottiers' situation in the landowners' scheme of things also fostered those habits that led to the filth, stench, and degradation of an Irish hovel. The dunghill beside the entrance to the cottage fertilized the potato garden in the rear. The pig was not to be consumed by the family but to be fattened and eventually sold in anticipation of "gale day," which came in May and November, when half the year's rent was due. This friendly but most untidy animal must have sensed its own importance in the family's scheme of things. Passing in and out of the cottage as freely as the children did, it nosed their legs out of the way in order to gobble up some potato leavings from the floor, dropped excrement when and where it pleased, grunted as if in conversation, and even slept on the straw between parents and children. The cabin was where it had the best right to be, to Paddy's way of thinking, since it paid the rent. Smelly, dirty, and unlovely, it was a necessary guest, one of the first living things the infant saw on opening its eyes on the squalid world of Ireland in the middle of the last century.

With England's help, the potato and the pig created and sustained the squalor, for when the latter was sold and the rent paid, anything left over was needed for the tithe (one-tenth the value of his produce) to the Anglican Church, to which he did not belong. As Lord Macaulay put it, "Between the poorest English peasant and the Irish peasant there is ample room for ten or twelve well-marked degrees of poverty."[1]

As a vegetable the potato is a potent source of calories—

those heat-producing units so needed in the 1800s by the
poorly clothed and sheltered Irish peasantry. It is also, if eaten
in sufficient quantity, a remarkable source of protein, amino
acids, and all the important mineral elements, such as nitrogen,
iron, calcium, magnesium, sulphur, chlorine, and potassium.
Even quantities of such elements as copper, boron, silicon,
manganese, flourine, and iodine, all of them necessary in small
quantities for health, are present in the potato. Moreover,
capable as it is of supplying all these necessities, it requires
little culinary preparation, either to heighten its flavor or to
extract its nutrients. A peck of unpeeled potatoes in a cauldron
of boiling water, and in half an hour the family had a meal.
Since no time was wasted between the cooking and the eating
of them, skin and all, little was lost of the food's essential
values. With a little salt, some crushed mustard seed, and possibly some buttermilk to add to its nutritional qualities, it was
capable of preventing scurvy, building and protecting sound
teeth, and supplying all the energy needed for a good day's
work.[2]

Sometimes on larger farms where there was a greater
variety and abundance of food, the potatoes would be served
in what was then a novel way. An immense pot of boiled
potatoes was emptied into a large wooden bowl, and after
their skins had been slipped off and put aside for the pigs and
fowl, the hot potatoes were salted and crushed with slotted
wooden spoons. As the crushing continued, about a pint of
diced, well-boiled onions was poured in, together with their
boiled-down liquid. Finally, a quart or so of fresh milk and
close to a pound of butter were added, and all the ingredients
were thoroughly mixed, mashed, and stirred until the whole
took on the appearance of a huge mound of thick cream—soft,
lumpless, delectable. Thus was born the now commonplace
dish called "mashed potatoes."

Arthur Young, an acutely observant early traveler in Ireland, described the partaking of an Irish meal this way: "Mark
the Irishman's potato bowl placed on the floor, the whole family upon their hams around it, devouring a quantity almost

incredible, the beggar seating himself to it with a hearty welcome, the pig taking his share as easily as the wife, the cocks, hens, turkies, geese, the cur, the cat, and perhaps the cow—and all partaking of the same dish. No man can often have been a witness of it without being convinced of the plenty, and I will add the cheerfulness, that attends it."

Young estimated that a barrel of potatoes containing 280 pounds would last a family of five persons, exclusive of its beggar and animal guests, a week, or eight pounds a person a day. Since three in the family would have been children, the father must have eaten twelve to fourteen pounds a day—more than enough, if shortly after they were cooked he ate them, skin and all, with some milk and an egg or two a day, to supply him with the necessary nutrients to be energetic, active, and healthy.

Though not a nutritionist, Young correctly disagreed with those who called the Irish potato, milk, and egg diet unhealthy. During his tour of Ireland he saw too many poor people "as athletic in their form, as robust, and as capable of enduring labour as any upon earth. The idleness seen among many, when working for those who oppress them, is a very contrast to the vigour and activity with which the same people work when themselves alone reap the benefit of their labour. To what country must we have recourse for a stronger instance than lime carried by little miserable mountaineers thirty miles on horse's back to the foot of the hills, and up the steeps on their own? When I see the people of a country, in spite of political oppression, with well-formed vigorous bodies, and their cottages swarming with children; when I see their men athletic, and their women beautiful, I know not how to believe them subsisting on an unwholesome food."[3]

In England, where the poor used their earned money to buy food—bread, cheese, and meat rather than potatoes and milk—and where they kept it under lock and key and consumed it with great economy, the English child had access to it only at mealtime, during which the parents were watchfully present. Under such conditions, everyone, including the children, soon learned the value of husbanding a penny out of every shilling; there was contact with tradesmen, a modest knowledge of the mercantile and social world.

In Ireland, on the other hand, the work done by the cottier or farm laborer was paid for not in wages but in the potatoes he was either given or allowed to grow in his own garden. Cash was so rare and so little understood that when a cottier, for some reason, was paid for his labor in money, he often pawned a pound note for a few shillings. It would scarcely have occurred to such a man to save one potato out of every twelve, as the English wage earner learned to save a penny out of every shilling.

The plentiful supply of potatoes during normal years and the willingness of the poor to live almost exclusively on them and a little milk led to a different kind of family life. The children helped themselves as hunger dictated; there were always a few extra potatoes being kept warm by the fire. They were neither counted nor put under lock and key nor missed when eaten. With always more about ready to be cooked, the family atmosphere was relaxed, hearty, and cheerful. Children going to school filled their pockets with cold lunch potatoes, the largest of which they often gave to their teacher. Laborers employed in digging potatoes were at noon allowed a "cast" of potatoes—as many large potatoes as they could roast on an open fire and eat at one sitting. Some Donegal fishermen had their wives weave special woolen stocking bags in which they carried mashed potatoes to be eaten at sea. Or they would take "live" turf into their boats with them on calm days and roast potatoes with fish at sea.

But the potato blight changed all that almost overnight. In and around every hovel and cabin, the stench alone of the rotting potatoes was enough to convince parents and children alike that they were caught up in an awful catastrophe. Many believed that God was punishing them for their gluttonous consumption of the potato during carefree years when it was plentiful enough to be used to manure the land. As the Irish landlord's daughter put it: "I can remember my mother (who was by no means superstitious) impressing upon us when children 'that it was the Hand of Providence destroyed the potato crop, for all the other crops prospered, and the very weeds in the stricken fields grew strong and green.' "

Speaking of the sudden change in the attitude of the people, the same woman said: "The distress was present at once, because in that hand-to-mouth existence on the potato there was no margin for failure. Even in good years, 'July' was known as 'Hungry July', for the winter supplies were often exhausted before the potatoes were fit to dig. . . ."[4]

As the pigs and chicken were slaughtered and eaten because the putrid potatoes were unfit even for them to eat, the tenant farmers, who had always bartered their eggs, chickens, and handiwork for other needed household items, who had seldom if ever seen money, let alone used it to buy necessities, became desperate in their efforts to feed their starving families. Seeing especially the young children dry up, waste away, and become almost lifeless fragments of family misery, they sold first the manure pile outside the cabin, then the family pig if the family was lucky enough to have one, for whatever they could get to buy oats, barley, or meal. When this food was consumed, they pawned their clothing, their furniture, their utensils, their agricultural and fishing equipment, to buy more food. Finally, with nothing left to sell or pawn, they begged or went into the fields for herbs.

One story told of a bailiff in Limerick who was driving his pony one evening to the west of town. Passing a country churchyard, he saw in the twilight a stooped figure moving amongst the graves. Thinking that someone was taking .old coffins as firewood or otherwise desecrating the dead, he stole in and, placing a hand on her shoulder, asked an emaciated woman sternly, "What are you doing here?"

"Oh, sir," she said, "my children are starving and the nettles grow so nicely here. I pick them at night unnoticed."[5]

This woman was not the only one who frequented graveyards during the famine. "I heard my own mother to say she saw the people travelling miles to the graveyards to gather the nettles that grew there," recalled an old man from County Cork in a handwritten manuscript. "They grew higher and better in churchyards than any other where."[6]

A wealthy and humane Englishman named James H. Tuke, traveling through Ireland during the famine, sent reports to the Central Relief Committee of the Society of Friends in Dublin, the Quaker organization that devoted so much time, money, effort, and thought to those starving in Ireland. After visiting Erris, a barony stretching along the northeast coast of Mayo, he wrote: "The culminating point of man's physical degradation seems to have been reached in Erris . . . the population last year was computed at about 28,000 . . . there is left a miserable remnant of little more than 20,000; of whom 10,000, at least, are strictly speaking, on the very verge of starvation. Ten thousand people within forty-eight hours journey of the metropolis of the world [London], living, or rather starving, upon turnip-tops, sand-eels, and seaweed, a diet which no one in England would consider fit for the meanest animal which he keeps . . ."[7]

The hunger and fear finally undermined the communal spirit of the people—of all people the Irish—who were naturally gregarious in their instincts, had much feeling for one another, and seldom wanted to be alone. A bit of luck, a misfortune, even a death in the family, had always been something the Irish shared with neighbors. It was a rare thing to hear a contemptuous word spoken to anyone poor; on the contrary, the sympathy expressed was often mingled with complaints of one's own poverty to avoid the sin of pride. Commendable, too, was the care with which the Irish attended their destitute relatives, the sacrifices they willingly made for them, the hope and joy they shared when things improved, no matter how slightly.

But now the ties of natural affection were broken; the weak and disabled became incapable of leaving their homes;

young mothers who had pawned their cloaks could not venture out to beg for bread because they were not fit to be seen in the streets; older people without enough clothing to cover their bodies had to give up going to Mass. People everywhere became more and more preoccupied with existence and how to make it continue; they turned inward and grew suspicious; they lost their sympathy for one another; the old scheme of survival had been shaken out of place. In the poorer parishes of Ireland, the peasant had lived with his wife and family almost solely on the potato; whole generations had grown up, lived, married, and passed away without ever having tasted meat. Now, with the entire potato crop destroyed, fathers and sons, and sometimes daughters, hunted or begged for food, while the grandparents and mothers squatted in their hovels, gathering their limbs together in any and every way to enable their rags to keep the cold air from their bodies.

"It didn't matter who was related to you, your friend was whoever would give you a bite to put in your mouth," recalled an old woman in a handwritten memoir. "Sport and pastimes disappeared. Poetry, music and dancing stopped. They lost and forgot them all. . . . The famine killed everything."[8]

The urgent need of every household to retrench led to dishonesty and exacerbated the already deep division between the gentry and the poor. Only the landlord and his guests, for example, were allowed to shoot game or fish for salmon and trout, and this ordinance was more strictly enforced as food became scarcer.

As one Irishman in Cromadh, County Limerick, described it: "The landlord of my home district forbade the keeping of greyhounds by farmers. This was to prevent the dogs' being able to kill hares, which . . . were shot in great numbers . . . by shooting parties from the 'big houses' in the neighborhood. These parties travelled by 'long car,' generally drawn by four horses, to the bogs. . . . As they returned, the grouse and hares which had been shot were hung from poles which projected from the long car. And the vast distance, the insuperable

chasm which separated us poor people from the finer parties of
men and women in the long cars was then felt by me even
though I was a child. I could not then clothe it in words, that
feeling, but I think it was something like hatred, I don't
know...."[9]

A decade earlier, a famous visitor to Ireland, Alexis de
Tocqueville, was reminded of these "ancient wrongs," by what
he called "a terrifying exactitude of memory among the Irish
peasantry.... The great persecutions [are] not forgotten."

Nor did the English, in Tocqueville's view, fail to recipro-
cate in kind: "All the Irish Protestants whom I saw . . . speak
of the Catholics with extraordinary hatred and scorn. The latter, they say, are savages . . . and fanatics led into all sorts of
disorders by their priests."[10]

Food became both a dream and an obsession, and the
scarcer it became, the more degrading and revolting were the
alternatives left to those trying to survive. In County Down, a
beggar woman and her two children went to the home of a
comfortable farmer asking alms. When they approached the
doorstep, they saw the pigs in the sty eating food. Before the
mother could stop them, or feel that she wanted to or had a
right to, the children ran over to the trough and, like pigs
themselves, gobbled up what the pigs had not yet eaten.[11]

Other Irish food hunters sought out edible bits even in the
offal of the fish market. They did it surreptitiously, using the
big toe of the right foot as a kind of tester. A woman, a man, a
boy (it made no difference, they were all barefoot and all used
their big toe in the same extraordinary way) would turn over
a lump of meat or fish offal, push it out of the way of any
guts or excrement, and poke at it with the toe in the hope of
finding something edible. When even the slightest hope was
roused, they would crook the big toe and lift the slimy morsel,
drop it, and lift it again, as if to try its substance. If the
message telegraphed from toe to brain was disappointing, they
moved on and started poking and testing some other piece of
waste. Only when the message announced a prize was the
morsel flung upward by that educated toe into the hands of

the food hunter, who immediately slipped it inside his coat and went off to share it with the family.[12]

The starving were everywhere and could not be avoided, even by veteran travelers like the Reverend S. Godolphin Osbourne. He and his English traveling companion were, later, on their way to Westport, in a cracked old coach with the paint worn off, a dingy harness, and a driver wearing the inevitable top hat and swallow-tailed frieze coat, when they became emotionally involved, against their will, with another seeker of food. This one, though, absolutely refused to lose self-respect in order to obtain it. The countryside between Limerick and Westport was wild, beautiful, hardly cultivated, with green mountains tinged with yellow and brown rising everywhere in the background. The brightly variegated plain seemed ideal for grazing purposes, but there were few farm animals and even fewer farms.

Suddenly a barefoot girl about twelve years old appeared —from nowhere, it seemed, for there were no trees and no cabins close to the road. Dressed in a man's old coat closely buttoned to conceal the fact that she was otherwise naked, she began running beside their coach, keeping pace with it whether it went very fast, as it did when the road was straight and level, or slowly, as it did around turns or up slippery grades. She did not ask for anything but with fists clenched kept running, matching her speed to the horse's so that she was always directly beside the two seated English gentlemen in the car and just behind the driver on his high seat.

Osbourne and his friend had by now reached the point where they refused all mendicants, including even those who, like this girl, were obviously not professional. From experience they had learned that by relieving them with the value of no more than a meal, they would be subjected to an eloquence of gratitude, spoken in every feature and gesture, invoking every office of Jesus Christ and the Virgin Mary, every pleading of the saints, to bless them throughout their lives and on into eternity.

Osbourne especially was firmly against giving alms to this barefoot girl in the threadbare coat, whose long blond hair bounced against her back as she ran, as though she was astride a trotting horse. He kept urging his friend to resist while they both kept telling her, again and again, that they would give her nothing.

But she never asked for anything, and in time they became astonished at her concentration, her stamina, the stoical expression that held in thrall her lovely features. She was a magnificent creature with a fine, expressive face going back to what had once been an Irish aristocracy, a face whose beauty now appeared almost improper in the daughter of a peasant. At any other time in Ireland, when singing and dancing and poetry reading in a warm commingling of families were weekly occurrences, the people watching such a girl in a jig would have said something like, "Faith, but that one mixes her legs well. Sure, while your back was turned, she could walk up your sleeve and build a nest in your ear."[13] She was that pretty, slender, and agile, but now her every feature showed such controlled determination that the two silent traveling companions grew more and more attentive to this unexpected and unwelcome contest. Osbourne, as he himself could plainly see, was much more irritated than his friend by her silent, wearying importunity.

The friend kept shaking his head at her in refusal, but with every quarter-mile traveled he did so with less and less conviction. His heart finally began to soften at the sight of her, asking for nothing but refusing to be denied, gasping for breath but clinging to some irreducible minimum of pride, literally running her heart out so she could go back to her mother and father (whose old coat she was wearing because hers had been new enough to pawn) and surprise them and her brothers and sisters with some food, or the money to buy some.

"The naked spokes of those naked legs, still seemed to turn in some mysterious harmony with our wheels," Osbourne said. "On, on she went ever by our side, using her eyes only to pick her way, never speaking, not even looking at us."

It was not until she had run at least two miles, a distance she would have to retrace on bleeding feet, that she won the day. Soaked with sweat, her eyes burning with salt, her mouth open and gasping for breath, she became very hot, coughed, and buckled over as if from stomach cramps. Still she ran with undiminished speed, absolutely determined to match the speed of the horse and remain parallel with the two Englishmen sitting in the carriage. Finally Osbourne's companion, fearful that her determination would destroy her, gave in.

"That cough did it," Osbourne said. "He gave her a four-penny: I confess I forgave him—it was hard earned, though by a bad sort of industry."[14]

The girl invoked neither the office of the Saviour nor the grace of the Virgin nor the pleading of the Saints to bless the English gentlemen. She took the money from them as she might have taken an apple from a tree or a fish from a lake, and walked slowly back with it along the road toward home. The fourpenny piece, equal to roughly half a day's pay for the lowliest worker, would buy enough meal to keep the family fed for another day or two. With it held tightly in her fist, she would enter, like sunlight, the darkness of the cabin and some-how reconcile everyone to it.

Chapter Four

Irish misery forms a type by itself, of which neither the model nor the immitation can be found anywhere else. In all countries . . . paupers may be discovered, but an entire nation of paupers is what never was seen until it was shown in Ireland. To explain the social condition of such a country, it would be only necessary to recount its miseries and its sufferings; the history of the poor is the history of Ireland.

—Gustave de Beaumont,
Ireland: Social, Political, and Religious

DAY, by day, more and more people, without money, credit, or anything left to sell or pawn, went hungry. Farm laborers who had been paid their wages in food were discharged because their employers were no longer able to feed them. Tailors, carpenters, shoemakers, and other artisans who had often accepted poultry, eggs, and milk as payment for their services now had no employment. Even beggars preferred the freedom of their precarious trade to the dismal certainty of death from disease in the workhouse.

"The people are killing off their hens and domestic fowl of all kinds," wrote one County Mayo man to the *Evening Freeman* in January 1847. "In every cabin hitherto there were kept a few hens. They were fed principally upon potatoes, occasionally getting some light grain, and their eggs were the source of no unimportant revenue to the poor. Now they must sell or eat them. There are no crumbs falling from the poor man's table these days. There *is* no refuse food. Hens cannot live, and a sentence of extermination has gone out against them."[1]

Those with a modest food supply and those with no food

supply at all became more daring and innovative in their efforts to remain alive. The son of a County Mayo farmer gave away his father's last pig, which was too starved to slaughter, for one ounce of gunpowder. "The gun-powder was intended, not, as our English friends may suspect, to bring down a landlord," a friend of the farmer explained. "The lad lived near a lake and had designs on the wild ducks."[2]

The stealing of sheep, shunned at first, spread to every county as the supply of food dwindled and the fathers of starving children became more willing to risk the severe penalties, of which the most common was transportation to Australia. Even these desperate fathers were reluctant to steal from any neighboring family whose few sheep represented its only hope of survival; they usually traveled to other districts where they were as unknown to the people as the people were to them. There they waited at night in mountain caves around which larger herds of sheep, belonging to more affluent farmers, gathered. It was of the utmost importance to be both silent and swift in the kill, and in the escape as well, for the farmers used sheep bells and often slept out on the mountainside, armed with rifles, with their herds.

The thief carried a knife as sharp as a fine-grit stone could make it, and as he dispatched the animal with it, he silenced the bell, which he left behind, along with the sheep's head, to inform the farmer that the sheep had not strayed. The carcass was then carried away, often to a graveyard, where it was skinned on a flat tombstone by candlelight or the light of the moon. The skin was buried in a bog on the way home, and the dressed flesh of the animal hidden in as many different places as there were different pieces. But the danger of being caught did not end there, for the smell of roasting meat was an immediate giveaway, meat being a once- or twice-a-year luxury even in the best of times. The different cuts of meat had to be taken to deserted places to be cooked, then carried back under the man's old frieze coat to the hovel, where he and his family devoured it, along with whatever wild herbs the children had gathered that day.

The same anarchy that prompted these destitute families to steal often led the victimized farmers to be lenient. Some shot over the head of a thief caught in the act of killing a sheep or trying to escape with it in the darkness. Others who witnessed the stealing of sheep refused to identify the culprits on the grounds that the country had reached the point where it was impossible for the poor to obey the law and remain alive too.

The Nation reported one case of a man in Doneraile who was arrested by the police for stealing a horse and killing it: "He and his wretched family were actually partaking of soup made of the carrion when he was taken. Without food for three days, he said that he was on the look-out for sheep, a pig, or cow, but was disappointed, as those animals are all secured by night and watched by day; so he had no recourse but horse flesh to satisfy the cravings of his appetite and the hunger of his starving children. . . ."[3]

Most farmers, though, treated thieves and trespassers as threats to their own survival. If they caught them, they beat them, had them jailed, or tied them to fence posts or cartwheels as a warning to others. When the thievery and looting continued, they built man-traps, deep pits eight to ten feet deep laid with spikes and concealed with brambles, grass, and weeds. As one Irishman looking back on those days put it: "Farmers lay in wait, and when the intruder fell into the trap and his feet were pierced, he was pounced upon and beaten to death with sticks. In some cases the trap held water and the robber drowned."[4]

Farmers, in an effort to protect their seed potatoes, those bearing the two or three eyes that represented the buds of the underground stems, buried them, as one might bury money, under the floors of their houses. Others were reluctant to sow the ground for fear the crop would either be stolen by the starving poor or seized by the landlord for rent. Those too weak from lack of food to sow a new crop of potatoes began to believe they were doomed to die. They stopped preparing, and with their clothing pawned could not prepare, to provide for the next year. Instead, in the desperate hope that public help would be forthcoming before they ran out completely, they began eating their seed potatoes. From an even deeper sense of insecurity, many killed and ate their miserable cows and sheep—even their horses. "If they don't eat them," reported one eyewitness, "they will be stolen, or will die of starvation. Cows are sold for fifteen or twenty shillings—cows which in better times would be worth four times the money."[5]

Where the slopes had been dotted with sheep and the low grounds crowded with herds of black cattle and troops of gamboling horses, there was now hardly an animal to be seen. Even the carcasses of diseased cattle were eaten, and the joints of starved horses shared, while starving dogs and rats devoured dead humans and attacked those still barely alive. A man in Mayo, near Balla, was forced to leave his wife at home and go out and beg. A few days later some of the neighbors went to the hovel of the feeble old woman and found her lying on a litter of straw in a corner, with the flesh of her shriveled arms and face mangled and eaten by the rats. She died a short time after.[6]

When it became a matter of eating or being eaten by the dogs and rats, the people killed, skinned, and ate the dogs and rats. Trapped rats were often chopped up, out of sight of the children, and the white, rabbitlike meat added to whatever gruel or herbal soup was cooking in the pot. At mealtime the children's hunger had no eyes, their savage teeth no discrimination.

Coroners were by now, in parishes throughout the country, attributing more and more deaths to actual starvation. Dying of hunger, the people were still restrained under laws enforced by a well-fed constabulary whose commissaries were replete with produce sown and harvested by the dying. For there was still food in Ireland; it was just not being used to relieve the suffering. As early as February 1847, the *Sligo Champion* reported that "the Coroner is still busily engaged in this country; the people are still dying of hunger, while the stores of the

Commissary General are full of corn, but political economy prohibits its being touched. The following inquests were held during the week on the bodies of Francis Kelly, Catherine Hoy, Maurice Conroy, John Caucurn, James Kilmartin, Michael Tighe, Patrick Conolan and Michael Hart. The Verdict, in every instance, was 'died of starvation.' "[7]

The condition of those still living deteriorated to levels that even eyewitnesses found frightful almost beyond belief. Once-hardy peasants suffered a steady decline in size, weight, and energy. Flesh and muscle wasted away until the bones of their frames became barely covered, insecurely jointed, brittle, and easily broken. The shoulders of even the strongest among them were thrown up so high that the thinned-out column of the neck appeared at once too delicate to support the head and too deeply embedded in the chest cavity to be a neck. The skin of their limbs dried and roughened to a crude parchment that hung in loose, sacklike folds where their arm and thigh muscles had been. Finally, as the delicate fatty tissue behind the eyes was broken down into food and devoured by the peasants' all-consuming constitutions, as the eye sockets grew larger and more cavernous with each day's diminution of lubricant and flesh, the eyes themselves appeared to be drawn backward, closer to the brain and into more intimate and painful communication with it.

Among the starved still-growing young, the deterioration was even more rapid. Having accumulated little excess fat to contribute now to the starvation process, their bodies went from lean to gaunt, their legs from firm to spindly. Their lips became blanched and shriveled; the skin over their chest bones and the upper part of their stomachs, so tightly stretched that every ridge and curve of the breastbone and ribs stood out in high relief. Their arms, the bones stripped of flesh, gristle, and muscle, made spastic movements uninfluenced by their minds or emotions.

Describing three such "entirely naked" children, "breathing skeletons" living in the outskirts of Skibbereen, one of Ireland's most devastated areas, an American philanthropist named Elihu Burritt, in a letter to the American people, wrote: "Had their bones been divested of the skin that held them together, and been covered with a veil of thin muslin, they would not have been more visible, especially when one of them clung to the door, while a sister was urging it forward, it assumed an appearance which can have been seldom paralleled this side of the grave. The effort which it made to cling to the door disclosed every joint in its frame, while the deepest lines of old age furrowed its face. The enduring of ninety years of sorrow seemed to chronicle its record of woe upon the poor child's countenance."[8]

Another visitor to Ireland, equally struck by the almost waferlike fragility of these children, said: "If you take hold of the loose skin within the elbow and lift the arm by it, it comes away in a large thin fold, as though you had lifted one side of a long narrow bag, in which some loose bones had been placed; if you place the forefinger of your hand under the chin, in the angle of the jaw bone, you find the whole base of the mouth, so to speak, so thin, that you could easily conceive it possible, with a very slight pressure, thus to force the tongue into the roof of the mouth. . . ."[9]

Most pitiable was the appearance of the heads of these children, for as the hair thinned and then gradually left the scalp in patches, the almost translucent pallor of the skin exposed the cranium so that it appeared too insubstantial to prevent a poking finger from entering the brain. At the same time, as if some cosmic joke were being played on them, hair grew from their chin and cheeks, a thick sort of down from their forehead and temple, making them look more like monkeys than children. Had only one child, or only a few children, been so afflicted, aid would have been immediately forthcoming, from relatives, neighbors, even strangers. But there were thousands of them, and they were everywhere, inside and outside hovels, in the towns, and along the roads. They no longer spoke, much less cried; they just stared with a gaunt, unmeaning vacancy, a kind of insanity, a stupid, despairing look that asked for nothing, expected nothing, received nothing.

The scenes everywhere were so stark that it was difficult to differentiate between the emotional extremes one observed inside a hut and the emotion one brought to it. Against a wall in Skibbereen, stood a row of cabins, built of stones gathered from the field and huddled together as their size and shape dictated. Each cabin was about seven feet square and five feet high, with a thatched roof as uneven as the innards of an old straw mattress and with a hole serving as door, window, and chimney. From the outside these cabins looked more like bundles of dirty rags than places where human beings lived, but through the hole in each passed light, smoke, children, and, when there were animals, chickens and pigs.

Of one such cabin, standing by itself in a hollow and surrounded by a moat of green filth, Elihu Burritt, in another letter from Skibbereen to America, wrote: "We entered with some difficulty, and found a single child about three years old lying on a kind of shelf, with its little face resting upon the edge of the board and looking steadfastly out at the door, as if for its mother. It never moved its eyes as we entered, but kept them fixed toward the entrance. . . . No words can describe this peculiar appearance of the famished children. Never have I seen such bright, blue, clear eyes looking so steadfastly at nothing. I could almost fancy that the angels of God had been sent to unseal the vision of these little patient, perishing creatures, to the beatitudes of another world; and they were listening to the whispers of unseen spirits bidding them to 'wait a little longer'."[10]

The famine had so rapidly leveled all parishes to an equality of destitution that the wonder among visitors was not that the people died but that they lived. Some claimed that in any other country the mortality would have been much greater, that many lives had been prolonged, perhaps saved, by the rigid training in poverty and destitution the Irish peasant had for so long undergone. Others attributed the general resistance to death to the people's custom of sharing their food with others, especially with helpless children, whose cries "The hunger! The hunger!" grew ever weaker as they took on the emaciated, ragworn look of century-old dolls.

"Look there, sir, you can't tell whether they are boys or girls," said an Irish physician to the visitor accompanying him into a cottier's cabin in County Cork in 1847. Taking up a skeleton child, he added, "Here is the way it is with them all; their legs swing and rock like the legs of a doll. They have the smell of mice." After they had seen a great number of these "miserable objects," the doctor said, "Now, sir, there is not a child you saw can live a month, every one of them is in famine fever, a fever so sticking that it never leaves them."[11]

The staring eyes of these children told the story, the unbelievable, incomprehensible story of an entire population, under the protection and dominion of Great Britain, whose shoreline was little more than a day's sail away, starving to death while their own country's produce, cattle, and wheat, oats, and barley were being shipped in British bottoms to British ports. During the winter of 1846–47 alone, while over 400,000 persons were dying of famine or famine-related disease, the British government, instead of prohibiting the removal of Irish food from Ireland, allowed seventeen million pounds sterling worth of grain, cattle, pigs, flour, eggs, and poultry to be shipped to England—enough food to feed, at least during these crucial winter months, twice the almost six million men, women, and children who composed the tenant-farmer and farm-laborer population. Even farmers with the grass of thirty cows were suffering; shopkeepers and others in town were contemplating going out of business. Incredible as it may seem today that such shipments from a famine-racked country were allowed, how much more incredible was it then that Irishmen with starving families were expected by the British to watch and be resigned to the shipments made.

At the same time, to make matters worse for the Irish and even better for what *The Nation* called "British Commercial Christianity," no relief food could be shipped to Irish ports,

from whatever country, except in British ships. Even the charity of other nations had to be turned to a profit by Great
Britain, whose Irish subjects had been paying taxes to the
British treasury ever since the so-called union with Britain in
1800.[12]

When Lord George Bentinck spoke in the House of Lords
on March 22, 1847 of "the ravages made in Ireland by famine
and disease . . . and attributed many of the deaths which had
occurred there to the neglect of the government to find food
and employment for the people," Mr. Labouchere, the Irish
secretary, protested in defense of the government against the
assumption that the loss of human life, which had unfortunately taken place in Ireland, was to be attributed to Her
Majesty's government. Every day's experience convinced him
"that the Government had pursued a wise policy in not interfering with the supply of food to Ireland in any way which
could compete with the efforts of private traders. . . ."[13]

This "wise policy" was better known as England's "political economy," one of whose most fundamental laissez-faire
doctrines was that "there must be no interference with the
natural course of trade." The starvation in Ireland, in short,
could in no way interfere with the shipping of that country's
abundant crops of grain and herds of cattle to England. The
traders and speculators had to realize a profit, the landlords
had to be paid their rents, the agents their commissions, and
the only way to accomplish these essentials of political economy was to carry on business as usual—that is, as though no
one had died or was dying of starvation in Ireland. In fact,
when private relief committees and charitable organizations in
Ireland showed a willingness to buy grain to feed the starving
(even at famine-inflated prices), some of the previously exported grain was shipped back to Ireland, laden with merchants' profits and the cost of being shipped twice in British
bottoms, for no other reason than that there was to be "no
interference with the natural course of trade."[14]

Lord Bentinck rebutted the Irish secretary in these words:

This political economy of non-interference with the import and retail trade may be good in ordinary times, but in times such as the present, when a calamity unexampled in the history of the world has suddenly fallen upon Ireland—when there are no merchants or retailers in the whole of the west—when a country of which the population has been accustomed to live upon potatoes of their own growth, produced within a few yards of their own doors, is suddenly deprived of this, the only food of the people, it was not reasonable to suppose that, suddenly merchants and retailers would spring up to supply the extraordinary demands of the people for food. Therefore, I should say that this was a time when Her Majesty's Ministers should have broken through these, the severe rules of political economy, and should, themselves, have found the means of providing the people of Ireland with food. . . .

When, every day, we hear of persons being starved to death, and when the [Irish secretary] himself admits that in many parts of the country the population has been decimated, I cannot say, that I think ministers have done all they might have done to avert the fatal consequences of this famine. . . . At this moment, we know that there are between 300,000 and 400,000 quarters of corn in stock on hand in the different ports of London, Liverpool and Glasgow. I want to know, then, what was to have prevented ministers from sending any part, or all of this food to the west of Ireland, to feed the starving people there? . . . It would have kept the retailers and forestallers in order, and prevented them from availing themselves of the Famine to obtain undue prices. What do we see with regard to Indian meal? Why Indian meal is, at this moment, selling in New York at three shillings, and at Liverpool and in Ireland at nine shillings per bushel.[15]

Even grain that remained in Irish bins could not be touched because in most cases it had the landlord's cross on it for the rent. In Galway, at Licknafon, a woman named Mary Driscoll, living on a small farm with her husband, father, and nine children, admitted at the inquest of her father's death that her family had been taking some of the barley, "about a barrel we had, and, God help us, we could not eat any more of the same, as the landlord put a cross on it, I mean it was marked for the rent." So while it remained there, with the landlord's cross and keepers on it, her father, Jeremiah Hegarty, died of starvation in a nearby ditch. Rather than risk the family's eviction for failure to pay the rent, he had resisted taking any more barley to sustain himself while breaking stones for roads designed by the public works to be of benefit to no one. Had he been paid in time by the public works to buy food, as his son-in-law testified, he might have lived. But instead he was found dead in a ditch, with his stomach and the upper part of his intestine (according to a post-mortem examination conducted by one Dr. Donovan) totally devoid of food.[16]

Ireland possessed within herself, in her thousands of acres of wasteland, the means of her own regeneration. But the money appropriated by the English government to Ireland's public works (money paid in taxes by Ireland to the English treasury) was not used to reclaim this uncultivated land. Instead it was spent on labor that the law decreed had to be unproductive—that is, on the construction of bridges and piers having no purpose or necessity and on roads that began where there was no need for them and led to nowhere in particular. Some of these monuments to the wisdom of the British government are still to be seen in various parts of Ireland—roads frequented now only by the daisy and the harebell, bridges where no rivers flow, and piers where ships are never seen.

The suffering, hunger, and wretchedness that had made the very name "Ireland" a universal synonym for poverty, disease, and humiliation had by now eaten into the souls of Irish intellectuals, who loved their country and its people with a passion equaled only by the enmity they felt toward England and the English. One such was John Mitchel, a fiery Irishman with a peculiar, distinctive character not unlike that of his archenemies on the editorial staff of the London *Times*. Indefatigable, fearless, determined, and gifted with a fine analytical mind, Mitchel wrote for *The Nation*, a leading Irish journal that became during these years a thorn in England's side. In response to the alarming number of deaths from starvation, Mitchel said in an editorial:

England takes away every year fifteen millions' worth of our produce; and of that store English merchants send in English ships a large quantity to their colonies . . . set down as "British produce and manufactures." "British produce" means *Irish* produce. In grain and cattle, England is not an exporting but an importing country; she has nothing of that sort to spare; and whatever provisions she sends to her colonies must be first brought into England from some other country. And when we remember that fifteen millions' worth of corn and cattle leaves our shores for England every year, we can be at no loss to conjecture whence this "produce" goes to [the colonies]. . . .

The rock of Gibraltar grows no corn, but the County of Cork does; and such is the admirable working of the Union [between England and Ireland] and the colonial system between them, that the garrison and citizens of Gibraltar live well, and feed abundantly, and care no more for the potato-rot than they do for a deficient date crop in Arabia, while in the County of Cork, in a place there called Skibbereen, families of men, women and children, are lying in heaps in the corners of mud hovels, some dead, and some alive, but the living "unable from weakness to move either themselves or the corpses". . . . Nay, the more exact and logical statement of this matter would be, that Skibbereen starves, and raves, and dies, *in order* that Gibraltar and St. Helena, and the rest of them, may be kept in good condition to support garrisons, and victual cruisers, and maintain the naval power of Great Britain in all the ends of the earth.[17]

The crisis, in this late fall of 1846, was of such a magnitude that the British government had to act with all the speed, power, and money at its command if it was to save the lives of hundreds of thousands of its subjects. Prime Minister Lord John Russell correctly called it a thirteenth-century famine affecting a nineteenth-century population, and, as the evidence will show, his government's response constitutes the blackest chapter in the history of Great Britain.

Chapter Five

On the roadside there were the humble traces of
two or three cabins, whose little hearths had
been extinguished, and whose walls were levelled
to the earth. The black fungus, the burdock, the
nettle, and all those offensive weeds that follow
in the train of oppression and ruin were here;
and as the dreary wind stirred them into sluggish
motion, and piped its melancholy wail through
these desolate mounds, I could not help asking
myself, if those who do these things ever think
that there is a reckoning in after life, where
power, insolence and wealth misapplied, and
rapacity, and persecution, and revenge, and
sensuality, and gluttony, will be placed face to
face with those humble beings, on whose rights
and privileges of simple existence they have
trampled with such a selfish and exterminating
tread.

—William Carleton,
The Black Prophet

INCREDIBLY, neither official reports nor published eyewitness accounts of conditions in Ireland did anything to stem or defer the eviction of tenants who failed to pay their rents on gale day. During the worst months of the famine, in the winter of 1846–47, tens of thousands of tenants fell in arrears of rent and were evicted from their homes. A nationwide system of ousting the peasantry began to set in, with absentee landlords, and some resident landlords as well, more determined than ever to rid Ireland of its "surplus" Irish. Potato cultivation having ended, at least for a time, because of the blight, tenant cultivators could pay no rents. Sheep and horned cattle could produce income, smart income at that, so the landlords decided to give the land over to them and clear it of its human encumbrances. And they were permitted to do so under existing laws that Parliament did nothing to amend despite the unprecedented circumstances under which almost every Irish family was living. A tenant farmer, no matter what the famine had done or was doing to preclude his ability to pay the rent, was subject to eviction by reason of his failure to pay it.

Resident landlords could see the famine's ravages among their tenants and in some cases refused to execute the eviction rights at their disposal. The absentee landlords, on the other hand, who during the famine represented the majority, neither witnessed nor had any emotional involvement in the eviction; they merely signed the necessary legal orders and had their agents in Ireland carry on from there. One such agent had the following notice posted all over the town of Cahir: "The tenantry on the Earl of Glengall's estate, residing in the manor of Cahir, are requested to pay into my office on the 12th of May, all rent and arrears of rent due up to the 25th of May, otherwise the most summary steps will be taken to recover same. John Chaytor 1st April, 1846."[1]

Another absentee landlord, in Templemore, had no sooner departed Ireland after paying a short visit to his estate than notices were served on his tenantry to pay the November rent. The tenants asked for time, saying they had only a few black potatoes left.

"What the devil do we care about you or your black potatoes?" replied the bailiff. "It is not *us* that made them black. You will get two days to pay the rent, and if you don't you know the consequence."[2]

Once the eviction papers were verified and signed by a magistrate in charge of such matters, the landlord's agent enlisted the protection of the British constabulary in Ireland, along with the help of some Irish housewreckers, and proceeded with them to the eviction site. Because so many in the same district were in arrears, the agent usually had eviction notices to present to a whole neighborhood on the same day. This saved time and made disposing of the matter much easier for both the sheriff, representing the law, and the stand-by constabulary, representing the power of the law. They needed each other, for the eviction process was an eradication not only of a family's dwelling but of its heritage—the family having lived there for so many generations that its very surname had come to identify the location itself. From one end of Ireland to another, with few exceptions, the eviction went this way in December of 1846, only a week or two before Christmas[3]:

The proper notices having been served on the parties concerned, the agent, on horseback, and his Irish housewreckers, in their bare feet, half of them armed with crowbars, arrive with sheriff and constabulary on schedule at the eviction site. There are perhaps eight dwellings situated in the same area close to a public road. Some are larger than others, but in appearance and structure they are much alike: two gables built of local stone connected by a thatched roof that overlaps each gable in a downward slant to some five or six feet from the ground.

The sheriff quickly goes through the form of putting the property in the possession of the landlord's agent, thereby giving the agent full power to turn out the people and pull down the dwellings. The relieving officer calls out the names of those to be evicted and, if he sees fit, offers them orders for admission to the workhouse. These orders are generally refused or, if accepted, not acted upon, on the mistaken assumption that there is still, even without shelter, more to be gained outside than inside the workhouse.

The impatient agent has by now given word to his "destructives"—the Irish housewreckers who have already been evicted from their homes and are now themselves desperately trying to survive—to begin tearing down the dwellings. The people inside, though, must first be dragged out, and with them, the bed, kettle, tub, spinning wheel, one or two stools, and perhaps an old chest. Because most of the furniture has already been sold to forestall starvation, few cabins have anything beyond this paucity of furniture, with the possible exception of the half-box, half-boat used as a baby's cradle, an item no longer in demand in a country where the stillborn now far outnumber the born.

Finally, when the families and their belongings are out in the road, a loud chorus of lament and self-vindication begins from those being ejected. Prayers and blessings are intermingled with reproaches, entreaties, threats, weeping. And as the ejections continue, the women beat their breasts and keen, embrace the knees of the agent's horse, try to climb, as if from perdition itself, the steps of the sheriff's car. To obtain mercy, they supplicate with waning smiles and weakly upraised arms as if about to die; to invoke vengeance, they spit out curses from a store of hatred gathered over centuries of oppression. Not only are they gifted with the powers of eloquence, but they move their bodies and gesticulate in ways that add to and blend with every soft entreaty or harsh vilification they utter.

Not even the most jaded landlord's agent can ignore this wild ballet that his appearance has provoked, but he has seen it before and now arrives expecting it, waiting for it, armed against it. The praying, groaning, and groveling of the evicted, like the torn-down thatch of their roofs, have long since become integral parts of a common roadside scene in Ireland—a scene accepted by the agent, sheriff, and constabulary as one of the famine's many unavoidable evils. "House tumbling," it has come to be called, as though it were a game invented by some toy manufacturer.

"Get on with it, boys," the agent says to his Irish housewreckers.

Two of them jump up on the thatched roof and have no trouble finding the supporting beam that extends from one gable to another. They fasten a rope around it and pass the rope through the door of the house to their workers on the ground. After a little action from a saw to weaken the beam, then from a crowbar to dismantle the wall plates at the gables' angles, a pull at the rope breaks the back of the roof, tearing it from its bearing at the apex of the two opposite walls. Down comes the roof in a cloud of dust, into the walled-in area it was meant to shelter. Sometimes a part will cling by threads to one gable, another part may rest with one end on the ground, the other leaning against a wall that is itself about to crumble. In every case the aim is the same and always accomplished: the cottage, cabin, or house is made uninhabitable.

So efficient have the Irish housewreckers become that all eight houses are destroyed in the course of three hours. The tenants, now homeless, are told that they may have the thatch and blackened wood of their fallen roofs but are warned not to linger long. The relieving officer advises them to get to the workhouse without delay, then takes his leave with the sheriff, agent, and constabulary—all British—and their Irish destructives. Left behind are the tenants, who sit beside their remaining furniture and contemplate their ruined homes. The moans and laments subside into silence; their despair becomes a kind of quietism now that it is only theirs to share.

The scene is at once wretched and picturesque, something to be captured by the brush of a Jean François Millet: the women with their long, dark hair, bare legs and feet, all wearing the emblem of Irish poverty, the tattered red petticoat, whose bodice is patched just enough to cover the bosom; the elderly, crouched together under a road bank or wall to escape the wind but also to watch, as if their survival hinges on it, the able-bodied dragging the smoke-blackened beams from beneath the thatch for use elsewhere; the younger children, half-naked, stumbling about the ruins, from which the bare gables point upward as if to reproach the powers above; the oddly precarious positions of the fallen roofs, as though the work of destruction had hesitated when it was already too late to put things right again.

Suddenly the silence is broken by the wailing of a child, who can be seen running round and round the flattened, fallen roof of one of the cabins. The child's cat is apparently trapped under the thatch of the roof and will die if not rescued. The women, believing the cat already dead, try to console her; for a moment her tragedy supersedes theirs. It comes almost like a gift from God, for by consoling her they are in effect consoling themselves as well. They are still trying to soothe the child when a scream of delight from other children announces the rise of a dusty kitten from a corner of the ruins. With the decorum so unique to her species, she proceeds to her toilette, cleaning herself with paw and tongue until she appears much less perturbed by the events of the day than those ejected.

For the children, the mere sight of her, the knowledge that she has escaped unharmed, the delight they feel in her existence, overcome for a while their sense of being homeless. But before long, as night draws on and the wind brings with it those cold sweeps of Irish rain, their tears and moans join those of the adults' chorus.

All over Ireland these evictions became so commonplace, so methodical, so legally impossible to prevent, that tenants whose homes were marked for destruction often helped to tear them down themselves on the promise that they would receive some gratuity for their labors. In almost every case recorded, the promise was not kept; instead, the tenants received contemptuous laughter for the effort they put into tearing down the very shelters they needed to survive. In late 1846, after witnessing several evictions just before Christmas, the Reverend Osbourne wrote in his notebook: "I took a statement from a clergyman, of one case, in which an old woman, actually worked her own house down, *with her own hands*, on the belief she was to have 5 s. for doing so. She had not however got it."[4]

Visitors to Ireland, reporters, priests, and clergymen, all asked in effect the same question: How could a government in Europe allow evictions of this kind to take place at a time when an entire nation was in the grip of famine? Josephine Butler, a humane Englishwoman who was living in Ireland at the time and personally witnessed the ejections, wrote: "Sick and aged, little children, and women with child were alike thrust forth into the snows of winter. . . . And to prevent their return their cabins were levelled to the ground . . . the few remaining tenants were forbidden to receive the outcasts . . . the majority rendered penniless by the famine, wandered aimlessly about the roads or bogs till they found refuge in the workhouse or the grave."[5]

When asked what effect the famine had in his district, one eyewitness replied: "My district was by no means regarded as a poor one, but the famine swept away more than half its population. The census of 1841 gave the families residing in it as 2,200; the census of 1851 gave them at 1,000."

According to the same eyewitness, "Only one landlord in the whole locality . . . did anything to save the people. . . . He asked no rent for two years, and he never afterwards insisted on the rent for those two years; although I must say he was paid it by many of his tenants, of their own free will; but, for the rest, he cancelled those two years' rents and opened a new account for them, as with men owing him nothing."

When the same man was asked what were the feelings of the other landlords with regard to their tenants dying of starvation, he answered with solemn emphasis: *Delighted to be rid of them.*"[6]

A very small portion of the English press sympathized with those being evicted to perish by the roadside. London's *Morning Chronicle* said in one of its leaders: "We shall here state at once our opinion, in plain terms, respecting this clearing system, by which a population, which for generations, lived and multiplied on the land, is, on the plea of legal rights, suddenly turned adrift, without a provision, to find a living where there is no living to be found. It is a thing which no pretence of private right or public utility ought to induce society to tolerate for a moment. No legitimate construction of any right of ownership in land, which it is for the interest of society to permit, will warrant it. We hold, at the same time, that to prevent the growth of a redundant population on an estate is not only not blamable, but is one of the chief duties of a landowner, having the power over his tenants which the Irish system gives. . . . He is to be commended for preventing overpopulation, but to be detested for tolerating first, and then exterminating it."[7]

After being evicted and seeing their homes tumbled, the

tenant farmers and their families still shunned the workhouse, where life with freedom ended and drudgery on schedule began. With the thatch from their roof and whatever beams and rafters they could salvage, they made their way to un-inhabited areas on the same manor or estate and built what in Ireland is called a "scalpeen." In England and America it would be called a "lean-to." Beams were so placed that they rested on one end on the ground and on the other end against a roadside bank or a natural stone wall somewhere off the road. Short sticks from the ruins of the original home were then set across the beams and the old thatch roof dragged up upon the makeshift structure. Stones and more wood were laid on the thatch to anchor it against the wind, then one end was closed off with more stone, dirt, and extra wood, and the other end left open for the family members to enter and leave. Into this miserable structure, measuring roughly fifteen by ten feet, crowded a whole family, sometimes with a *lodger*, if the latter was able to beg or find enough food every day to share as his or her "rent."

Other evicted families lingered around their tumbled homes for days after the authorities had left. Their parents, grandparents, and great-grandparents had lived and died there, were buried in consecrated ground not far away; leaving now would be like casting aside their identity. These people waited until finally, at night, they made crawl-in shelters within the same walls and between the same gables of their tumbled homes, keeping them low enough to avoid detection. They crept into these sites and tried to live, until desperation forced them out or they died of starvation and were discovered by some agent of the landlord's agent, who had their bodies carried out.[8]

Ireland's absentee landlords—about 70 percent of the total number—avoided these horrors, spending what money they had left in London and Paris and meanwhile putting their famine-encumbered estates up for sale to the highest bidder, who always turned out to be another Englishman. The differ-ence now, with the ongoing famine, was that the new absentee landlord, along with most resident landlords as well, wanted his land occupied by cattle rather than by the people who had been living on it for generations. The whole maneuver, like the government's response to the famine itself, represents the ugliest chapter in the history of Great Britain. Landlords who were not native of and had no attachment to the land on which they were speculating were allowed by their government in London to rob the indigenous Irish of their last dignity.

"It is common to hear all the evils of Ireland attributed to absenteeism," wrote a French visitor to Ireland only eight years earlier, "but this is to mistake a consequence of the evil for the evil itself. The aristocracy of Ireland is not bad because it is absentee; it is absentee because it is bad, because nothing attaches it to the country, because it is retained there by no sympathy. Why should it, loving neither the country nor the people, remain in Ireland, when it has England near, inviting it by the charms of more elegant and refined society, which attract it back to its original country?"[9]

What could Parliament do by way of legislation to bring together the rich and the poor of Ireland when religious antagonism so hopelessly separated them? Who or what was to unite the landlord and his tenant, the conquerer and the vanquished, the Englishman, who with Henry VIII became Protestant, and the Irishman, who remained Catholic? The laws were made by and for Protestants, enforced by a Protestant constabulary, and carried out by Protestants in Irish courts. The magistrates, the lawyers, and most of the jurors chosen were well-to-do Anglo-Saxon Protestants, while ninety-eight out of a hundred defendants were Irish Catholics.

No wonder the gallows in Ireland were familiar and ever-present features in front of every jailhouse—no higher from the ground than an ordinary second floor. Unlike England, where the gallows were brought out at the last moment before a scheduled execution and then immediately removed, they were in Ireland permanent fixtures—iron balconies with their fallen floors still hanging down from the last execution for all

Irish Catholics to see and contemplate. In one small Irish town named Mullingar, the British constabulary went out of its way to impress the people: the iron balcony was made to hang two at a time. About ten feet above each trap floor was a horizontal iron beam from the end of which hung a large iron cast of a skull. A ring attached to the bottom of this skull received the rope from which the condemned man swung.[10] And the magistrates and lawyers had the presumption to bemoan the unreliability of Irish witnesses, who would, on taking the oath in court, kiss their thumbs while pretending to "kiss the book."[11]

"I have been present at many criminal trials in Ireland, and it is impossible to describe the painful feelings with which such a spectacle filled my mind," wrote Gustave de Beaumont eight years before the onset of the great famine. After spending months in Ireland in 1839, he called the legal procedure "a lie of forms," the deliberation of judgment "a preparation for vengeance." On every side, he added, "are displayed the prejudices and malevolent passions of which the accused is the object; they may be heard in the accent of the judge, seen in the emotions as well as the passiveness of the jury; the very language of the counsel for the defense reveals them. It is difficult to form an idea of the tone of contempt and insolence in which the members of the Irish bar speak of the people of the lower classes . . . the judge and jury treat the accused as a kind of idolatrous savage, whose insolence must be subdued, as an enemy that must be destroyed, as a guilty man destined beforehand for punishment. . . . Who will be astonished that in Ireland this hatred of the law is universal?"[12]

Seven, eight, and nine years later, during the famine years when the wealthy Protestants who sat as jurors spent most of their time out of Ireland, Catholic jurors could not be peremptorily set aside as usual by the clerk of the Crown. Some had to be chosen if a quorum of twelve was to be met, with the result that British jurisprudence suffered some funny Irish spasms.

For example, in a case at the Roscommon assizes involving a man charged with stealing a cow, the judge, on swearing in the jury and being informed that the prisoner was unrepresented by counsel, said to him: "I must tell you that you are charged with a very serious offense, and if convicted you may be sent to prison for a considerable time. Surely you have at least a solicitor to say something for you?"

"Not a soul, me lord," replied the prisoner. "But I've several good friends among the jury."[13]

Another story involving the jury occurred at the trial of a Kilkenny man charged with attempted murder. A landlord had been fired on from behind a hedge, where the police found an old blunderbuss and near it a finger, evidently torn from the hand of the intended assassin by the defective firing of the weapon. A tenant farmer was arrested as a suspect, not only because he had a missing finger, but because it had obviously not been missing for long. The prisoner was nevertheless found not guilty by the jury and released.

"What shall we do with the finger, my lord?" asked the prosecutor.

"Why, return it to the owner," said the judge, "the man who has just left the dock." Thus did the judge show his opinion of juries made up of Irishmen who knew they and the accused might soon exchange roles.[14]

In Ireland it was with good reason that no one was more despised than an informer, no one more universally cursed with the words "May the hearthstone of hell be his bed rest forever." During the years leading up to the Act of Union of 1800—"the union of a shark with its prey," Byron called it—Dublin was honeycombed with spies in the pay of Dublin Castle; members of the Irish Parliament were bribed to vote for union; the country was being divested of political power through deceit, fraud and corruption. "Do not unite with us," Dr. Samuel Johnson had confided to an Irishman in 1779. "We should unite with you only to rob you."[15]

One and a quarter million pounds (the equivalent today

of about sixty million dollars) was spent in bribing the Anglo-Irish politicians who controlled seats in the Irish House of Commons. As Lord Castlereagh, the chief secretary of Ireland, later explained, it was necessary, given England's urgent need to settle the matter, "to buy out and secure to the Crown forever the fee simple of Irish Corruption." Jonah Barrington, an Irish Protestant, called it "one of the most flagrant acts of public corruption on the records of history."[16]

Many years later, the awakened conscience of England would express itself in the words of William Gladstone, the Liberal prime minister of Great Britain, who advocated Home Rule for Ireland and called the union of 1800 "a paper Union obtained by force and fraud, and never sanctioned or accepted by the Irish nation." Still later he attacked it as "the offspring of tyranny, of bribery and fraud." Oxford professor Albert Venn Dicey, the leading authority on constitutional law, characterized the union as "an agreement which, could it have been referred to a court of law, must at once have been cancelled as a contract hopelessly tainted with fraud and corruption."[17]

A century of misery and religious persecution preceded union; now in its wake came famine, hopelessness, and defeat. When Catholic emancipation was still denied, no one in Ireland among the Catholic majority was more honored than a juror refusing to find a neighbor guilty, no one more respected than a witness in court (considered by all Catholics enemy territory) willing to perjure himself for a relative or friend.

Still, in 1847, even the absentee Anglo-Irish landlords might have been impelled toward some benevolent action had they been in Ireland and witnessed what the famine was doing to the people who had for decades supported them. The resident landlords did witness the famine's devastation, from their carriages or mounted horses, and did in fact, in many if not all cases, do everything they could to save the lives of their tenants. They remitted their rents, or half their rents, kept their servants busy and their stoves hot long hours every day in an attempt to feed the hungry. Both Catholic and Protestant clergymen of the lower rank tended the sick and dying, shared their bread with them, and often themselves went to bed supperless. All these good people did what they could, many losing their relatives and friends, sometimes their own lives, in what everyone now believed was a doomed country.

Chapter Six

Large numbers had some variety of fever along
with dysentery, and often scurvy or famine
dropsy as well, and so did not die of one disease
but from a combination of causes. . . .

—Sir William MacArthur, M.D.,
The Great Famine,
Edwards and Williams, eds.

DURING normal times, the plentiful supply of the potato, its nutritional properties, and the gargantuan quantities in which it was consumed made scurvy unknown in Ireland. Now all the symptoms of the disease, caused by a deficiency of vitamin C, appeared among the poor, in many cases completing the work that hunger had begun.

The gums of both child and adult turned purple, swelled, became spongy and ulcerated, bled at the slightest touch; crablike tumors sometimes set in and destroyed the lips. The teeth loosened and eventually fell out or were lost while the person was trying to chew some herb taken from the field. Deep sloughing sores formed on the inside of the throat, creating a loathsome, putrid stench that emanated from their persons as if the decomposition of their vital organs was anticipating death. As the disease progressed, purplish patches appeared on the skin from massive effusions of blood into the muscles and joints, causing severe pressure and pain. Bruiselike spots erupted all over the body, and a hemorrhage from the mouth was often followed by a hemorrhage from the bowels. The legs too became affected, as blood infiltrated tissue around the ankles and worked its way upward until the legs turned black up to the middle of the thigh. Because of the ghastly effect of this internal bleeding, in rural Ireland the disease was called "black leg."[1]

The lack of other food elements, vitamins and minerals needed for a proper balance of fluid in the body tissues, led to famine dropsy, a disease, like scurvy, limited to the starving poor. It showed itself first by a tumescence in the lower extremities, an unsightly swelling that gradually worked itself upward through the legs until the pathetic victim became completely waterlogged, the skin of his legs eventually breaking open from the pressure within. To see such a person, a loved one, literally bursting, not only from the rags covering his or her body, but from the very skin enveloping that body's flesh and bone, to watch the liquid ooze out through the torn and broken skin and form a glazed puddle of body fluid at the victim's feet, was to experience something like the end of comprehension.[2]

Typhus, the most deadly of the famine diseases, appeared sporadically at first, but as the people grew weaker and more despondent from lack of food, it spread and engulfed the entire country. By then the destitute had lost the power and even the desire to wash themselves, let alone the rags they called clothing, which they wore night and day while huddling together for warmth. In every cabin where peat was burning, and especially where turnips, nettles, weeds, and herbs were being cooked, old and young—men, women, and children—crowded together like so many pigs or dogs, without any covering but the rags on their persons, all indescribably filthy, some dead, others dying, all gaunt, yellow, and hideous with famine and disease. The foulness, the stench, the crusty residue accumulating in these cabins, the unwashed bodies and unchanged clothing, and the crowding together provided ideal conditions for the propagation of lice, those wingless parasites that live on human blood and multiply most prolifically when their hosts are most defenseless.[3]

With their mouthparts adapted for sucking blood, the lice

crawled over these exhausted people, going from one to another for their blood meals until they sucked the blood of a typhus-infected person, whose high body temperature and prostration made him an even more tempting host. Typhus is a disease of the small blood vessels, which are extensively damaged by an invasion of various bacterialike microorganisms of the genus *Rickettsia*.

When a louse sucks an infected person's blood, the rickettsiae in the blood invade the cells lining the louse's intestines. If this invasion of rickettsiae resulted in the sudden death of the louse, there would be no epidemic of typhus. But the infected louse, like the infected person, lingers; there is ample time for the louse to crawl from the infected person from whom it has sucked blood to the uninfected person from whom it wants to suck blood. While this migration from one human host to another takes place, the rickettsiae in the louse's intestinal cells multiply and become so jammed that the cells swell to enormous proportions and ultimately burst. The rickettsiae thus set free in the louse's intestine soon pass out of it with the louse's feces—onto the skin of the still-uninfected human host.[4]

From lack of soap and with a daily accumulation of crust, filth, urine, even the remains of their own excrement on their bodies, the skin of these people was cracked, sore, irritated. The coarse frieze material they used to cover their bodies was alone enough to cause abrasions wherever it rubbed against the skin. The infected louse therefore did not have to bite the next victim in order to spread the disease; once the louse's droppings were deposited on the skin, the rickettsiae in its feces invaded the bloodstream through the scratches and abrasions all over the victim's body.

But even in the rare cases when the skin was undamaged and the louse's excrement dried to a fine powder without penetrating the skin, the rickettsiae remained active long enough to be carried by the air and inhaled or brought by a fingertip to the eye, nostril, or mouth. Sometimes, because the bite of a louse is painful and irritating, the victim would slap and crush it to death and then violently scratch the area with his nails. By doing so he not only ruptured the louse's intestines, thus releasing the rickettsiae microorganisms, but put scratches in his skin at the very spot where the rickettsiae were released.

The louse did not live long after becoming infected; on the eighth day it sickened; on the tenth day it could barely crawl; on the twelfth day, as its tiny body turned red with blood forced out of its distended bowel into all the surrounding tissue, it died. But eight days gave it ample time to infect other people, whose own body lice were then also destined to become infected. Even when these newly infected lice, after infecting others, sickened and died, they continued to spread the disease, for the rickettsiae that had killed them remained active long enough in the fine dust of their remains to become part of the very air the people breathed.

Thus thousands of people, millions of lice, became infected, and as the latter multiplied and carried the deadly germ from one host to another, as the number of infected people increased, so did the odds that more and more people would become infected. The lice were carried along roads, from town to town, cabin to cabin, by people looking and begging for work or food—anything that would keep them and their families alive. It was so generally accepted that the fever was spread in this way, from infected towns or districts to others previously healthy, that it was often called "road fever."[5]

Wherever food was to be distributed, or a government road job paying wages (seven pence a day) was going into operation, these people congregated, crowded together in their desire not to be left out. The waiting time—hours and sometimes even days—was such that the lice had all the opportunity necessary to crawl from one person to another. A man who was uninfected when he left his cabin in the morning might return infected in the evening. He did not transmit the disease directly to his family; the lice they shared during the night did. It made no difference whether the infected person was on his feet, still incubating the disease, or already prostrate, suffering the severe headache that usually signaled the first sign of danger. Once a louse took blood from a person infected with typhus, whether the disease was in an incipient or developed stage, the louse became a transmitter of the disease.

The people soon became expert at recognizing the deadly symptoms, and since no one knew what caused the disease or how it was transmitted, their fears were increased a thousand-fold when they saw a loved one suddenly seized with rigor, headache, back pain, and fever. On about the fifth day the victim suffered body chills; a rash appeared across the abdomen and on the soft white skin in front of the shoulder joints; then came the aching pains and congested face, the clouded mental state that many at first mistakenly associated with drunkenness, then the muscular twitchings, the delirium, and finally the deep stupor caused by the leakage of blood from the small blood vessels that fed oxygen to the brain.

During the fourteen days of fever that in over 70 percent of the cases ended in death, the skin took on a dusky hue—the term *fiabhras dubh* (black fever) is still heard in Donegal. So fearfully well known were those words, *fiabhras dubh*, that they were once used by spurned mendicants as a malediction. There is recorded, for example, in documents written during the comparatively minor famine of 1816, the true story of a lady of wealth ignoring the importuning of a beggar woman for alms. The beggar cursed the woman, shouted after her, called on the black fever to strike her down. That same evening the lady came down with typhus and died a week later. Her husband, infected while nursing his wife, died a few days later, adding credence to the superstitions about the power of a beggar's malediction—and no doubt money as well to the pockets of all of Ireland's beggars.[6]

Had the progress of typhus been rapid and the resulting deaths quickly reached, as is the case with cholera, survivors would have suffered a greater initial shock and perhaps even a temporary paralysis of will. But in time they would have found the strength to see the funeral through and move on back into

life. With typhus there was a tedious and lingering train of
affliction, misery, and distress for the victim and a steady claim
on the attention, sympathy, and love of those trying to nurse
him or her back to health. The disease moved toward its conclusion so slowly and gradually that all the details of prolonged human suffering and struggle had to be endured, all the
depths of love, misery, regret, and hopelessness reached. There
was ample time for the victim to suffer long nights of racking
pain and for those around him, while themselves contracting
the disease, to brood over all the phases of the life that was
passing away. In the end, when the person died and the fever-
racked body began to cool, the lice, needing body warmth for
their existence, deserted it and crawled onto the still-warm
bodies of those not yet dead.

Neighbors and friends began avoiding all contact with a
cabin where typhus was suspected. In some instances, brothers
and sisters, and even mothers and fathers, would leave a
stricken loved one alone in a cabin they believed to be infested
with the disease. It was not desertion so much as quarantine,
for once or twice a day these people would feed the ailing one
inside by tying a can of water and a bit of hot gruel to the end
of a long pole. The person inside would remove the food, tie
an empty spare can to the end of the pole, and give the pole a
tug as a signal that it should be withdrawn. It was only when
there were no more tugs on the pole, when the food was left
tied to the end of it, when shouted queries and entreaties went
unanswered, that the whole cabin was pulled down over the
dead person and set afire. Though these people had no inkling
that the louse was the carrier of the disease, though they were
themselves louse-ridden, many avoided infected lice in this
way and survived.[7]

Soap, the boiling of all clothing, and a thorough disinfect-
ing of the cabins and hovels might have saved thousands of
lives. But even doctors did not know what caused or transmitted the disease, and many of the more dedicated ones
among them became fatally infected themselves from treating
the poor in their cabins and hovels, where the very air was

contaminated with the powdery feces of infected lice. In 1847 in the rural districts of Ireland, each doctor served the needs of over fifteen thousand men, women, and children. He traveled the country roads on a horse almost as starved as the people he was trying to treat.

"Here in the parish of Schull there are scarcely any gentry, and none rich," wrote one eyewitness. "What can one physician do amongst 18,000 people in such a state, with oats for his horse dear? What can the . . . local clergy do? They cannot visit 1-10th part of the sick, even if they had horses, and oats to feed them, which some of them do not. Can Dr. Traill be expected to carry meal to the people in the mountains across the pommel of his saddle, as he has done? Can Mr. McCabe, the curate, be expected to push in the door and look for a vessel, and wash the vessel previous to putting a drink into it for the sick, who are unable to rise, as he has done?"[8]

Typhus was without doubt the most devastating of the famine diseases; it killed the most people because its vector was the louse, and most of the people—that is to say, the poor and destitute—were louse-ridden. The gentry and wealthy landowners had soap, the habit of using it, and the inclination to avoid contact with those who did not. Besides, it was common knowledge during the famine that the poor and starving were alive with body vermin, so even well-fed maids and gamekeepers were kept at a distance. But if the famine was indeed the work of God, as the London *Times* and so many English lawmakers believed, then it must have been God who devised a way of transmitting the famine's deadly rickettsiae to the wealthy as well.

There were literally millions of typhus-infected lice whose feces had turned to a fine powder on the skin of the poor, in the folds of their clothing, in their beards, their pubic hair, the hair in their ears and nostrils. This fine powder retained its deadly microorganisms, and it was the powder, not the lice, that infected the upper classes.

A magistrate, say, sitting in court during trials determining the fate of horse, cattle, and sheep thieves, food rioters, murderers, would be in the same room for hours with hordes of the defendants' relatives and witnesses, many of whom would be carrying the deadly powder in the creases of their skin and clothing and in amongst their various body hairs. It took merely the opening of a door or window, the creating of a draft, the wafting of the powder on a current of air toward the bench, for the magistrate (or one of the lawyers present) to breathe it in or catch a grain or two in his eyes or nostrils.

The mystery was why, once he was stricken and put to bed at home, no one else in his family came down with the disease. Since no one at the time linked typhus to the louse, much less to its feces or to the fine powder the feces turned into, it would have taken a medical Sherlock Holmes to explain why, in the homes of the upper classes, where there were no lice to transmit the disease to others, there was in almost every case only one victim, whereas in the homes of the poor, where the lice crawled at will from one to another, virtually everyone in the family came down with it.[9]

In scoring the mortality from typhus during the famine years, Sir William Wilde (father of Oscar Wilde) said in effect in the Tables of Death, which he compiled, that while almost every upper-class victim died of the disease, many of the poor, with their built-in immunity from having lived in the past with both lice and milder forms of the disease, survived at least long enough to come down with some other deadly disease or starve to death.[10]

People all over Ireland were by now, in the late spring of 1847, committing petty crimes in the hope of being sent to prison, where there would at least be food. At Tralee gaol, Dr. Crumpe, the medical officer, witnessed these crowds of petty thieves, some sick, some healthy, jammed into gaol, where they were fed and then, just as quickly, carried off by fever. The most exhausted and worn-down among them often died within a few hours of admission. Many were louse-ridden, and these spread the fever to previously healthy prisoners who had never suffered from starvation. When the attendants too came down with it, the place became a "horrid den" in which the sick, the feverish, the dying, and the dead were haphazardly stretched together.

"So insufferable was the atmosphere of the place," recalled Dr. Crumpe, "so morbidly fetid and laden with noxious miasma, notwithstanding constant fumigation with chloride of lime, that on the door being opened I was uniformly seized with the most violent retching."[11]

Meanwhile, outside the prisons and workhouses, famine diarrhea became almost universal, for almost everybody was starving. But when bowel spasms were followed by painful straining and the feces began to show signs of blood and mucus, the poor victim did not have to be told that "the looseness" (dysentery) had taken hold. He or she grasped for the threadbare hope that things would improve, until there came the passage of blood and mucus only, which meant that the dreaded dysentery was progressing toward its final stage, when gangrene of the intestine would set in and the stools would resemble water in which raw meat had been washed. In Ennis, a Dr. Cullinan said that such patients had from twelve to twenty intestinal evacuations in an hour, "consisting of serous bloody fluid, often without a trace of mucous or faecal matter."[12]

When post-mortem examinations of these dysentry victims were made, as they often were in Cloughjorden, by a pathologist named Dr. Purefoy, the mucus membrane of the rectum was found in protracted cases to be "literally honeycombed by an innumerable number of ulcers, many of them very minute, and a few as large as a four-penny piece, and so deep in some instances as to have completely laid bare the serous covering of the bowel."[13]

In some hospitals, dysentery patients were isolated; in others they were excluded because the overworked staff could not clean up after their frequent and uncontrollable evacuations; in still others they were admitted and placed beside louse-ridden patients suffering from typhus or relapsing fever,

raising even higher the odds against anyone's surviving. Either
the fever was added to dysentery, or fever existed and dysentery supervened.

It was dangerous enough to enter a hospital, either as
doctor, patient, or nurse; but to enter the homes of the poor,
where most of the victims of the famine's diseases preferred to
remain, was to risk immediate infection and eventual death. In
Schull, a Dr. Lamprey found a quick and simple way of determining whether the people in any given cabin were suffering from dysentery. If the dirt floor was marked and spattered
with clots of blood, he knew that everybody in the family had,
or would soon have, dysentery. With so many uncontrollable
bowel discharges on the ground both inside and outside the
cabin and everybody walking about barefoot, infection was
inevitable. For the spattered clots of blood and mucus were
highly infectious, literally swarming with dysentery bacilli
transmitted, like those of typhoid fever, by fingers and flies,
not to mention food so contaminated. Once swallowed, these
bacilli multiplied in the intestinal wall, creating inflammation,
bowel colic, painful and exhausting straining, violent diarrhea
with the passage of blood and mucus, and, finally and fatally,
gangrene.[14]

It was at once disgusting and heartrending to see human
beings losing their power to resist destruction in this way. A
boy dying on the floor could not be helped because those
around him were too close to his own weakened condition to
stand. Yet the father of such a family walked, or tried to walk,
in his bare feet six to ten miles to the public works in order to
obtain the necessary food to keep his wife and children alive—
until he too fell and died, often with the food his family
needed in a bag beside his body.

Because of the government's concentration on these useless roads rather than on cultivation, the unworked and un-
seeded land sent up foul weeds everywhere. So much now was
utter waste that there was little evidence on the surface that it
had once been otherwise. The absence of pigs, the disappear-

ance of dogs, and the rarity of a cackling chicken outside a cabin were remarkable features to eyes and ears accustomed to Ireland. This famine silence, as it came to be called, seized the imagination of visitors and gave them a deeper feeling of the country's devastation than anything else they encountered. It was as if the entire country had become an open tomb, with voiceless specters moving about under a shattered sky whose thunder and rain alone made any sound.

Chapter Seven

The moment the very name of Ireland is
mentioned, the English seem to bid adieu to
common feeling, common prudence and common
sense, and to act with the barbarity of tyrants
and the fatuity of idiots.

—Sydney Smith

THE growing, incontrovertible evidence of Ireland's desperation did nothing to quell the animus of the London *Times*, notorious throughout Europe for its supercilious attitude toward the Irish. Its most arrogantly inhumane editorials were printed in early 1847, during the very weeks and months when the Irish were reduced by hunger to a state of indifference and despair, when the poorest and weakest were being evicted from their homes, when every week thousands were literally starving to death or dying of some famine-induced disease, when those still trying to survive were so exhausted and feverish that they could not get to their feet, let alone walk on them long enough to search for food. Not bothering to investigate the effects of disease and starvation on the will of those suffering both or to ask the opinion of English physicians, who without doubt would have concurred with Irish physicians, *The Times* in March of 1847 wrote: ". . . The season has come when not only the herb of the field should shoot forth, and the tree should blossom, but the hopes of men also bring forth their fruits. But in Ireland, alas! the voice of nature strikes upon listless ears and sluggish hearts. In vain has spring returned to men of idle hands and nerveless purpose. In vain has the iron tongue of experience spoken its warning to men who hug their indolent misery as a treasure, far more precious than the wages of unaided industry. They have tasted of public money, and they find it pleasanter to live on alms than on labor. The alternative raises no feeling of shame or self abasement. Deep, indeed, has the canker eaten. Not into the core of a precarious and suspected root—but into the very hearts of the people, corrupting them with a fatal lethargy, and debasing them with a fatuous dependence! . . . Thus the plow rusts, the spade lies idle, and the fields fallow."[1]

Three months before this editorial appeared in London, an Irish reporter for the *Cork Examiner*, a newspaper read and sometimes even quoted by editors of the London *Times*, explained in moving words why no seed was sown: "A terrible apathy hangs over the poor of Skibbereen; starvation has destroyed every generous sympathy; despair has made them hardened and insensible, and they sullenly await their doom with indifference and without fear. Death is in every hovel; disease and famine, its dread precursors, have fastened on the young and old, the strong and the feeble, the mother and the infant; whole families lie together on the damp floor, devoured by fever, without a human being to wet their burning lips or raise their languid heads; the husband dies by the side of the wife, and she knows not that he is beyond the reach of earthly suffering; the same rag covers the festering remains of mortality and the skeleton forms of the living, who are unconscious of the horrible contiguity; rats devour the corpse, and there is no energy among the living to scare them from their horrid banquet; fathers bury their children without a sigh, and cover them in shallow graves, round which no weeping mother, no sympathizing friends, are grouped; one scanty funeral is followed by another and another. Without food or fuel, bed or bedding, whole families are shut up in naked hovels, dropping one by one into the arms of death."[2]

The London *Times* in January, February, and March of 1847 avoided the above account and any mention of the fact that the roads of Ireland were still dotted with animals being driven to the sea for export—always now with an escort of armed constabulary to prevent an attack by the few Irishmen still strong enough to lift a stick or throw a stone. "While millions of Englishmen and Scotchmen are fed upon grain and meat which Ireland sends them . . ." reported *The Nation*, "the people of Ireland, the enormous agricultural population who remain vegetating here, are fast sinking into an indiscriminate mass of poverty and misery. . . ."[3]

The Times was either blind to such considerations or contemptuous of them, for it continued to use the harshest and most brutal phrases with which to infect the Saxon mind with hatred, loathing, and contempt of everything Celtic and Catholic in Ireland: "We do not doubt that, by the inscrutable but invariable laws of nature, the Celt is less energetic, less independent, less industrious than the Saxon. This is the archaic condition of his race. But, after all, these generic distinctions of blood, though not caused, are yet modified by laws and institutions. . . . Had Englishmen been, like the Irish, alternately goaded by oppression and stupified by neglect, they would have sunk into the same lethargy that has deadened the Irish soul. They would sit, like the Irish, with folded arms, on the edge of subterranean and untried wealth, or in the face of anticipated but unrepelled famine; they would lounge, like the Irish, on the shore of a sea whose produce they never sought, and cumber the surface of a soil whose fertility they never cared to augment. But kind Heaven has blessed them with a nobler fate and more auspicious laws: they can, therefore, afford to look with contemptuous pity on the Celtic cottier suckled in poverty which he is too callous to feel, or too supine to mend."[4]

The English magazine *Punch*, taking its cue from the *Times*, did its utmost to create for its readers something humorous from the Irish crisis. Despite reports reaching London every day about the disintegration of virtually every family, village, and town in Ireland, it said, under the headline "Emblem for Ireland," that "different nations have different representatives, derived from the animal creation. There is the British Lion, the Austrian Eagle, the Gallic Cock. The emblem of Ireland ought to be the Hyaenna, the creature—according to Wombwell's natural history—'wot kindness cannot conciliate, nor hunger tame.' "[5]

Almost weekly *Punch* published cartoons portraying the Irishman as a dumb brute, a lazy lout, a liar, or a filthy beggar who spent whatever money he collected on weapons with which to assassinate the British. Even the *London Spectator* was moved to offer solutions for settling matters with Irishmen agitating for better living conditions. With the potato still blighted and the flight from Ireland still in full swing, this conservative publication told its readers "How to Roast an Irish Patriot: Pick out a young one; speakers or editors are very good. Tie the arms behind the back, or close to the sides; but not too tight, or the patriot will be prevented from moving, and the ribs will not be done. Skewer down to the pile. You will want a strong, steady fire. Dry pine makes a very good blaze. When the fire gets low, throw in a little oil or fat. When nearly done, a little gunpowder thrown in will make the patriot skip: some cooks consider this important."[6]

All this, and much more, despite the statement in the Tables of Death that "no pen has recorded the numbers of the forlorn and starving who perished by the wayside or in the ditches, or of the mournful groups, sometimes of whole families, who lay down and died, one after another, upon the floor of their miserable cabins, and so remain uncoffined and unburied, till chance unveiled the appalling scene. No such amount of suffering and misery has been chronicled in Irish history . . . and yet, through all, the forbearance of the Irish peasantry, and the calm submission with which they bore the deadliest ills that can fall on man, can scarcely be paralleled in the annals of any people. . . ."[7]

Admittedly, it was difficult to relieve a country like Ireland, trapped in a poverty brought upon her by British laws enacted to make her poor and keep her so. Under these laws and the uncertainty of tenure they perpetuated (something the London *Times* should have investigated), the tenant farmer was deterred from improving his condition by the knowledge, founded in experience, that if he built a better cabin and improved his farm, he would be forced to pay an increased rent or evicted for not paying it, in either case receiving nothing for his trouble.

Countless were the cases of tenants renting uncultivated poor ground at the foot of the mountain at a few shillings an acre. After a few years, when by their own labor they had raised the value of the land, they were forced to leave their farms and move higher up the mountain to begin again on uncultivated land. This went on until those who began to cultivate the soil at the foot of the mountain were, by progressive removals, forced as near the top of the mountain as the land allowed. They were thus defrauded of the fruits of their early hard labor and forced to end their days in want and misery, with the added mortification of daily seeing the ground they had in their youth brought into cultivation occupied by others. Yes, it was difficult to help a country whose laws made a mockery of self-help and instilled in the peasantry the conviction that it was better to leave squalor well enough alone.[8]

James H. Tuke, an Englishman who had visited the United States and spent several weeks in Ireland in 1847, had this to say about a tenant farmer's chance of success in Ireland: "I have asked the emigrant Irish farmer in America, why he does not toil at home, from 'sunrise to sundown' as he does there, and I have asked the emigrant about to leave his native shore for the unknown west, why he did not employ his little capital and labour in improving the land of Ireland. The answer invariably has been that they would much prefer toiling and expending their little capital at home, if they had land at a fair rent, and leases which would enable them to enjoy with certainty the fruits of their labour. The small farmers of Ireland are, too generally, rack-rented tenants at will, and have no confidence in the justice or mercy of those who have the land in charge."[9]

But in the spring of 1847, even more pressing than the uncertainty of tenure was the widespread hunger and disease. Given every sign and warning that an extreme emergency existed, that starvation, pestilence, and death would result if immediate steps were not taken, England's politicians continued to stitch and patch and pin and paste and shorten and lengthen and straighten and widen endless reports, arguments, resolutions, and decisions. Commission after commission came into being—the Scientific Commission, the Dublin Castle Commission, the Poor Relief Commission, the Police Inquiry—and these went on analyzing, printing, distributing thousands of pounds of query sheets, and making reports to be sent to London for further evaluation long after it was proved beyond all doubt that the food of the Irish people had been irretrievably lost.

The man-hours spent in preparing and collating all this paperwork were of course English, not Irish, man-hours, so that while England boasted of the money she was spending to alleviate the suffering, a substantial portion of it was going back either to the English, in the form of wages for all the paperwork, or to members of Ireland's Anglo class, who were employed as commissioners, superintendents of work, inspectors of work, and so forth. In 1847 ten thousand government servants were administering relief to the poor, from the same government fund from which their salaries were drawn.[10] What remained of the fund after salaries were paid constituted a small portion indeed of the relief needed. Even when the fund was supplemented by private donations and by the unstinting, unsalaried dedication of the Quaker Society of Friends, it was scarcely enough to stem the number of deaths, which every day kept increasing.

The Irish had for generations been paying taxes to England and tithes to her alien church, but no longer was it Irish money the English were spending to allay the distress; it was now, by some sleight of hand at the exchequer's office, English money. Wrote Lord Cloncurry, the lord mayor of Dublin, in a public letter: "Was there ever heard of such a thing as the almost yearly famine of this country, abounding in all the necessities of life, and endeavoring to beg or borrow some of its own money to escape starvation?"[11]

Instead of using the old-fashioned remedy of keeping the food in the country where it was needed by closing all Irish ports against the exportation of food, the British government opened the ports. This meant that the Irish, threatened with famine, were to eat not the wheat and oats sown and harvested by their own hands in their own soil but imported American maize, or Indian corn, which the prime minister himself later admitted was an acquired taste, a food he feared the Irish could not be induced to use. The abundant oat crop in Ireland was more than sufficient to feed the whole tenant population, and for over a year the Irish and their leaders, Daniel O'Connell among them, had demanded that it be kept in the country for that purpose. There were cries for the prohibition of exportation, particularly of oats; a demand that whiskey distilleries be prohibited from buying grain as long as the potato blight lasted; a consensus that the people should part only with their surplus food and not sell what they needed for themselves. To sell wheat and oats and oatmeal and flour with one hand, they said, and buy American Indian corn with the other to avoid starvation, while the excess grain in their own country was being distilled into whiskey, made neither common nor economic sense.[12]

But this is precisely what the British government under Sir Robert Peel, and then under Lord John Russell, forced Ireland to do. The wheat and oats were staple ingredients in the diet of the English, and the maize from America would never do as a substitute, temporary or otherwise, for *them*. Besides, the market value of Ireland's wheat and corn far exceeded that of maize, and there were shipping profits to be made, England's workers to be fed what they were used to eating, and whiskey distilleries to be kept in operation. The British government could have purchased Ireland's wheat and oats and stored them in Ireland for Irish use during the famine; the landlords would thus have been paid and the people kept alive and strong enough to prepare for the next harvest. But this solution ran counter to England's sacrosanct political economy, whereby all crops grown in Ireland, with the exception of the potato, were earmarked for consumption elsewhere.

Speaking of this regrettable dependence of the Irish on the potato, Sir Robert Peel said in a speech before the House of Commons on January 22, 1847, "I wish it were possible to take advantage of this calamity, for introducing among the people of Ireland the taste for a better and more certain provision for their support than that which they have heretofore cultivated."[13]

Nothing could have been more deceitful than this, coming from a man who knew perfectly well that the Irish had cultivated the potato out of sheer necessity, that no other crop, given the minimum amount of land allotted to them for their own use, could have sustained them from year to year. As for introducing them to something better, at what better time could he have introduced them to a taste for their own home-grown wheat, barley, and oats, a taste they had long since acquired without his help? But these crops were needed in the markets and on the cupboard shelves of England, so the Irish would wait in vain to be introduced to them by Sir Robert. For the foreseeable future, they would have to do with the more abundant, cheaper, and harder-to-prepare maize. Even the *Quarterly Review*, a Tory periodical, protested: "*Opening the Irish Ports!* Why the real remedy, had any interference with the law been necessary, would have been to close them— the torrent of food [is] running *outwards*."[14]

The fact is that while the London *Times* was exhorting the Irish, crumbling from starvation and disease, to get off their duffs and back to work, the Irish themselves did not know what was happening to them, what to think, what to do. With their minds darkening, their feelings becoming calloused, blunted, and apathetic, and their energies leaving them, they welcomed death but resisted suicide in the belief that it meant

eternal damnation. From the edge of being they cried for release from life, cried but still waited for God to take them when
"it pleased Him to do so."

"I have visited the wasted remnants of the once noble Red
Man on his reservation grounds in North America, and explored the 'Negro quarter' of the degraded and enslaved African," wrote one English traveler in a letter from Ireland in
1847, "but never have I seen misery so intense, or *physical*
degradation so complete, as among the dwellers in the bogholes of Ireland."[15]

Priests began administering extreme unction to whole villages at once; all were dying of starvation. Overworked and
exhausted coroners protested being called so often to examine
frightful corpses whose entire alimentary canals, from mouth
to anus, were completely empty. At inquests, "death by starvation" verdicts became so commonplace, despite the efforts of
the Board of Works to prevent juries from reaching such conclusions, that magistrates in many cases stopped holding inquests.

A rider added by the jury to the usual verdict in Waterford stated that "death was caused through the negligence of
the government in not sending food into the country in due
time."[16] In Bantry, County Galway, where the deaths from
famine were estimated at four thousand up to the end of April
1847, the Dublin *Freeman's Journal* reported on the foreman
of another jury announcing a unanimous verdict in these
terms: "From the multitude of deaths which have taken place
in this locality, and the number of inquests which have already
been held, without any good resulting, he thought, with his
fellow jurors, that they ought to bring in a general verdict,
inculpating Lord John Russell [who had replaced Sir Robert
Peel], as head of the Government. That minister had the power
of keeping the people alive, and he would not do so. Notwithstanding the fatal consequences which had attended his policy,
he had expressed his determination to persevere in the same
course, and therefore [the jury] thought that he was guilty of

this death and of the rest. He [the foreman] would bring in no verdict but one of *wilful murder* against Lord John Russell."

When it was suggested that the verdict should simply state "death from starvation," with an appended opinion as to how far it was attributable to the neglect of Lord John Russell in yielding to the interests of greedy traders, shippers, and speculators, a rider expressing the willful-murder opinion was added to the verdict of death from starvation.[17]

Long before death came from starvation, the victim suffered unquenchable thirst, delusions, madness, and a feeling of weakness and fatigue so complete that it took a concentrated effort to open an eyelid. Whatever strength remained was spent in yearning for life to end, and for some it did with merciful speed. For others, the famine's diseases led to even more horrible varieties of human suffering before death came and rescued them. The youngest and strongest nevertheless clung to survival, and these exerted their will over their ever-diminishing physical resources in the belief that help would come—as it finally did—from the United States.

Chapter Eight

The chief source whence the means at our
disposal were derived was the munificent bounty
of the citizens of the United States. The supplies
sent from America to Ireland were on a scale
unparalleled in history.

—Transactions of the Central Relief Committee
of the Society of Friends during the Famine
in Ireland in 1846 and 1847

WHEN the first accounts of the Irish famine reached
America in early 1847 and were soon authenticated by English eyewitnesses visiting America, a sympathetic and generous response was at once excited, in sharp contrast to that
shown by the British government, whose responsibility it was
to give immediate and sufficient aid to its own starving subjects. The "timidity" on the part of Parliament to intervene in
the operation of its own political economy is still being defended today, in words like these: ". . . It needs patience to
realize that what is obvious and uncontroversial today was dark
and confused a century ago to many persons of good will. . . .
In earlier famines men died unnoticed by their rulers, but the
new humanitarianism of the nineteenth century gradually
forced upon reluctant minds a more delicate appreciation of
the sufferings of others."[1]

This kind of reasoning founders first on the issue of the
scale of the famine affecting all of Ireland, and second in view
of the humanitarianism shown by the United States in response to the same crisis. Beginning with Boston, New York,
and Philadelphia, meetings were held in cities and towns

throughout the country to devise the best and speediest means of helping the starving people of Ireland. All through the states an intense interest and a noble generosity were shown. Railroads carried free of charge all packages marked IRELAND. Public carriers undertook the gratuitous storage and delivery of any bundle or box intended for the relief of the destitute Irish. Even the U.S. government intervened, allowing its ships of war, with their guns removed to afford more room for stowage, to hurry to Ireland's shores with supplies. Everything was put at the disposal of the Society of Friends, the great Quaker organization in Ireland whose sole aim and every energy during the famine centered on helping the starving.[2]

The British had by the spring of 1847 been forced by world opinion to allow foreign ships carrying relief to go directly to Irish ports. No longer were these ships required to add to the profit of British shippers by having their cargoes transferred to British bottoms before the cargoes could be unloaded in Ireland. In 1847 alone, as a result of this change in policy, one hundred and fourteen ships (two of them American ships of war, the *Jamestown* and *Macedonia*, for whose cargoes of provisions no freight was charged) carried close to twenty thousand tons of provisions to Ireland, the money value of which was about two hundred eighty thousand pounds, or one and a half million dollars—a figure equal to about thirty million dollars today.[3]

When these shipments of clothing, flour, meal, and Indian corn began arriving at Irish ports from America, the London *Times*, leaving out of consideration the Irish-grown wheat and oats that were still being shipped from Ireland to England, consoled itself in another editorial: "We will confess to a passing sensation of wounded pride when we hear of our fellow subjects [the Irish] becoming objects of republican [U.S.] benevolence, and our social sores being exposed in the cities of New England. But if we are unable to rescue Ireland from the grasp of famine, as confessedly we are, it does not become us to resent the assistance of a generous kinsman and friend. Whoever is to blame, most true it is that Ireland does not prosper in our hands. We must, therefore, submit to be commiserated and helped in our task."[4]

Other humane and generous visitors to Ireland, both English and American, did not see how such a vast, neglected amount of wretchedness could exist within less than two days' sailing time of English ports, how even an absentee aristocracy, its religion and heritage aside, could have allowed such a mass of evil and corruption to accumulate in a country entrusted to its care. The people really seemed, as they themselves believed, doomed to extermination, and London newspapers complacently agreed that the opinion "in political circles" was that two million would perish before the next harvest. This represented one-fourth of the country's entire population, but the British government, in all its official correspondence, continued to refer to the Irish crisis as a "local distress," a "scarcity" rather than a nationwide famine, just as in all its actions it continued to carry out a policy suited to a minor rather than a major calamity.[5]

Meanwhile, scornful criticism of the Irish grew in both volume and frequency as their degradation deepened. It was during the height of the famine, in March 1847, that Lord Monteagle in Parliament spoke "deploringly and earnestly of the idleness of the Irish people, of their reliance on others, their mendicant propensities."[6]

Lord Monteagle would no doubt have spoken differently had he taken the trouble to visit parishes throughout Ireland. In the parish of Tartaraghan, for example, in the County of Armagh, weavers were working seven days a week, each weaving a web of sixty yards and thereby earning only two and a half to four and a half shillings, not nearly enough at the famine price of food to support even a weaver without a family.[7]

An English traveler in Ireland named Henry Ingles disagreed with Lord Monteagle: "We certainly have no proof of a want of will among the Irish peasantry to work, in the thousands who travel every season from the remotest parts of Ireland, to earn a pound or two at laborious harvest work [in the

Low Countries or in England]; and who carry back, sewed up in the sleeve of their ragged coat, or elsewhere, these hard and far-sought earnings, to pay the rent of their cabin, and a bit of potato land."[8]

Despite the poverty and deprivation in every corner of Ireland, well-dressed visitors like Ingles could travel from parish to parish secure in the knowledge that they would suffer no reprisal or harm. "I walked back to Kilkenny from Callen in the evening, without any fear of robbery, in a country where half the people are starving . . ." he said. "A traveller is in less danger on the highways of Ireland than in any other part of the British dominions."[9]

The French visitor de Beaumont went even further: "In no part of the world can a stranger travel with more safety than in Ireland."[10]

Most visitors to Ireland during this period were journalists and men of wealth who "crossed over to see for themselves." The most skeptical among them, those determined to cut through the exaggeration and set the record straight, were often the most graphic in their reports. Like their predecessors, they too were accused of exaggeration.

One such man of means, William Bennett, wrote several letters during a six-week stay in Ireland in 1847, in one of which he reported: "My hand trembles while I write. The scenes of human misery and degradation we witnessed still haunt my imagination, with the vividness and power of some horrid and tyrannous delusion, rather than the features of a sober reality. We entered a cabin. Stretched in one dark corner, scarcely visible, from the smoke and rags that covered them, were three children huddled together, lying there because they were too weak to rise, pale and ghastly, their little limbs—on removing a portion of the filthy covering—perfectly emaciated, eyes sunk, voice gone, and evidently in the last stage of actual starvation. Crouched over the turf embers was another form, wild and all but naked, scarcely human in appearance. It stirred not, nor noticed us. On some straw, sodden upon the ground, moaning piteously, was a shrivelled old woman, imploring us to give her something—baring her limbs partly, to show how the skin hung loose from the bones. . . ."

William Bennett entered over fifty of these cabins, where he found remnants of families crowded together, orphaned little relatives, and sometimes even strangers taken in by families almost equally destitute, their kindness to one another true to the very end. In one cabin he found a dying girl lying next to her dead brother. She said nothing, did not complain, but when asked, "What is the matter?" she gave the same universal answer: *"Tha shein ukrosh"*—Indeed the hunger.

"We truly learned the terrible meaning of that sad word 'ukrosh' . . . ." Bennett wrote. "Some of the scenes have retained their grasp upon the imagination day and night. Such a state of things as has long existed in Ireland would not have been suffered by England in any foreign country, without pouring forth its missionaries. Such abandonment of duty and responsibility would not have been endured in England. I have elsewhere written, that if the *animals* had been anywhere allowed to live and die off in the manner of these poor people, the nation would have been up in arms against the owner of that estate."[11]

Not all observers, however, were critical of England's handling of the crisis, and these included many of the Protestant bishops and ministers with parishes in Ireland. These Anglican churchmen received salaries made up not only by the country's Protestant, mostly wealthy minority, but also by every Irish Catholic, who by law had to tithe to the Anglican church, in whose doctrines he did not believe.

The tithe law had for decades been criticized by both Catholics and enlightened Protestants. As early as 1783, in the Irish Parliament, Henry Grattan scorned every parson taking tithes from a starving peasantry. Such a man, he said, "exacts contribution from a pauper, gleans from wretchedness, leases from poverty; he fattens on hunger, raggedness and destitution."[12] A well-known visitor to Ireland during these years, Arthur Young, agreed by describing tithe proctors as "vultures ready to strip and skin the peasant."[13]

Fifty years later, in 1833, with the tithe still in force, the Protestant Episcopal Church in Ireland not only owned five million acres of land, from which it derived a revenue of a million pounds a year, but also collected every year, from the tithe charge, over six hundred thousand pounds—an enormous sum in those days, equal to about a hundred twenty-five million dollars today—extracted with efficiency and dispatch from an impoverished peasantry. John Mitchel, editorial writer for *The Nation* in Dublin, called it "the wealthiest church in the world quartered upon the poorest people, who abhor its doctrines and regard its pastors as ravening wolves." An Englishman, Lord Thomas Macaulay, agreed with him when he called the same church "the most utterly absurd and indefensible of all the institutions now existing in the civilized world."[14]

No Protestant bishop in Ireland received less than four thousand pounds a year, and some got as much as fifteen thousand, whereas in England many bishops were still receiving less than three thousand a year. Small wonder, then, that there were few Protestant ministers critical of the mother country, whose tithe law amply supported their residency in Ireland, even though they too, like the landed gentry, were mostly absentee.[15]

There were so few Protestants in the south and west of the country that in 151 parishes the minister was without a single parishioner. The Catholic peasants, who attended and supported their own church, were nevertheless compelled to support in luxury and idleness a class of men from whom they received nothing but contempt and hatred. Even the passing in 1838 of the Tithe Commutation Act, which levied the charge against the landlord rather than the tenant, did nothing to relieve the tenant; the landlord merely raised the rent to make up the difference, so the tenant still in fact paid.[16]

A decade later, during the famine, the more affluent Protestant ministers attributed the starvation in Ireland not to England's failure to act in time with sufficient concern, vigor, and effort but to the hand of Providence. While scientists were offering as the cause of the blight the Insect Theory, the

Weather Theory, the Parasitical Theory, the Electrical Theory, the Fog Theory, and the Fungus Theory, Protestant theologians were claiming that Roman Catholicism, better known in England as "popery," was the true cause of the potato blight. The prolonged and seemingly ineradicable presence of Catholicism in Ireland, coupled with England's guilt in allowing it to perpetuate itself, had brought on God's punishment.[17]

Wrote one Protestant journalist: "As Popery is idolatrous, any treaty with it must be opposed to God's will, and call down his wrath upon those nations who have commerce with it: more particularly upon nations like Ireland wherein its hideous deformities are most signally manifested. . . ."[18]

Another, after quoting Old Testament examples of how God punished idolatry, claimed that "[idolatry] is just as true of the millions of Ireland as it was of the millions of Judah: 'They worship the work of their own hands, that which their own fingers have made.' . . . Ireland is scourged . . . and England's guilt is measured in the manner in which she allows 'priests to defend, and practice, and perpetuate, this corrupt and damnable worship in this realm.' . . ."[19]

In St. Jude's Cathedral in Liverpool, the Reverend Hugh McNeill called the blight a rod that was meant to scourge England for tolerating popery: "That it is a sin against God's holy law to encourage the fables, deceits, false doctrines, and idolatrous worship of Romanism, no enlightened Christian—no consistent member of the church of England can deny. . . ."[20]

In Ireland, some Protestant ministers even went so far as to laud the poor Irish Catholic peasant for accepting the fate that God had meted out to him. This nineteenth-century doublethink is beautifully expressed in a letter written in February 1847 by one Reverend Woodward, Protestant rector of Fetland, County Tipperary: "A poor man joined me on the road in the County of Mayo, about the middle of October last, and entered into conversation with me. He spoke of the prevailing famine and of his own privations, and then exclaimed, 'but patience is a fine thing. I had rather die in a ditch than do anything out of the way.' And then, after some pause, he added, 'and if a man were to die patient, what could be better for him than that?'"

If Paddy had been trying to pull the reverend's leg, as is most likely, he succeeded, for the reverend pompously goes on: "Now if you can think that such a reflection, under such circumstances, does not seem to argue a Christian spirit, however clouded its apprehensions may be of many important doctrines, all I can say is, that, in my judgement, to him belongs the charge of bigotry and superstition, and not the patient sufferer, at whose door he would be disposed to lay it. The country is full of such instances of meek submission to the will of a chastising Providence. . . . It is impossible for anyone who . . . has had an opportunity of witnessing the conduct of these patient sufferers, to withhold his testimony to the bright example they are now setting of (I will say) pious resignation to the hand that smites them. . . ."[21]

There is no historical evidence implicating the British government in a conspiracy to exterminate the population of Ireland, but many government officials, as well as those advising them, looked upon the famine as a God-sent solution to the so-called Irish question. One such was Nassau Senior, professor of political economy at Oxford and a staunch supporter of the views of the British treasury. Senior did not hesitate to express himself on the Irish question, and after doing so to an Oxford colleague named Benjamin Jowett, the latter remarked: "I have always felt a certain horror of political economists, since I heard one of them say that he feared the famine . . . in Ireland would not kill more than a million people, and that would scarcely be enough to do any good."[22]

This cool regret that the famine would do away with only a million (instead of the earlier estimated two million, which turned out to be closer to the mark) was shared by those in government as well, who spoke publicly of the Irish as though they were unfit to be included in the human race. Poulett

Scrope, a member of Parliament, said that traveling from England to Ireland was like going back through history "from an age of civilization and science to one of ignorance and barbarism." Even Thomas Macaulay, who criticized England for not "elevating" the Irish, called Ireland a perverse and obstinate exception to the progress shared by her European neighbors—"a marsh saturated with the vapours of the Atlantic."[23]

Sir Charles Trevelyan remarked in 1846 that "the great evil with which we have to contend is not the physical evil of the famine, but the moral evil of the selfish, perverse and turbulent character of the people." He then turned not to "popery" or to the "idolatry" of the Roman Catholic Church but to God Himself, that Great Disposer of Events, whose intentions were as unfathomable as they were holy and unassailable, and attributed the famine to Him. Since the Almighty had willed it, the English government would be presumptuous indeed to attempt any rash or precipitous solution. The Irish problem and overpopulation were, in his eyes, one and the same, and "being altogether beyond the power of man, the cure had been applied by the direct stroke of an all-wise Providence in a manner as unexpected and as unthought of as it is likely to be effectual."[24]

Later, in 1848, he admitted that the matter was "awfully serious," but added, "we are in the hands of Providence, without a possibility of averting the catastrophe if it is to happen." By then, though another half-million Irish had died, what Trevelyan perceived as catastrophe had still not happened. Obviously prepared to see the entire population wiped out, he said, "We can only wait the result." He even went so far as to pity the Irish for not appreciating the hopelessness of their situation: "It is hard upon the poor people that they should be deprived of knowing that they are suffering from an affliction of God's providence."[25]

The idea that the famine in Ireland was the work of Providence gained more and more adherents among Anglican churchmen and government officials as the crisis deepened and the deaths from starvation and disease increased. God was blamed for the British government's sins of omission, its own dismal failure to act in time with a power and purse commensurate with a disaster that was soon to be ten times greater then the Great Plague of London in 1665, when the Black Death killed off between sixty thousand and a hundred thousand people. Four hundred thousand had already died in Ireland, the deaths were on the increase, and the government was still calling it a "local distress." Nor was it forgotten by the Irish that after the Great Fire of London, in 1666, when a blaze lasting five days virtually destroyed the city, including St. Paul's, the Irish contributed for the relief of distressed Londoners twenty thousand fat cattle, whose value in 1846–47, when the Irish were starving, far exceeded the relief sent to Ireland from England *and* Europe.[26]

Trevelyan's "affliction of God's providence" remark was made during 1847, the very year that a government statistical commissioner, Captain Larcom, found the total value of the agricultural produce of Ireland for that year to be £44,958,120, enough to feed, at least during the desperate famine months, not only the eight million people living in Ireland but another eight million besides. Trevelyan could not have been unaware of what happened to this produce. In every harbor in Ireland during this period, a ship sailing in with Indian maize from America passed half a dozen British ships sailing out with Irish wheat, oats, and cattle. But in Trevelyan's eyes, and in the eyes of most members of Parliament, England was exonerated from any guilt because all agreed "that there must be no interference with the natural course of trade."

"They call it God's famine!" cried a distraught Bishop Hughes from a pulpit in New York City. "No!—No! God's famine is known by the general scarcity of food which is its consequence. There is no general scarcity. . . . But political economy, finding Ireland too poor to buy the produce of its own labor, exported that harvest to a better market, and left the people to die of famine, or to live by alms."[27]

France, Belgium, Holland, Germany, and Russia all suffered a potato blight in 1846–47. But unlike British-ruled Ireland, they stopped all other food exports to make up for the loss. With virtually its whole population starving, Ireland under self-rule would have done the same thing. Indeed, the Irish Parliament of the eighteenth century, before the union with Britain in 1800, had more than once in times of distress prohibited the export of grain. But Ireland under British rule was powerless to counter the blight as other countries did. The potato had become the crucial food because all other food produced in Ireland was destined under Britain's economic scheme to be eaten elsewhere. It was the scheme, rather than the lives the Irish were losing, that British government officials held sacred.

Trevelyan had not even taken the trouble to visit Ireland and see with his own eyes the degradation he discussed with such glib simplicity and lofty detachment. Another Englishman who did take the trouble, William Bennett, vehemently contradicted Trevelyan's attempt to exonerate England by attributing the havoc to God's will. The west of Ireland, he said, "exhibited a people not in the center of Africa, the steppes of Asia, the backwoods of America,—not some newly-discovered tribe of South Australia, or among the Polynesian Islands,—not Hottentots, Bushmen, or Esquimaux,—neither Mohomedans nor Pagans,—but some millions of our own Christian nation at home . . . living in a state and condition low and degraded to a degree unheard of before in any civilized community; driven periodically to the borders of starvation; and now reduced by a national calamity to an exigency which all the efforts of benevolence can only mitigate, not control; and under which thousands are not merely pining away in misery and wretchedness, but are dying like cattle off the face of the earth, from want and its kindred horrors! Is this to be regarded in the light of a Divine dispensation and punishment? Before we can safely arrive at such a conclusion, we must be satisfied that human agency and legislation, individual oppressions, and social relationships, have had no hand in it."[28]

Even English writers and poets were among the critics of the Irish, and if they refrained from rejoicing in the famine's decimation of the people, they did not hesitate to wish that the troublesome island would somehow go away. When Alfred Nobel invented dynamite in Sweden, England's poet laureate, Alfred Tennyson, calling the Irish "furious fools" who "live in a horrible island and have no history of their own worth the least notice," hit upon what he apparently considered a splendid idea: "Could not anyone blow up that horrible island with dynamite and carry it off in pieces—a long way off?"[29]

These harsh expressions of suppressed English guilt increased as the situation in Ireland became more desperate. Instead of wishing Ireland blown up and carried off in pieces, the English could have given the horrible island back to the Irish. Had they done so, there would have been no starvation, at least not in Ireland, where the produce earmarked for consumption in England would have been beyond the capacity of the Irish to consume themselves.

But Ireland was too close and, after suffering seven centuries of oppression, too hostile to be set free. She was at once a vital and gangrenous member of the British Empire, a backyard dominion whose people under any other flag would be a constant threat. Besides, England continued to profit from the arrangement, while Ireland continued to display the same deep and hideous wounds. The wheat, barley, oats, and live cattle, sheep, and pigs continued to flow in only one direction —from Ireland to England. In the other direction flowed the manufactured goods from England, the clothing, saddles, harnesses, soap, and machinery that only 10 percent of the Irish population could afford to buy. From 1800, when the union was formed, to the time of this terrible famine, manufacturing of all kinds, and especially of cloth (an Irish specialty), was systematically discouraged until Ireland became an agricultural country dependent upon the manufactured goods of England. Irish farmers continued to use and mend their old farming tools and equipment; their wives still wove cloth and made coats for their children, but manufactured goods came mostly from England, at the expense of Ireland's economy and to the advantage of England's.[30]

As one old, foresighted Irishman put it during these awful years of the famine: "Ah, the answer is in the tea leaves, if only you will wait for them to settle."[31]

Chapter Nine

To whatever part of the world the Englishman
goes, the condition of Ireland is thrown in his
face . . . by every worthless prig of a philosopher
. . . by every stupid bigot of a priest. . . .

—*The Times*, March 22, 1847

THE jingoistic fervor of the London *Times* notwithstanding, English lawmakers began in early 1847 to bend
under the mounting worldwide criticism of England's treatment of Ireland. That spring, the government passed the Poor
Relief Bill, which advanced a loan of ten million pounds, one
half to be expended on public works, the other half for outdoor
relief in the form of soup kitchens. By the end of April 1847,
the relief works had under its employ no fewer than 730,000
Irish fathers (or mothers if the fathers were dead), who with
their children represented well over half the country's population of roughly eight million. These starving men and women
walked barefoot five to ten miles over cold, sodden ground to
work all day long for tenpence, without so much as a morsel of
food, on roads and bridges that British law decreed had to be
unproductive in accordance with laissez-faire doctrine opposing
governmental interference in economic affairs. Women with infant children could be seen breaking stones for bridges where
there was no water, or for roads that led nowhere, benefited no
one, and to this day have never been used.[1]

"Sometimes you might see a half naked poor woman holding a child to her breast with one hand, while she, the famish-

ing mother, is endeavouring to break stones with the other, in order to earn the price of a quart of meal," wrote the Very Reverend Vaughan to the *Tipperary Vindicator*.[2]

By being thus forced to spend their time on unnecessary and unproductive works—projects that created no revenue even to pay back the expenses incurred—the heads of these families were prevented from farming the land, working on needed railroads, reclaiming the thousands of acres of fertile wasteland, or building piers, harbors, and curing houses along the coast, whose surrounding waters were alive with a more than abundant supply of fish—enough to feed twice the population year after year. The money would have been spent on these self-sustaining projects had Irish statesmen in Parliament been heeded, and in the long run much less relief would have been required, while thousands of lives would have been saved.

But the British government insisted upon substituting useless for useful labor, with the inevitable result that Irish industry was paralyzed, the land allowed to go unheeded, and, most important, the natural inclination of the people to help themselves undermined. This British system of relief led neither to an increase of food nor to the production of goods that could be exchanged for food. It did what it was intended to do: diminish the capital of Ireland, increase by a proportionate amount the poverty of her already starving people, and coerce them to leave their own country. As Sir Charles Wood, chancellor of the exchequer, said in his letter to Lord Monteagle, a landlord in Ireland: "I am not at all appalled by your tenantry going. That seems to me a necessary part of the process. . . . We must not complain of what we really want to obtain."[3]

The Poor Relief Bill served this scheme perfectly by its inclusion of two clauses written by Lord William Henry Gregory, a name destined to be forever despised in Ireland. The first of the two clauses, written in the interest of landlords wishing to clear their land of surplus people, addressed itself to the assistance such people might need to get out of the country and settle elsewhere. This assistance never exceeded by more than a few shillings the cost of the fare to America, so that the people leaving would be arriving virtually penniless.

The second clause became infamously known as the "quarter-acre clause," whereby any farmer wishing to obtain "outdoor relief"—that is, food—for his wife, children, and himself had first to surrender "all rights to any land over and above . . . one quarter of a statute acre." The head of a family who occupied one foot of ground over one-fourth an acre was thereby denied, along with his family, outdoor relief no matter how desperately he and they needed it.

"And if any person," the clause went on, "having been such occupier as aforesaid, shall apply to any Board of Guardians for relief as a destitute poor person, it shall not be lawful for such Guardians to grant such relief, until they shall be satisfied that such person has, *bona fide*, and without collusion, absolutely parted with and surrendered any right or title which he may have had to the occupation of any land over and above such extent as aforesaid, of one quarter of a statute acre."

The first of the Gregory clauses made it easier for those willing to relinquish their land to board a ship; the second, the quarter-acre clause, made them relinquish their land whether they wanted to or not—or die of starvation. A more Machiavellian device was never conceived, and because it was written and implemented in the guise of something else, its success was assured. Everything was being done, Britain kept telling the world, to help the distressed Irish, while the same Irish were being told in effect to leave their country.

For it must be remembered that Ireland was one of those rare countries—the only one in Europe, in fact—where there was a surplus of both population and food. Since the surplus food was earmarked for consumption not by the "surplus" Irish but, rather, by the industrialized British, who did not produce even enough, much less surplus, food and who as a result did not want an industrialized Ireland, something had to be done to get rid of the "surplus" Irish. In Parliament, no mention was ever made of the "surplus" British, whose food had to be imported, who would have starved had they not been supplied with the very surplus Irish food that the Irish were denied even during the famine years when the potato, their food, turned up rotten in every field and garden.

Immediately after the two Gregory clauses became part of the Poor Relief Bill, the whole Irish-famine policy of the government was attacked in the House of Commons by Lord Bentinck, the prime exponent of putting the destitute Irish to work on Ireland's sorely needed railroads: ". . . Never before was there an instance of a Christian government allowing so many people to perish without interfering. (Great confusion and cries of 'Oh! Oh!' among the members.) Yes, you will groan; but you will hear this. The time will come when we shall know what the amount of mortality has been; and though you may groan, and try to keep the truth down, it shall be known, and the time will come when the public and the world will be able to estimate, at its proper value, your management of the affairs of Ireland."[4]

A new Irish Relief Act became law on February 26, 1847. It dealt with soup kitchens and how and to whom food would be distributed. The Irish would no longer have to enter a workhouse to receive food; they would simply have to be destitute, helpless, or impotent. The able-bodied could also receive if they were both destitute and without land, or if they were both destitute and holders of less than a quarter-acre of land. Every workhouse had long since become jammed to the walls anyway, with crowds of people waiting outside to be let in, one by one, as the people inside died and were carried away, one by one. Now, at last, kitchens were to be built and the people given food, hot food, something susceptible to being cooked in one huge cauldron and served in bowls.[5]

Since millions were to be fed in this way—and cost was uppermost in the minds of those in the exchequer—soup was naturally chosen over a bulky and substantial stew, the latter of course being what the people really needed to survive. Indeed, the cost of dispensing even this infinitely cheaper, watered-down food became so moot in Parliament that the lawmakers turned to their own favorite *chef de cuisine*, Mon-

sieur Soyer of the Reform Club in London, where they spent
so many evenings sipping not soup but wine, while enjoying
Monsieur Soyer's many nutritious entrées of fish, meat, and
fowl. The ludicrous result was that the British government
solemnly appointed Monsieur Soyer of the Reform Club the
"Head Cook to the people of Ireland, with ample instructions
to provide his soups for the starving millions of Irish people."[6]

It was soon announced that the soup to be served had
already been "tested" by Soyer—that is to say, served to the
patrons "of his noble art of gastronomy in the Reform Club. It
was not served as soup for the poor, but as soup furnished for
the day, in the *carte*." No mention was made by the *Sunday
Observer* of the other courses served to these patrons who
declared Soyer's soup "excellent." The soup itself could not
have represented more than one-tenth of the food these
patrons consumed, but Soyer nevertheless took it upon himself,
with the British government's blessing, to feed and keep alive
all the starving in Ireland with one serving of this soup each
day. One hundred gallons of it was to cost only one pound
sterling, and yet it was to supply, according to Soyer, enough
nourishment "for the poor of these realms" to assure that in
Ireland there would be no more deaths from starvation.[7]

Soyer had by now concocted soup recipes with and without meat. For the former, every two gallons of soup was to
include four ounces of beef, two ounces of dripping fat, eight
ounces of flour, and one-half ounce of brown sugar, with a few
onions, turnip parings, and celery tops thrown in to help
flavor and color the water. Broken down, each quart, the
amount to be allotted to each person, was to cost three
farthings (three-fourths of a penny, which at that time represented 1/240 of a pound) and contain the essence of one-half
ounce of meat. This amounted to only one of the many morsels
of meat eaten by British lawmakers at the Reform Club every
day in London. Yet it was proclaimed by Soyer to be sufficient
to sustain life, and the British government, goaded by an
exchequer shocked at the cost of trying to save so many Irish
lives, concurred.[8]

When another chef, Monsieur Jaquet of Johnson's Tavern in Clare Court, expressed doubt in a *Times* column that Soyer's almost meatless soup had any intrinsic value, much less enough to justify an experiment on the "destitute poor" of Ireland, Soyer replied with the stamp of the British government's authority that he had made two gallons of excellent soup without any meat at all, that he now had three soups, "on taste," two with meat and one without, and he defied Monsieur Jaquet "to tell which was which." He went on to say that "the meat I consider of no more value than the other ingredients, but to give a flavour by properly blending the gelatine and the osmazone, for in compounding the richest soup, the balance of it is the great art."[9]

Jaquet countered by saying that he had never doubted Soyer's ability to make a tasty soup with little or no meat; he was talking not about taste but about nutrition. He then challenged Soyer by saying that if an analysis of Soyer's recipe number 1 proved that it contained the necessary nutrients to sustain life, he would apologize. This suspended the controversy but did not end it.[10]

On April 5, 1847, fully eight months after the blight had destroyed Ireland's entire potato crop, a model kitchen and food distribution center built according to Soyer's specifications opened its doors in Dublin. The wood-framed canvas building, erected near the main entrance to Phoenix Park, was forty-eight by forty feet, with an entrance at one end, an exit at the other. In the main apartment were a three-hundred-gallon steam boiler and an oven capable of baking one hundredweight of bread at a time, both heated by the same fire. In front of this equipment were rows of tables eighteen inches wide, in which holes were cut to hold a white-enameled quart basin, to which a metal spoon was attached by a chain.

Soyer planned for the people in need of his soup to file into a zigzag open-air passageway capable of holding one hundred persons outside the tent. When a bell rang, these first one hundred would enter the main apartment and occupy benches at the one hundred bowls of soup set in the tables.

Grace being said, they would use the chained spoons to consume the soup (the "Poor Man's Regenerator," Soyer called it), until another bell signaled that their soup time was over, whereupon, as they filed out the exit in the rear, they would each be given one-quarter of a pound of bread or savory biscuit.[11]

About a minute later, or just as soon as the bowls and spoons had been swabbed with a sponge and another quart of soup poured into each bowl, the bell at the entrance would invite another hundred people in from the zigzag passageway. Soyer estimated that each cycle would take six minutes, allowing him to feed one thousand people every hour. But opening day, April 5, 1847, was a special event not so much for the hungry, who were impatient to be fed, but for the gentry, who had come for a wee nip of the famous soup and to watch the hungry fed.

"His Excellency the Lord Lieutenant was there," reported the *Dublin Evening Packet*, "the ladies Ponsonby and many other fair and delicate creatures assembled; there were earls and countesses, and lords and generals, and colonels and commissioners, and clergymen and doctors; for, reader, it was *a gala day,—a grand gala*."[12]

Another Irish reporter said bitterly that he "envied not the Union flag the position it occupied as it flaunted in triumph from the chimney top of the soup kitchen; it was its natural and most meet position; the rule of which it is the emblem has brought our country to require soup kitchens,—and no more fitting ornament could adorn their tops. All the parade I could have borne, but indefensible was the exhibition of some hundreds of Irish beggars to demonstrate what ravening hunger will make the image of God submit to."[13]

For the privilege of watching the hungry eat, the gentry were expected to donate five shillings each, which was to be distributed by the lord mayor in charity. "Five shillings each to see paupers feed!" wrote one reporter. "Five shillings each! To watch the burning blush of shame chasing pallidness from poverty's wan cheek! Five shillings each! When the animals in the Zoological Gardens can be inspected at feeding time for sixpence!"[14]

By this time, Monsieur Jaquet's challenge to Soyer had been taken up by *The Lancet*, England's famous medical journal. After making a scientific analysis of Soyer's soup, the journal declared without hesitation or doubt that it was worthless:

The mass of the poor population of Ireland is in a state of starvation. Gaunt famine, with raging fever at her heels, are marching through the length and breadth of the sister island. . . . The British public, under the form of clubs, committees, and relief associations, are actively engaged in sending food to the famine districts. All this is done without boasting or ostentation. But parliament and the executive, in the midst of the best intentions, seem to be agitated by a spasmodic feeling of benevolence; at one time adopting public works, at another preaching a poor law . . . and then descending to M. Soyer, the chief cook of the Reform Club, with his ubiquitous kitchens and soups, at some three farthings the quart, which is to feed all hungry Ireland.

As this soup quackery (for it is no less) seems to be taken by the rich as a salve for their consciences, and with a belief that famine and fever may be kept at bay by M. Soyer and his kettles, it is right to look at the constitution of this soup of pretence, and the estimate formed of it by the talented but eccentric self-deceived originator.

The given proportions of beef, fat, flour, sugar, and water provided, *The Lancet* said,

less than three ounces of solid nutriment to each quart of soup à la Soyer. Of this its inventor is reported to have said to the Government "that a bellyful once a day, with a biscuit, will be more than sufficient to maintain the strength of a strong healthy man!"

To bring this to the test, organic chemistry proves to us that the excretae from the body of a healthy subject by the eliminatory organs must at least amount to twelve or fourteen ounces; and organic chemistry will not, we fear, bend to the most inspired recipes of the most miraculous cookery book, to supply the number of ounces without which the organic chemistry of the human body will no more go on than will the steam-engine without fuel. M. Soyer, supposing each meal of his soup for the poor to amount to a quart, supplies less than three ounces, or less than a quarter the required amount, and of that only one solitary half ounce of animal aliment, diluted, or rather dissolved in a bellyful of water. Bulk of water, the gastronomic may depend, will not make up for the deficiency of solid convertible aliment. No culinary digesting, or stewing, or boiling, can convert four ounces into twelve, unless, indeed, the laws of animal physiology can be unwritten, and some magical power be made to reside in the cap and apron of the cook for substituting fluids in the place of solids, and *aqua pura* in place of solids in the animal economy.

It seems necessary to bring forward these facts, as M. Soyer's coup has inspired the public mind with much satisfaction—a satisfaction which, we venture to say, will never reach the public stomach.

Marquises and lords and ladies may taste the meagre liquid, and pronounce it agreeable to their gustative inclinations; but something more than an agreeable titillation of the palate is required to keep up that manufactory of blood, bone, and muscle which constitutes the "strong healthy man."[15]

Queen Victoria's physician, Sir Henry Marsh, without once mentioning Soyer by name, demolished him thus on the subject of food and health: "Our attention must not be too exclusively directed to soups and other semi-liquid articles of food. These pass away too rapidly from the stomach, are swallowed too hastily, and violate a natural law in superseding the necessity of mastication, and a proper admixture with the salivary secretion. Restricted to such food the carnivora cannot maintain life; nor can man, being half carnivorous, if laboriously employed, long preserve health and strength of food of such character. . . . Food, to be at once sustaining to the labourer, and preventive of disease, must have bulk—must possess solidity—must not be rapidly digestible, and must contain, in varied proportions, all the staminal ingredients of nutriment."[16]

Perhaps nothing during the famine years more appropriately symbolized England's "helping hand" to Ireland than Soyer's Dublin soup kitchen, for it was there, on April 5, 1847, with the beating of drums and the sounding of horns, with the Union Jack proudly flying from the kitchen's smoking chimney and a splendidly attired gentry nodding its approval, that the British government fed the Irish a soup incapable of keeping a newborn cat alive. As one old Gaelic proverb aptly put it: "Beware of the horns of a bull, of the heels of a horse, of the smile of an Englishman."[17]

It was with an English smile that *Punch* again tried to make a joke of the whole thing by saying that M. Soyer had been nicknamed by the Irish "the broth of a boy." In a subsequent issue, the same magazine remarked that "a gentleman of taste, who had dipt rather deeply into M. Soyer's soups, says the Irish would certainly relish the soup all the more if there was a bit of Irish Bull in it."[18]

All the same, when copies of *The Lancet*'s criticism of the soup were distributed and the Queen's physician's opinion of watery soup as a sustaining food got abroad, Soyer decided to resign as "Head cook to the people of Ireland" and return to England. After being given a dinner and a snuff box by the Dublin gentry who had watched the hungry fed on the "gala day," he boarded the first outgoing ship, never to return to the country he had vowed to save. Just before leaving, he published a sixpenny cookbook called *Charitable Cooking or The Poor Man's Regenerator*, in which he said: "It requires more science to produce a good dish at trifling expense than a superior one with unlimited means."[19]

One week after opening his soup kitchen in Dublin, he was back in the more congenial atmosphere of the Reform Club, where he continued to delight his English patrons with "superior dishes made with unlimited means"—that is, with beef, veal, lamb, and pork brought over from Ireland on the same Liverpool steamers whose upper decks were jammed with Irish emigrants.

Shocking as it may seem today, neither Soyer's nonsensical soup, nor *The Lancet*'s criticism of it, nor Queen Victoria's physician's remarks on soup in general did anything to change the famine diet the English offered the Irish. Parliament had passed the Irish Relief Act, the bureaucratic process had been put in operation, and the food to be distributed determined. When the kitchens or distribution centers were built in different parts of Ireland, therefore, the same diet was given daily to those who were certified as having given up all but a quarter-acre of land and as being in danger of perishing from hunger. Appearing on the verge of perishing from hunger was not enough; recipients of outdoor relief had to be certified by the commissioner of the district as having no means of support, no animals to eat or sell, and a potato patch utterly laid to waste by the blight. In addition, all but children under nine years of age and the ill and disabled had to be present to receive the food allotted.[20]

The ration was to consist of one pound of biscuit, meal, or flour; or one quart of soup with a quarter-pound of bread, biscuit, or meal. When bread alone was baked and issued, one and a half pounds were allowed. But since no strict nutritional standards were set, the soup often turned out to be worse than Soyer's—anything, everything, or nothing, depending upon who was in charge at any given location. At one center it might be wholesome, with chunks of meat, vegetables, and rice; at another, thin, almost worthless gruel; at still another, nothing more than greasy water.

"Do you call that soup?" cried one recipient after finishing his allotment. "Why, ye only get a quarter of water and boil it down to a pint to make it stronger."[21]

When something substantial like bread was given along with the soup, the recipient could at least wet and warm the bread by dipping it in the hot liquid. But even then, by coming miles for it the people often expended more energy than the food restored. Then from America came Indian meal, a food new to the Irish, which was boiled in a huge cauldron of salted water, sometimes with rice, until with periodic stirring it thickened and bubbled like hot lava. If eaten daily after being cooked long enough to break down and soften its rough fibrous content, this "stirabout," as the Irish called it, was capable of preserving life, if not health. In 1847, when it became the main substitute for the beloved potato, the English applied to its distribution the "cooked food test" to prevent any abuse of their generosity, which in fact could no more be called "generosity" than a bank loan could be.[22]

For the money expended by the British treasury was not an outright grant to relieve the suffering of a people living under British rule, a people who year after year contributed to the British treasury, but a loan that was to be paid back, with interest, by the same people in later years.[23] In any case, the "cooked food test" and the introduction of stirabout as a substitute for the potato went hand in hand with the vote in Parliament to advance the necessary money to continue building food depots to relieve the distress. The reasoning went this way: first, the pound ration swelled by the absorption of water to three or four pounds; second, it became thick enough when cooked to be easily carried away by the cottier or farm laborer and his family; third and perhaps most important, it turned sour if it was not promptly consumed. Hence it could not be converted into cash by anyone who needed, or thought he needed, tea, tobacco, or whiskey more than he needed the stirabout. Paddy was not likely to apply for it, they decided, if he did not want it for his own consumption.[24]

The system was beneficial to the Irish for reasons never considered by the English, for in their efforts to prevent abuse they did indeed distribute thoroughly cooked Indian meal to the needy. The trouble was that the kitchens were scattered too far and wide for people living in isolated districts to walk every day the many miles to reach them—sometimes to find the stirabout all gone. Niggardly guardians and their aids kept the rations to minimum amounts even after the Board of Health recommended that one pound twelve ounces of Indian meal be given to an adult and a half-pound to a child under twelve years of age.[25]

Many persons waiting on line to receive rations were literally dying of starvation, and in some areas, where guardians struck the poor off the lists for the least reason, it was necessary to appear that starved in order to receive. At Ennistymon, for example, anyone imprudent enough to look healthy was refused and had his ticket taken from him. In one case a woman was struck off the list for giving a few spoonfuls of her ration to the children of her starved brother, who had been struck off the list. She was reinstated only after the magistrate presiding at her dead brother's inquest intervened on her behalf.[26]

At another distribution center, there appeared a miserable skeleton of a man whose distress distinguished his case from the rest. He lived several miles from the center of town, in one of the rural districts, where he found himself on the verge of perishing with his family of seven small children. Making one last effort to save them, he had fastened his youngest child to his back and, with four more by his side, staggered the five miles from home, a hopelessly defeated and maimed athlete of survival, up to the door of the food distribution center. With his beard nearly as long as the hair hanging from his head, his cheeks caved in, his jaw so distended that he could scarcely articulate a word, and his withered left arm close to his side like a man carrying a parcel, he waited patiently for help, hoping it would come but not demanding it.

Meanwhile, his four children sat on the ground by his feet, nestling together, their distended little bellies drooping like half-filled sacks, their shriveled limbs hanging about as if they did not belong to their bodies, their dripping rags as coarse in appearance as horsecloth or sacking. They were children who would never grow up to be men and women, and how they had stood on their feet and walked five miles remained a mystery to all who saw them at the distribution center. One visitor who was there said that "their paleness was not that of common sickness. There was no sallow tinge in it. They did not look as if newly raised from the grave and to life before the blood had begun to fill their veins anew; but as if they had just been thawed out of the ice, in which they had been imbedded until their blood had turned to water."[27]

So many had been starving for so long that when they

were given food—that is to say, an ample amount—the danger
of death actually increased. The body by then could neither
absorb nor assimilate so sudden an intake of the nutrients it
had been craving for so long. Like a shut-down factory suddenly put back into full production, it suffered breakdowns
everywhere. The heart especially could not withstand the
added workload of a sudden increase in the body's metabolic
rate. "Carthy swallowed a little warm milk and died,"[28] was
the simple statement in Skibbereen of one man's death from
starvation. With slight variations as to the kind of food consumed, the same statement might have been made for thousands of deaths in Ireland in 1847.

"If they get any strong dose at all, they die off at once,"
said one man connected with the Quaker Society of Friends.
When asked what he meant by a strong dose, he said, "If they
get a full meal it kills them immediately."[29]

In time, because the distances between food distribution
centers were so great and accidents with the hot liquid so
frequent, the Indian meal from America was also distributed
dry and uncooked, as well as given as wages to those working
on the public works. When these people arrived home with the
dry meal, they were too close to starvation to sit around and
chat while it cooked down to the nutritious porridge it was
meant to be. The hungry children cried, the exhausted father
grew impatient, until they all began dipping their tin mugs
into the half-cooked and only partially digestible stirabout.
Because of their weakened condition and their bodies' sus-
ceptibility to internal abrasion, the rough meal brought on an
irritative diarrhea, which prepared the way for dysentery and
eventually gangrene.

Three years earlier, in the House of Commons, Benjamin
Disraeli offered this opinion of British-ruled Ireland: "A starving population, an absentee aristocracy, an alien church, and
the weakest executive in the world."[30]

Chapter Ten

I have been assured . . . that a young healthy
child well nursed is at a year old a most
delicious, nourishing and wholesome food,
whether stewed, roasted, baked, or boiled, and I
make no doubt that it will equally serve in a
fricassee, or a ragout. . . .

   . . . I grant this food will be somewhat dear,
and therefore very proper for landlords, who, as
they have already devoured most of the parents,
seem to have the best title to the children.

—Jonathan Swift,
A Modest Proposal

IF the first and most pressing problem for the living was how
to remain alive, the second was how to dispose of the dead. For
though there were virtually no births and therefore few infants
less than a year old (pregnant women being too starved and
emaciated to carry, much less feed, a fetus), the deaths from
starvation, typhus, relapsing fever, famine dropsy, scurvy, dysentery, or from combinations of any of them became so frequent and numerous, the dead so common everywhere, that if
the driver of a cart felt a bump at night, he knew he had ridden
over a body stricken on the highway.[1]

Next to food, clothing, and medical help, families stood in
need of coffins, and as they became too expensive to buy, and
then almost impossible to obtain at any price, a sad and hu-
miliating change took place in the way the Irish put their dead
to rest. Before the famine, the poorest farmer believed in and
strove for the credit and respectability attached to a good,
large, well-conducted funeral. Many saved for no other pur-

pose than to have the necessary money to buy a coffin, finance
a wake, engage professional keeners, and hire the horse-drawn
hearse that hundreds would follow on foot to the grave. No
custom was more firmly rooted in Ireland's pagan past or
more resistant to Roman Catholic criticism. The priests had
always inveighed against the more obvious excesses of an old-
fashioned Irish wake—the mock marriages among children,
the sexual exhibitionism, and the drunkenness—but with only
limited success. In Ireland the pagan and Christian rituals had
become so intertwined as to be inseparable.[2]

About the importance of a coffin, however, there was no
argument from either side. In everyone's eyes the coffin represented the dead person's ultimate seclusion, his final and inviolable private room. To be without one at the end was to
lose respect and to cast shame on those you left behind. It was
so important that in 1847, when deaths outnumbered burials
and unburied bodies began to accumulate, relatives of the
dead pulled old family chests apart to make coffins. When the
chests were gone and the people kept dying, tables and boats
were torn apart, warped coffin boards were stolen from old
graveyards. In Armagh, County Tyrone, where people knew
the art of basketry, basket coffins were made for the dead
when wood became unobtainable. In other districts the dead
were wrapped by their relatives in sheets, sacking, or straw
mats or in barrel staves bound up with straw ropes. One
woman brought her wasted dead husband, wrapped in a sheet,
on her back to Kilsarcon churchyard to be buried. The edges
of the sheet were held together by "scannans," thin bogdeal
spars worked in and out through the edges of the sheet.[3]

Finally, a new kind of reusable coffin, called a "trap
coffin," came into use. Built sturdy enough to withstand the
wear and tear of hundreds of funerals, it was fitted with a
hinged bottom that swung open like a trap door when released
at the graveyard, whereby the dead person was dropped into
the grave. The man who owned it also owned the horse and
cart that carried the dead person to the graveyard. He made
several trips a day, always with the same coffin and often to

the same grave, which was filled with as many as six bodies, the topmost one being very close to ground level, before the grave was closed and covered over. This explains why starving dogs, so starved that they could no longer even bark, raided graveyards at night and why one famine graveyard in Cashel, County Tipperary, was later, after the turn of the century, barbarously and contemptuously called "The Shank Yard."[4]

As the manner and means of burial became uppermost in everyone's mind, some starving and exhausted people, knowing they had a short time to live, sought admittance to the poorhouse. They wanted not so much aid as the coffin and decent burial that their families and friends could not afford them. Others, not so desperate but expecting a death in the family, rushed to the carpenter's and ordered a coffin ahead of time for fear there would be no lumber left when the death occurred.

"In every village the manufacture was remarkable at the doors of the carpenters' houses, and in the country parts I often met coffins, and boards for making coffins, carried on the backs of women," wrote the Reverend F. F. Trench in a letter dated 1847. "At Glengariff, the Roman Catholic Chapel is turned into a place for making coffins. . . . I entered . . . and said to one of the carpenters, 'What are you making boys?' 'Coffins and wheelbarrows, Sir.' "[5]

Funerals became as common as changes in the weather; they went unnoticed, were seldom attended. In churchyards where years before a hundred people would attend a burial, lonely, emaciated survivors dug scarcely deeper for burying their dead than they would for planting potatoes. Even in the few areas where wood was still available, the coffin itself came to be hastily and carelessly built. A carpenter who earlier had spent a week building a coffin with dovetail corners and an inlaid lid was now making eight to ten raw-wood coffins a day. It was as if all the bonds of natural affection and respect were loosening under the pressure of incessant death and burial—as if the entire population were being forced to load and unload some macabre carrousel that refused to stop turning.

One eyewitness reported that in County Cork "a hearse piled with coffins—or rather undressed boards, slightly nailed together, passed through the streets, unaccompanied by a single human being, save the driver of the vehicle."[6]

In Galway another resident said, "Coffins are to be seen carried in every direction, so that to number the dead is now gone beyond possibility; a general consternation has seized everyone."[7]

But not everyone ended with a funeral, even an unattended one, much less with a coffin. If a husband of a woman died and she induced relatives or friends to bury him, and then days or weeks later the relatives or friends died, and then finally she died, who was to coffin and bury her? Such was the case in many parishes where destitution and disease wiped out hundreds in weeks, where indeed there was no official burial procedure to prevent the spread of disease and reduce the number of deaths.[8]

"On Wednesday the body of a poor woman was found dead in a field adjoining the town of Castlebar," a resident reported on May 12, 1847. "A child belonging to the deceased had piled some stones around the body to protect it from the dogs and rats."[9]

The men who spent their days carrying the sick, the dying, and the dead in their horse- or donkey-drawn carts were callous by nature as well as from practice. Remembered to this day with hatred and contempt, they were paid so much a body by the local authorities, and their routes were usually the same every day: first with the sick to the fever or workhouse hospital, then with the dead from the hospital to the cemetery. One such driver, according to an old resident in Ballina, was nicknamed "Sack-em-up" because of the way he handled those he took to the hospital. The patient was put in a sack, feet first, and the sack was tied closely around the neck and labeled. Up to seven or eight patients were laid out in the body of the cart, which then set off on its bumpy journey to the workhouse hospital. Few ever returned. But the cart did not return empty, for at the hospital the coffins were already tenanted and nailed down, and when a coffin was not available, the corpse was sewn in white cloth—ready for the driver to carry to the graveyard. In most cases the relatives were not even notified of the deaths.[10]

One driver became infamously known as "Paddy the Puncher" when stories circulated about his treatment of the dead and dying. As one person put it: "He would dispatch to eternity those poor people who were at death's door. He received so much per body, and consequently his whole interest lay in the number of his burials." The same person said that another driver, who found himself one morning with no dead bodies to take to the cemetery, "went around to the fever hospital to see if there were any dying or likely to die. He saw one person in a very poor state and asked the attendants to release him on the grounds that the dying man would be dead before he reached the graveyard."[11]

There was also the story of the driver who was only temporarily nonplused when the "corpse" he was trying to bury protested, at the graveyard, in a barely audible voice, that he was still alive. The driver regained his composure as quickly as he realized that the man had been declared dead at the hospital from which he'd taken him. In the driver's eyes this made the burial legal and proper, an assignment he had the right and responsibility to complete. Besides, the man was dying; he was close to death and would certainly be dead by the time they returned to the hospital. So the driver buried him anyway and collected his fee.[12]

Another story told of a man who was still alive enough and strong enough to refuse to be buried, and who for years after the famine publicly castigated the man who had tried to bury him.[13] In County Cork there were two accounts of the boy who was to be buried with several corpses in a pit in the Abbey graveyard outside Skibbereen. The gravedigger's spade broke the boy's legs before he cried out and was found to be alive. After the famine he became a living legend to the people of West Cork, whose ancestors to this day talk of his crooked legs and the verse honoring him that begins:

I arose from the dead in the year '48
Though a grave in the Abbey had near been my fate . . .[14]

James Mahony of Cork, an artist commissioned by the *Illustrated London News* to draw sketches of conditions in
Skibbereen, said that "All sympathy between the living and the
dead seems completely out of the question; and the revolting
practice will, doubtless, go on until it works its own remedy . . .
so hardened are the men regularly employed in the removal
of the dead that I saw one of them, with four coffins in a car,
driving to the churchyard, sitting upon one of them and smoking with much apparent enjoyment. . . ."[15]

In Skibbereen, when the coffins ran out and whole families continued to die, monster graves, called by the people "the
pits," were dug in the churchyard of Abbeystrowry. The dead
were dropped coffinless, without mourning or ceremony, into
these pits in the middle of the night by relatives trying both to
elude observation and to be present the next day at the public
works—their only means of obtaining the money or food to
survive. So many were buried in this way that the dead bodies,
like some monstrous produce of the place, became hard to
distinguish. Each pit was kept open for days, sometimes for as
long as a week. The corpses arrived one by one, and as each
was laid in the pit, the only thing resembling interment was a
sprinkling of sawdust over the body. Then came another
corpse and a fresh sprinkling of sawdust, until the pit received
its full complement of tenants and was covered over with dirt.
In a year and a half, a whole generation of Skibbereen's people
was buried in these pits in the churchyard of Abbeystrowry, a
place where today a visitor enters, becomes rapt in its lonely
seclusion, and thinks with sorrow and indignation of its dark
and terrible history.[16]

In the more remote parts of Ireland, the bodies of the
dead were too filthy and diseased, their stench too disgusting,
and their faces too often ravaged by starving dogs and rats for
strangers among the living to treat them with respect, much
less to care whether they were taken to the nearest graveyard.

In most cases they were buried beside the road where they lay or dragged to nearby ditches and covered with brambles and stones. A young man named Stephen Regen, in Kenmore, County Kerry, one day met a dog dragging along a child's head. After a struggle he took the head from the dog, buried it, and set a heavy rock over it. The family to whom the child belonged was getting outdoor relief for the child and for that reason did not report its death.[17]

When a whole family died in its thatched hut and the diseased bodies were discovered, burial was effected simply by knocking the cabin down over them and setting it afire. Only when a dead person had a living relative dedicated and strong enough to carry, drag, or cart the body to the graveyard was he or she buried in the consecrated ground that every Irish Catholic hoped would be his or her final resting place.

A woman named Mrs. Thomas O'Brien, who was seventy-one years old when she was interviewed in Kilworth in 1945, told this story of death and burial:

My grandfather was at work cutting wheat and my grandmother was with him binding. My mother was a young girl at the time [1847], and she was with them in the field. They saw the man coming along the road—Scannlon was his name—and a load on his back. My grandmother asked him what had he there, and he said t'was his wife that was dead and he was taking her to Leitrum graveyard to bury her. He had her sitting on a board fastened over his shoulders, and she was dressed in her cloak and hood just as she'd be when she was alive. His little son was with him. My grandmother went into the house and brought them food and milk. Scannlon would't take anything; he said it would overcome him and he wanted to have his wife buried before the dark. The little boy drank the milk.

Everytime my mother would talk about that she'd cry.[18]

Those too weak to carry their dead to the grave tried other means. The dispensary physician of the parish of Kilmore, Dr. McCormick, told of seeing a man tottering along the road with a rope over his shoulder and at the other end of the rope, streaking the ground, the bodies of his two dead children. The man, held upright as much by the strain on the rope as by his own strength, was with difficulty dragging them to the grave.[19]

But this man was extraordinary, one of the few who somehow found determination in the few hours of life left to him. Most were too empty and weak to care whether they were buried or left lying where they died. They had already lost the ability to experience regret, to think of past pleasure, to long for relief of their distress, or even to try, much less wish they could try, to bury the dead child lying next to them on filthy straw strewn with feces and saturated with blood from their own uncontrollable dysentery. In those thatched huts and mud cabins, whose stench from death, disease, and excrement burned like phosphorus in their nostrils, the famished Irish experienced a hell destined not by God but by the British government's willingness to lay the blame for that hell on God.

In those days it was acceptable to turn to the hand of Providence as the possible explanation of great human catastrophes. No one accused England of causing the potato rot. But English, French, and American visitors to Ireland, and some members of Parliament as well, did accuse the English government, with justification in the light of what is now known, of supercilious and even criminal neglect of millions of starving people less than two days' sailing time from English ports, many of which were filled with food taken from Ireland in British ships.

This one last story, corroborated in a courtroom in Ireland, perhaps suggests the depths to which the Irish were driven during the famine—the same depths that a century and a half earlier led a still-renowned Irishman, Jonathan Swift, to suggest, in a brilliant satire called A Modest Proposal, roast baby as the only humane alternative to Ireland's food problem. In Belmullet, County Cork, a starving woman lay in her hovel next to her dead three-year-old son, waiting for her husband to return from begging food. When night fell and his failure to return led her to imagine him dead in a ditch, she lay there in the faint light of the fire's dying embers, caressing with her eyes her dead son's face and his tiny fists, clenched as if for a fight to get into heaven. Then slowly, with death searching her, and now with her own fists clenched, she made one last effort to remain alive. Crawling as far away from her son's face as she could, as if to preserve his personality or at least her memory of it, she came to his bare feet and proceeded to eat them.

When her husband returned and saw what had happened, he buried the child, went out, and was caught trying to steal food. At his trial, the magistrate from his immediate district intervened on his behalf, citing the wife's act as a circumstance deserving special consideration. The baby's body was exhumed, the flesh of both its feet and legs found to have been gnawed to the bone, and the husband released and allowed to return to his wife.[20]

It was time, it was long past time, to get out of Ireland. But the British Empire had its fingers everywhere—in every continent and on most of the stepping-stone islands in between. But there was one exception, one enormous exception: the United States of America.

II

Escape

Chapter Eleven

. . . It was just like a big funeral . . . and the last parting . . . was indeed sad to see. . . . The parents especially were so sad, as if the person leaving were really dead. . . . You would rather not be there at all if you would be any way soft yourself.

—Manuscript 1411, Irish Folklore Department, University College, Dublin

THE Irishman's love of his homeland and of the Irish way of life, despite the hardships imposed by the misbegotten union with Britain in 1800, had always, until the famine, limited emigration. The peasant's desperate hold upon his land, his passion for survival at home, his love of the Gaelic language, and his fear of puritan America's hostility to Catholicism had created a kind of psychological moat confining him to Ireland. But emigration had been used in the past as a remedy for hard times by adventurous Irishmen whose imagination had been fired by stories of America, by letters from emigrants who rode their own horses and spoke of being so far west in America that they had to crouch to let the sun go down.

"I wish to heaven all our countrymen were here," wrote one such emigrant from the Chicago area. ". . . The labourer can earn as much in one day as will support him for a week. The richest land in the world may be purchased here or in Wisconsin for $1.25 an acre—equal to 5s 3d sterling—pure alluvial soil, over 30 feet of surface. . . . If I could show them the splendid prairie I am looking on, extending in wild luxuriant verdure far as the eye can reach—virgin soil that will stand the wear and tear of ages without requiring a shovel full of manure—how different would their situation be from what it is! How gladly they would fly with their families! . . ."[1]

Such letters had always, even in good times, induced some Irishmen to emigrate. Indeed, long before the famine, many Anglo-Irish landlords, given the eviction rights at their disposal, had done their best to turn the country into a kind of nursery for raising humans for export. But never before had so many been swept by the same impulse at the same time. Now, with the worst famine in recorded history far outstripping Britain's lame efforts to mitigate its effects, thousands saw emigration as the only remedy. No longer was it a question of whether to go, but of when and how to leave.

People on their way to ports where outgoing ships lay at anchor were reluctant even to linger with relatives and friends, knowing that any expression of affection or loss would only weaken their resolve to leave before it was too late. Hope was before them, nothing was behind them but the misery they were leaving. Their kinships, ties, songs, dances, fairies, leprechauns, and wakes would come back to them later, with powerful impact and special significance, in terms of their lives as a whole. Many did not know it then, but with them also went a terrible bitterness and sense of wrong: the memory of a protracted, seemingly endless struggle against blighted harvests, increasing taxation, and rack-rents that rose inexorably every time a man tried to improve himself and his family by working harder; the witnessing of death by starvation, of long lines of people waiting for the flavored hot water that Monsieur Soyer called soup, of evictions of entire families, some with sick children, in the middle of winter; the sight of carts hauling foodstuffs bound for England through villages reeking with death. None would ever doubt or stop proclaiming (no matter where in America they finally settled) that under the shade of England's laws and her administration of them famine had been the chief crop.

But tens of thousands were too poor to afford passage, too weak from starvation to reach embarkation points, or too far gone with disease to be allowed on board even if they had the passage money. At least fifty thousand of the almost quarter of a million who fled in 1847 were those the country could least afford to lose—the moderately successful farming families whose parents wanted their children to have a chance at life in America. Although in rare cases an entire family tried to make a bargain and go "for the whole in a lump" on the same ship, most families were forced to separate, in many cases permanently, because of grandparents too old to travel, parents emotionally incapable of leaving Ireland, or—the most common reason—lack of money.

If a family could raise only enough money for one passage, the ticket would be bought in the name of the eldest son or daughter. When that son or daughter arrived in America and got a job, money would be sent back to Ireland to help the family pay the rent and eventually to buy another passage ticket for a younger brother or sister. This remittance system of "one bringing another" was to become so firmly rooted on both sides of the Atlantic that sister would follow brother, and brother sister, until the children of an entire family were reunited in America. Because of the peculiar strength of Irish family relationships, one newspaper used Goldsmith's Traveller, who "drags at each remove a lengthening chain," as a symbol of the Irish emigrant. "But the emigrant's chain does not draw him back," the paper went on, "but pulls forward those he has left behind."[2]

The days leading up to the departure of a family's oldest child put a terrible strain not only on the parents and the one leaving but on all the other children as well. The parents knew they would never see their eldest again, the younger children hoped they would, either in America or, later, in Ireland, after their parents died. Meanwhile, the emigrant suffered through a torturous push and pull. Pushed by the fear of hunger and poverty out of the country, away from his family, friends, everything he knew and loved, he was also pulled by the uncertain hope of plenty to a strange land where he had no

family, friends, or ties and where no one spoke Gaelic. If he
was also leaving behind a girl he loved and wanted to marry,
the torture leading up to his departure became almost unbear-
able.

All sorts of subterfuges were used to ensure the continuing
love of the emigrant until his return to Ireland or his sweetheart's joining him in America. A few strands of the girl's pubic
hair would be surreptitiously cut during the night by the sister
with whom she slept and sewn into the garment of the young
emigrant about to depart for America. Or if the one leaving
was a young lady, the man she was leaving behind would
often bribe or otherwise induce an intimate or sister to procure
his loved's one's pubic hair, which he kept as a love charm,
sometimes wearing it on his genitals, to ensure her virginity.
One rustic midwife said she made a love charm for any girl
whose sweetheart was going into emigration by taking the
"seed" (menstrual fluid) of the girl, staining a small piece of
linen with it, and having the linen secretly sewn into the garment of the emigrant. His love would thereby be made constant until she emigrated and joined him in America.[3]

There were many songs written and sung to com-
memorate those painful separations. One was called "A Youth
and an Irish Maid":

I

As I roved out one evening
In the summer time,
To view the fields and meadows,
All nature seemed delight.
The thrushes and the blackbirds' notes
Invited and I stayed,
To hear the conversation
Of a youth and an Irish maid.

II

The young man broke the silence first
And to his love did say:

Oh Molly, lovely Molly
No longer can I stay.
For the ship is waiting at Queenstown
And her anchor now is weighed.
But where I be I'll think of thee
My lovely Irish maid.

III

When you go o'er to Yankee shore
Some Yankee girls you'll see.
They'll all look very handsome
And you'll think no more of me:
You'll forget the vows and promises
That you to me have made
You'll forget them all you left behind
And your lovely Irish maid.

IV

When I go o'er to Yankee shore
Some Yankee girls I'll see,
And they'll all look very handsome
But to remind me still of thee;
For there's not a flower or a shady bower
Or a place where we have strayed,
Wherever I be I'll think of thee
My lovely Irish maid.

V

These two fond hearts together drew
Into a last embrace,
And tears like falling dew drops
Came rolling down each face;
"There is not a day while you're away
But I'll visit this dark cool shade
Where first you stole away the heart
Of your lovely Irish maid."[4]

On the night before the departing one was scheduled to make
the trip to port and board ship, the family held what later

became known as an "American wake," a custom unique to Ireland. Although practiced as early as 1830, when emigration was uncommon if not unheard of, it did not become widespread until the vast exodus of the late 1840s and early 1850s, when the country lost through emigration almost what it had lost through starvation and disease.

The practice was a natural extension of Ireland's pagan-derived ritual of "waking" the dead: watching over the dead person during the night prior to burial to prevent evil spirits from entering the body. Since departure was a kind of death, especially during sailing-ship days when a voyage across the ocean lasted two to three months and the prospect of a return voyage was beyond imagining, the emigration ceremony was inevitably associated with waking the dead. Indeed, if birth, marriage, death, and burial were the four most important events in Ireland's peasant society, the American wake would have to be ranked a close fifth. It even took on the elements of all four, though not in the same order: death was departure; burial, the boarding of the ship that sealed for life the separation; birth, the emigrant's arrival in America; and marriage, the subsequent letters sent back and forth across the ocean.

Although the ceremony itself was substantially the same throughout Ireland, the name for it differed in some counties. In parts of Galway it was called the "farewell supper"; in Mayo, the old people referred to it in Gaelic as the "feast of departure"; in Kilkenny and Tipperary it was unflinchingly called a "live wake"; in Antrim and Derry, a "convoy"; and to those in Donegal who had not taken Father Mathew's pledge, it was known as an "American bottle night" or a "bottle drink." But the generic term became "American wake" as the custom became more similarly structured and practiced throughout the country.[5]

During the week preceding his departure, the emigrant would make calls throughout the parish and beyond to inform his friends and neighbors of his intentions. In every cabin, cottage, or farmhouse visited, there would be a minor tempest of regrets, blessings, and good wishes, followed by questions about departure time, embarkation port, and where in America the emigrant's ship was headed. Sandwiched in all this talk and hubbub was an invitation to attend the American wake at the home of the emigrant's parents on the night before he was scheduled to leave. Those invited were not obliged to attend, but almost all did, just as they attended funerals. It was something like a point of honor, and those absent without good reason would receive the same response when one of their own died or went to America. As one old Irishman remarked, "In those days, people made very little difference between going to America and going to the grave."[6]

In the famine year of 1847, very few families could afford the kind of American wake that included dancing and ballad singing, festivity, drinking, eating, and ribaldry. With no food, drink, or tobacco to share, the American wake became an evening spent in somber discussion of the United States, a sharing of opinion about emigration, an exchange of hints and warnings from those who had already arrived, and a final giving of advice by the old to the youth leaving, along with letters he was to deliver personally or mail from New York or Boston to previous emigrants who had arrived safely.

But in every district there were a few modestly successful farming families who could afford to give their departing child a real American wake, and other families were proud or rash enough, given the importance and finality of emigration, to finance the affair "on tick"—that is, on credit. "Long ago you had to get a whole lot of things on tick," explained one man whose father had been through the experience. "And we'll say you did not pay for three or four months, then you had to pay more than the price of the stuff. Interest, the shopmen called it. Well then, if you got money from America you would be sure to pay off all debts like that at once, for every day it was costing you more."[7]

In most cases, the debts incurred by a family's holding an American wake could not be paid until the money came from America, from the very emigrant who had been waked before his departure. The emigrant accepted this responsibility and

lived up to it as quickly as possible, knowing that every day
lost added to the cost. He considered the hardship suffered in-
significant compared with the honor bestowed and the memories won.

The basic elements necessary for a successful American
wake were those that had for generations enmeshed the par-
ticipants in their parish and village way of life—neighborli-
ness, friendship, respect, warmth, reminiscence, dancing, singing, food, liquor, and a shared feeling of loss and regret at the
permanent departure of a loved one. Clay pipes and plenty of
tobacco, a luxury reserved for the most important functions,
were offered to the men and women. The tobacco was bought
in town for a penny a "finger," the measure being the middle
finger of the right hand from the tip to the third knuckle, and
any wake deserving the name saw many "fingers" consumed
before the night was over.[8] If there were more guests than
pipes, man and wife would share one or the packed and
lighted pipes would be passed around. In those days in Ireland
smoking was prevalent among the older women, who found
solace in the habit in their declining years. One grandmother,
asked when she first took to the pipe, replied, "I tuk to it as a
bit of divarshion after me poor old man was tucked under the
daisies. A better husband niver lived."[9]

Whether the liquor served was "Big Still" (shop whiskey),
or poteen, a clear and highly potent spirit distilled illegally
but extensively from potatoes, it was neither expected nor
offered during the early hours of the wake, when those who
could gave the emigrant contributions to his sea stock of provisions—a box of hard-boiled eggs, some crocked butter, or a
supply of rye or oatmeal patties dried and hardened to last but
still tasty and nutritious when dipped and softened in a cup of
hot tea. A close relative might present him with a few loaves of
"frog bread," made by killing, roasting, and pulverizing an
ordinary frog and mixing the powder in with the bread dough.
By eating this frog bread during the voyage, the emigrant, it
was believed, would be immunized against fever.[10]

In Ireland, where fairies, banshees, and leprechauns were part and parcel of everyone's imagination, where the people were highly emotional and addicted to superstition, there were many such beliefs. Another common one held that anyone born with a caul (the fetal membrane that sometimes covers the head of an infant at birth) would be forever safe from drowning. This belief, apparently based on the caul's protection of the embryo in the watery world of the womb during pregnancy, gradually led in the mind of the Irish peasant to an extension of the caul's powers. When an infant was born with one, it was carefully removed, and if a family attending an American wake had had a child born with a caul, the lucky emigrant might be asked if he would like to borrow it for the voyage. The emigrant, who had no doubt been searching the parish for one, would accept with great appreciation, embrace the child whose caul it was, and promise to return it to the family posthaste for someone else to use.[11]

Guests who could not afford to give the emigrant material gifts gave verbal ones. An arriving guest, for example, might address him—adding the affectionate "-een" to his Christian name—with "When you reach America, Mikeen, may the devil fly away with the roof of the house where you're not welcome."[12]

The evening started quietly, with peasant stories made up by and for peasants, stories from an endless repertoire that was added to and handed down by each succeeding generation. Some dealt with the mysteries of the Christian faith in a reverent but playful way, as though the author were trying to explain one of the more abstruse mysteries to himself:

> Three folds in my garment,
> Yet only one garment I bear,
> Three joints in a finger,
> Yet only one finger is there,
> Three leaves in a shamrock,
> Yet only one shamrock I wear,
> Frost, ice, and snow,

These are nothing but water.
Three persons in God,
Yet only one God is there.[13]

Others touched upon the Irish peasant's sometimes critical attitude toward the Church's abiding interest in wealth and material possessions: "There was a priest in the chapel one day, and there came in a young, fine-looking, well-combed man and stood at the door. 'You sleek lad yonder,' says the priest, 'come here till I see have you your Christian Doctrine. Tell me how many deadly sins there are in it.' 'Six,' says he. 'Musha, there were seven in it last year,' says the priest. 'There were,' says he, 'but now we leave covetousness to the church.' "[14]

These stories would gradually lead to the main topic of conversation: the United States and that country's inexhaustible wealth. A man would say that he had heard of a river so full of fish in upstate New York that "if you were to boil the water you'd take out of it, you'd be getting the taste of salmon in your tea." Going one better, a woman guest from another parish would tell of two men who left her village and went to New York. "When they landed in that city and were walking up the docks from the boat, one of them saw a sovereign lying on the ground. He was bending down to pick it up when his companion caught him by the arm and said, 'Not at all, John, don't bother with one. Come on to the heap.' "[15]

Along with these imaginative concoctions about America's riches, there were true anecdotes about the mishaps and good fortunes of previous emigrants. For example, the nephew of a woman who had emigrated to the state of Delaware told this story:

I have an aunt Biddy, a sister of my father's, and herself and Mary-in-Jacks, a Callaghan girl, went to work in a big house in Wilmington. Every winter the man and woman who own the big house went down to Florida for two or three months, and when they left there was nobody in the house except Aunt Biddy and Mary-in-Jacks. They were setting at the fire one night talking about old times when they heard a noise at one of the windows. They were frightened, for they knew it was a burglar and, as the house was off by itself, they could get no help. Then my aunt said to Mary, "Do you know what we'll do? We'll sing a song, and let on to him that we are not a bit frightened."

At that the both of them started, and though Mary-in-Jacks could not sing a note, she kept chiming in. . . . Suddenly the noise at the window stopped and they could hear the man going back down the ladder. . . .

A few days after that they got a postcard delivered to the house. It was from the burglar, who said that the song they were singing was the song his mother had sung to him back home in Ireland. . . . When he heard the song and was reminded of his mother, he could not go on with [the robbery]. It must have been God put the old song in their heads, for there's no knowing what that man would have done, maybe even killed them.[16]

Then perhaps a girl would pass around a photograph of her older sister, who had found a situation in New York, earning what to the guests were unheard-of wages. In the photograph, a daguerreotype very popular in America at the time, Noreen, the older sister, is wearing a large hat swept round with feathers, a flowing gown worthy of a queen, a fur boa around her neck, and slippers whose severely pointed toes peep from beneath the gown. On her wrist is a bracelet, which everyone agrees must be gold.

The older people shake their heads in wonder and doubt at so rapid a transformation from the Noreen they knew to the one in the photograph. Gone only a year, she now looks like someone who would not set foot in the parish, let alone the cabin where she was born. Cathy, Noreen's sister, senses the faint disapproval and says, "Sure, a year in America would speed us all up."

But the elders have not yet accepted speed as one of life's ideals; having lived their lives with the vicissitudes of nature rather than with bosses and clocks, they relate time to social activity and seasonal change, both of which determine its value and set its pace. A summer twilight is not announced by the hands of a clock but by "the time when the dew is thinking of falling." With nature telling them pretty accurately what time of day it is, they seldom if ever look at a clock. Besides, they are too old now to change, so they continue to sigh and shake their heads, as committed to their side of the confrontation as Cathy is to hers.

"I say nothing against America," declares an elderly man who has just returned from Boston. "Why should I? For well enough I did while there. I don't deny but it's a fine life, but there are things you earn too hard. Men get better wages, true; but they earn it harder and spend it faster. It's better to have a minute or two now and then to yourself, and time to be sitting down even if it's to put your feet beside the burning turf, than to be going from morning till night. I'd rather have a little peace than all the money I might earn there. Sure, money's a needed thing, but it's not everything."

Emboldened by this speech, another old man says, "All the world knows that Yankee hates Paddy."

This further arouses Cathy, who cannot wait to receive her passage money to emigrate, who no longer looks upon America as a foreign country but as one capable of making Ireland one of its states. "Isn't it better to be looking as Noreen does now," she asks, "than to be slobbering barefoot through the mud with a tub of turnips for the pigs? Let people say what they think proper, but America is going to be one of the greatest countries in the world. The bowing and scraping and making a god of the landlord, *Yes, your Honor, No, your Honor*—that's all played out over there. The mayor and the city sweep get the same amount of respect. If you put your hand to your hat to a man you'd be the laugh of the neighborhood, or stand a chance of being put in the newspapers. I tell you, America is going to lift up the poor man and woman and put them on a level with the so-called gentlemen and ladies. And as Noreen keeps saying from New York, 'The younger you are when you get here, the better.'"

"Sure, that one loves her youth," whispers one old woman to another.

"And so do I, old as I am," says her friend. "Just as she will, again, one day."

The two old women have been through the gamut of time and want to be young again, not as Cathy is young, but as they were once young. For it is their own youth in Ireland that they remember, talk about, and every day relive, not the ever-present but remote youth she represents. Cathy, on her side, does not want to be old and finds it hard to believe she ever will be. All the same, she is as linked to them as birth is to death—as daunted by what faces her in America as they are by being too old now to forsake Ireland. There is no real envy or animosity between them. The aged even find room to pity her inability to recall and share all the triumphant, sad, meaningful, and exquisite experiences of the long-gone past. They are close to the end of the road and they know it, so while she continues to defend her point of view, never realizing that she is taking part in what for her will fifty years later in America be a memorable experience, they continue to shelter their youth as carefully as they do their senescence. Still possessing the capabilities of youth—love, tenderness, warmth, friendship, even sex—they are cautioned in the presence of youth to keep their true impulses a secret if only to protect themselves from disbelief or even ridicule.

Everyone had something to say about America, most of it based on letters received from relatives living in the United States. But given the Irishman's facility of speech, his fatal desire to please, and his ability to embellish, alter, and distort, an actual letter from America, raised high like a prize at the American wake, then reopened for the hundredth time as though the envelope were as precious as its contents and finally read aloud, was considered more authentic and reliable. No doubt the letter would contain ornamental details of its own, but these would at least be coming directly from America, unadorned by a second or third party.

It was from the actual letters that the listeners gleaned

such comments as "No female that can handle a needle need be idle," "A man is a man if he's willing to toil," "If some of our hardy men were here . . . what a fortune would be open to them," "Every man is his own landlord in this country—'Jack is as good as his Master.'" And finally, from a moderately successful emigrant: "America is a country for every man of energy and industry to rise to respectability and independence in."[17]

From the letters, stories, and talk developed the overwhelming consensus that the United States was "the mainstay and the hope" of the Irish people, a "ready-made Republic" where they would pay no tithe to an alien church, cultivate the soil without paying rent, earn high wages without being servants, and have a stake as voting citizens in the country of their choice. But given the famine conditions under which they were living, the most powerful and appealing attraction was the money paid for the work done. Freedom and citizenship would come later, when they found the time and strength to think of something other than survival.

The older guests could see that Ireland was on its way to becoming "one vast American Wake," as one journal was to put it,[18] that the qualities they had lived by were not those behind the impetus to emigrate. The famine had destroyed the communal spirit that had kept families living in the same place next to the same neighbors for generations. People from the same parish were not pooling their resources and emigrating together; they were doing so separately, sometimes even secretly. Every unmarried youth was out for himself in his quest for the high wages America offered; every married man was out for himself and his immediate dependents. Neither would forget those he was leaving behind, but in his determination to reach his goal he exhibited an individualism until then unknown in the communal life of the Irish peasant.

Just witnessing Cathy's eagerness to leave Ireland provoked in the elderly a certain resentment toward the country she was trying to reach. With their own peasant world crumbling, their most ancient and long-cherished customs disregarded, their children and grandchildren leaving, and their burial in Irish soil not too far off, they began to look upon their lives as a total loss, upon the values they had lived by as no longer useful even to those staying. A great social watershed, which they could neither define nor fathom, was in some crucial way dividing their lives from the lives of their children. The young, driven from the land in Ireland, would have little or nothing to do with the land in America; they would become city dwellers, while in Ireland the donkey and the goat, symbols of poverty, would come to be neglected and in some areas despised. Even the gifts of nature so essential in helping the poor survive the famine—the wild berries, the cresses, and the edible seaweed and fungi, the ubiquitous eel, hare, and rabbit—would be shunned for the painful memories attached to them.

The famine, the exodus, and the changes both were bringing about soured the elders' memories, set them to wondering about what they had thought were eternal verities, robbed them in many ways of their past. Brought up to believe that the past never dies, that it lives on buried in the minds of men, they could see that it was doomed to disappear in the aftermath of this terrible calamity. If only they had died before this beginning of the end of their era, they would not have lost that sense of continuity, which would now forever elude them.

It was no wonder that the American wake brought so many conflicting emotions into play, for if departure was a kind of death, so was being left with the conviction that your country and your way of life were finished. The liquor and the gregarious nature of the Irish helped bring to the surface these emotions. One person would cry for some private reason with a friend; another would express openly, tearfully, his or her thoughts on the country's plight. The evening gradually became cathartic for everyone except the intending emigrant and the members of his family, who knew that every hour passed brought the moment of permanent separation nearer. Like a man attending his own funeral, the emigrant seemed to be trying more and more desperately to relate what was happening to him to something habitual in the past that his imagination might at least pursue. He knew he was alive and looked the same, but the guests kept treating him with the respect and consideration reserved for someone lying in a coffin. As the night wore on, his relationship with these people, with his own parents, brothers, and sisters, became faultless, even ideal, for being in the very process of ceasing to exist.

"It was a wake in every sense of the word," an old native of County Mayo recalled, "though not of a dead person, but of a living one, who next day would be sailing for the promised land."[19]

Finally, at three or four in the morning, as if concentrating in one act the love, sorrow, and loss everyone was feeling, the emigrant's father would stand and say, "Get up here, son, and face me in a step, for likely it will be the last step ever we'll dance."[20]

As father and son faced each other, arms akimbo, legs springing in triple rhythm, each one trying as never before to make it a jig to remember, there would not be a dry eye in the house. The partnership they expressed in their timing, the ascendancy of their concentration over their sorrow, and the note of courage and hope in their exuberance, brought what everyone was feeling to the surface and broke down all restraints. It was this shuffling of festivity and sadness that heightened the importance of an American wake, for the combined pleasures of song, dance, and melancholy were nowhere so appreciated as in Ireland, a country whose people had centuries of oppression behind them and no reason for hope in the future. Joy, however intense, was never separated by more than a membrane from the memory of misery and never more than a glance from misery's continuing reality. The American wake was an interchange of conflicting emotions, a time when happiness and sadness, hope and defeat, passed to and fro as through a beaded curtain.

If the family had invited a professional keener, an old woman of the parish noted for her ability to wail and lament, she would wait until father and son had finished, then, swift as a witch, drawing on the emotion generated by their dance, start keening over the "dead" person—the emigrant. With prolonged wails that carried the guests back through time to the days when their pagan ancestors were faced with the mystery of death, she would expound on the virtues of the person leaving, on the suffering both he and his parents were undergoing. Whether or not she felt or believed what she was saying, the mournful effect of her high-pitched lament, similar to that of one of Shakespeare's witches, took hold of everyone present. Her extravagances of voice and movement dissipated overcharged tensions, brought to mind ancestral spirits, and helped keep alive, at least for a time, one of Ireland's oldest customs. Long before she was through bemoaning the loss of the "dead" one, the women guests, along with their weeping husbands, joined her in a chorus bereft of inhibition—a chorus so elemental and infectious that the emigrant's parents, and at last the emigrant himself, joined in.

It was a harrowing experience, and everyone showed its effects in the light of dawn, when the guests stepped outside to allow the departing son to bid his parents his last farewell in private. The parents did not want to embarrass their son; they tried, in fact, to appear calm, but this was the end of the American wake, the closing of the coffin, and as the seconds passed, a kind of family torment webbed the air and made it hard to breathe.

"Be sure and write, lad, as soon as you can," the father would say, rather than wait speechless for the inevitable.

"I will, Da. You can rest on that."

"Did you pack your . . . ?" the mother would add. She had worn her husband's jacket during childbirth in the Irish belief that he would thereby bear some of the pain. Whether or not he did then, they were both bearing equally the pain of departure now.

At last, with the kindness of efficiency, the drained and exhausted son tried to leave. Embracing his father, kissing his mother, making quick, solemn promises to take care of himself and send back money, he turned as if expecting his mother to release him. The father too, his pent-up sorrow killing him, tried to shorten the ordeal, but the mother, with her instinct for the truth of the situation, would have no part of it. She knew that she would never see, be with, talk or listen to her son again, that once she released him from her grasp, he would be as good as dead as far as the rest of her life was concerned. All the untouched time between her and her son, all of it still to be lived, would now and forever be lived in separation.

The son knew what she was going through. Her naked grief tore at his heart, and to end it once and for all he used his utmost strength and his father's help to free himself. With tears streaming down his face, he turned and ran out, waved good-bye to the remaining guests, and joined the convoy of youths chosen to accompany him to port or to the next town on the way to port. But as so often happened, the mother at the very end broke free of her husband's grasp and, with a deafening wail, ran out of the cottage to lock her arms once more around her son. She clung, she hugged, she sobbed, her concern for appearances completely deserting her. Shrouded in the privacy of a cell, she could not have been more willing to expose her grief, her tears and swollen eyes, the agony in her voice as she cried out, "Oh, Tommy, don't go! God bless you, Tommy! God preserve you! The lord in heaven protect you! Tommy! Don't go!"

Without meaning to or trying to, she told everyone present, in language as true as the emotion it expressed, that there is no greater pain in all of life's ills than permanent separation not caused by death itself. She and her husband would retain their full consciousness of loss and their full strength to suffer, knowing as they would that their son was still alive but forever gone, never to be seen, touched, or spoken to again.

For the son it was a ghastly experience, one that other young men in the audience swore they would at any cost avoid. Many of them in fact did by stealing off to America without their parents' knowledge.

"You would rather not be there at all if you would be any

way soft yourself," one man said. "As they say, the sight would take a tear out of a stone."[21]

One of these final partings was witnessed by a writer named Harriet Martineau, who frowned upon grief openly expressed and reacted accordingly, with a peculiarly British blend of sympathy and disdain, prejudice and an assumption of moral superiority: "The last embraces were terrible to see; but worse were the kissings and the claspings of the hands during the long minutes that remained. . . . When we saw the wringing of hands and heard the wailings, we became aware, for the first time perhaps, of the full dignity of that civilisation which induces control over the expression of emotions. All the while that this lamentation was giving [me] a headache . . . there could not but be a feeling that these people, thus giving vent to their instincts, were as children, and would command themselves better when they were wiser. Still, there it was, the pain and the passion: and the shrill united cry . . . rings in our ears, and long will ring when we hear of emigration."[22]

The convoy of brothers, sisters, and close friends never took a near cut, or short cut, on the way to port, for the same reason that a funeral procession in Ireland never took a near cut to a graveyard: if you hastened the dead one's departure, you jinxed his arrival. Eventually, though, either in the next village or the one beyond that, the time came for the emigrant to continue on his own. Those who had been carrying his bags and chest of clothing and provisions would hand them over to him. There would be handshakes and good-byes, promises, hopes, blessings, and perhaps at the very end a rhymed or proverbial toast to the departing one:

> Here's wishing good health and long life to you,
> And the choice of the girls for a wife for you,
> And the land without a penny of rent to you.
> If these three blessings are sent to you,
> Then they'll be peace and content to you.[23]

Finally, with all the weight on his own back, the emigrant would trudge on along the road, which by now would be radiant with sunlight as it passed by and over many streams running bright through emerald meadows. Farther ahead would probably be a country cart, with its load casting a huge shadow, and farther still, in the extreme distance, the clear cold outline of some mountains. The sky would be an Irish sky, with white clouds tumbling and stretching in the wind as though in some fairy-controlled harmony with the landscape below.

The convoy would stand there, with an unbroken stillness, watching and waiting for the young emigrant to pass forever out of sight. But just before that happened, he would, as they knew he would, turn around and wave.

Chapter Twelve

From my earliest youth, I have regarded the
connection between Ireland and Great Britain as
the curse of the Irish nation; and felt that while
it lasted, this country could never be free or
happy. . . . I was led by a hatred of England, so
deeply rooted in my nature that it was rather an
instinct than a principle. . . . The truth is, I hate
the very name of England. I hated her before my
exile and I will hate her always.

—Wolfe Tone,
Autobiography

THE exodus was by now being discussed in all the newspapers and on every village corner; there were signs everywhere of panic and hysteria and of the opportunistic greed
that even in the midst of famine feeds on both. Shipping
agents fanned out over the whole Irish countryside, extolling
the safety and spaciousness of the ships whose 'tween decks
they intended to jam with emigrants—a cargo much more
profitable to the shipping companies than crates and bales.

No matter its age or tonnage, a vessel was always "first
class," replete with "superior accommodations," "fast," "expressly built for the passenger trade" or "admirably adapted"
to it.[1] In Limerick, more than one ship captain, whose go-
ashore manners were put on with his go-ashore clothes, was
paraded through the streets as though he were part of the
ship's fittings. If he happened to be an American to boot, his
knowledge of the United States became another selling point,
though during the voyage he would have as much contact with
the steerage passengers as he would with the bilge of the
ship.

The agents nevertheless trumpeted the understanding and experience of the captains and crews, the reasonableness of the steerage rates, the abundant allotments of drinking and cooking water. At every chapel gate they posted flaming placards to be read by parishioners on Sundays, giving sailing dates, embarkation points, and destinations as though not a minute were to be lost by anyone considering emigration.[2] Throughout Dublin and for fifty miles around, they tacked handbills telling the people not to turn their backs on prosperity, that only fools were remaining in Ireland, that in America the stranger would find a welcome, the exile a country, the landless a farm, the evicted a home, the laborer employment, the naked clothing, and the hungry food. To share in this inexhaustible American abundance, the only giant step necessary was onto a ship, away from the poverty of Ireland.

The farmers and cottiers had been warned by their priests, by travelers returning to Ireland from abroad, and by Irish journals like *The Nation* against the extravagant stories of America told by agents who stood to profit by their going. The utopia of every shipping agent's imagination, they said, was not the United States of anyone's experience, least of all any Irishman's. As one saying put it: "If you have potatoes and salt at home, stay there and be happy."[3] But the emigrants were influenced not so much by the misrepresentations of shipping agents or the bright coloring of their own imaginations as by their immediate past experience, their own personal tragedies, their intimate knowledge of what the famine had done and was doing to them. As early as September 1846, cottiers in Sligo had written to their relatives in America, "For God's sake, take us out of poverty and don't let us die of hunger."[4]

No doubt the agents gave impetus and a certain brassy clamor to the exodus in 1847, but it was the famine, the whole complex of physical, emotional, social, and family suffering it created, and what Britain did and did not do about it that changed the attitude of the people toward leaving. Emigration was no longer a banishment but a release. In severely stricken areas, like Bantry and Schull, anyone with the means to emigrate was looked upon as reprieved from almost certain death.[5]

From every parish these escapees could be seen on their way to embarkation points with bags, bundles, boxes, and chests of clothes, bedding, cooking utensils, and sea stores of provisions for voyages to the New World, from which none would return. Some had carts, and a few of these were fortunate enough to have a beast to pull them, but most were forced to carry their belongings on their backs and rely on the power of their own legs. Since every Irish port served roughly a fifty-mile land radius around it, the emigrants had to walk thirty, forty, and sometimes fifty miles over dusty and rutted roads to reach their embarkation points.

Along the way they passed not only the debris of torn-down cabins, some still smoldering, but also the naked ruins of monastery and castle, relics of Ireland's medieval past and the destruction and decay she had suffered under British rule. It was as if they were leaving a country still at war, where the only new, still-standing buildings in the macabre landscape were the British soldiers' barracks and the prisons.

Many had never traveled more than twenty-five miles from where they were born or ridden in a fishing curragh, much less an ocean-going ship. They had been bound all their lives to the land, to one village and one parish. That parish and its village represented the one place by which they knew and understood themselves and others; the one place whose skies, soil, rocks, woods, waters, roads, houses, church, burial ground, and people they knew better than they did their own hands; the one place from which they could never separate themselves in spirit no matter where or how long they lived.

The sight of these people—many of them up in years, fathers broken by prolonged misfortune, elderly youths who had failed to free themselves of farming as a livelihood, women with ragged children clinging to their red petticoats—had a shocking, uprooting effect on all those watching them. Though the Catholic Church as a whole deplored the flight of its own people from their own land, though the priests had been warned in the press that they too would be forced to emigrate or become "shepherds without flocks" if the exodus continued, the priest in every parish was out on the road to see his parishioners safely out of Ireland. The emigrants gathered round him with smiles of affection while he gave a word of advice to Pat, a caution to Nelly, a suggestion to Mick, and a promise to Dan to take care of the "old woman" until the five pounds came to send her over to America. The tears and lamentations that followed, when the emaciated old and young got down on their knees around him and he asked God to protect them during their long journey, left an indelible impression on the minds of everyone present.

Those remaining behind experienced a peculiar loneliness coupled with a contagion of fear that they were procrastinating, losing their last opportunity. Having always regarded emigration as the answer to the problems of others, they were at last forced to consider it as an answer to their own problems as well. The many straggling columns of gaunt men with their old people, wives, and little ones, all loaded down with belongings, raising dust from the roads as they wound their way to Dublin, Belfast, Cork, Limerick, Galway, Sligo, Kilrush, Tralee, Waterford, Kinsale, and Youghal to take ships to America, were an insistent reminder that emigration might end their struggling year after year merely to exist. Some called it a weakening of spirit, a failure of morale, another step toward the total disintegration of the country. But whether it was one or all of these things, thousands of people who had given no thought to leaving began feverishly trying to raise the money and husband the food (ten pounds sterling and a sea stock of oatmeal and biscuit) to arrange their own departure.

The amount of small capital in famine Ireland surprised not only the shipping agents but all those who thought they alone had the wherewithal to emigrate. Neighbors and friends were amazed when destitute cottiers, some of them evicted from the land and their cabins torn down, said they were emigrating and dug from their tattered clothing the ticket to prove it. In Ireland money was a possession always hidden and never talked about. Among the poor it was mostly coffin, burial, and wake money, held on to for so many years that it was looked upon not as money so much as a secret, inviolable part of their selves. Now it was being used not for burial but to escape untimely death in Ireland.

In Kerry and Tipperary, many comfortable farmers, emigrating more in fear of the future than because of any immediate pressure, financed their departure by selling their cattle, furniture, and farming equipment. They had the means to survive another year or two, but were on the one hand repelled by the growing devastation around them and on the other convinced that they would become part of it if they remained in Ireland.[6]

In the towns, the middle classes shared the same general reluctance to stay it out; among those sailing were provisions merchants, artisans, shopkeepers, hardware dealers, confectioners, bakers, contractors, even pawnbrokers. In Cork, smaller farmers, acting under the same prevailing panic, sold their sheep, lambs, and wool; others, with little or no livestock, put up for sale everything they owned, including their dunghills and old iron. Those lucky enough to get the landlord's consent took only their personal effects and sold the "good will" of their holdings, their "tenant rights," for which they often received high prices. Other tenant farmers gave up their land in return for passage money from landlords determined to consolidate their small farms, do away with the tenants' cottages, and turn the tillage plots into grazing fields for the cattle, sheep, and swine needed for export to England and Scotland.[7]

When the landlord did not offer passage money, the tenant often asked for it. "Honoured Sir," wrote two sisters in 1847 to their landlord, "The humble petition of Mary and Kitty Quinne, of Lanagan, humbly showeth, that their Father and Mother departed this life and that they have No Means of Support, or to Continue any longer in this country. They request that, by their bequething their home and giving up their land to your Honour, that you will give them the help to

Emigrate to America, and by your doing they poor female orphans will for him forever pray. Mary and Kitty Quinne of Lanagan."[8]

In the repeatedly expressed opinion of the landlords, the exodus was voluntary; not the slightest pressure was put on the tenants to leave; the cries of "extermination" in the press were senseless and defamatory; the departure of the "surplus" tenants was essential to both their own survival and the estates on which they lived. But if the tenant had a choice, and some tenants deluded themselves that they did, it was more fallacy than fact. For the Irish landlord and his tenant were in no way partners, nor did they make up a feudal relationship in which benefits and responsibilities were shared by each. The tenant, having lived his entire life on the same bit of land in the same country that the landlord's ancestors had taken by force from his ancestors, still had no legal rights to it, no power to bargain for or with it, no judicial remedy to the landlord's "suggestion" that he now pack up and leave. Hungry and destitute, struggling to keep himself and his family alive, with no money to see him past gale day and the bailiff hounding him, he was not about to refuse an offer of passage out of his predicament—that is to say, out of his own country. If the landlord was kind enough to offer not only passage money but a few shillings over, the tenant no doubt told himself that the choice was his without bothering to ask himself what alternative he might have chosen instead.

The alternative, of course, was eviction, which came to no choice at all, for eviction meant that the tenant left with nothing, while emigration included free passage, provisions for the voyage, and the right to sell or take with him his household effects. It is true that there were landlords whose philanthropy equaled or at least tempered their self-interest, who gave thought and consideration to the tenants and cottiers they could best do without. In their eyes emigration was the solution of a complicated question, a balancing of good and evil, the only alternative to what would otherwise have become extermination through neglect. In nothern Ireland, Lady Hassard, in the county of Armagh, offered every tenant who wanted to emigrate five pounds an acre. Farther south, in County Monaghan, a landlord named Powell Leslie did all he could to help his tenants sell their interests to adjoining holders of land on his estate.[9]

Still, the underlying object of assisted emigration was not, as the landlords claimed, to help the tenants and cottiers but to rid the estates of the worst of them while retaining the best. The landlords discovered, as one Irishman put it, "that the best plan would be to get completely rid of those who were so heavy a burden upon them, by shipping them to America; at the same time publishing to the world, as an act of brotherly love and kindness, a deal of crafty, calculating selfishness—for the expense of transporting each individual was less than the cost of a year's support in a workhouse."[10]

Those selected for emigration were thus the poorest, the weakest, and the most unskilled and untrained—all those least likely to survive the voyage and, if they did, most likely to be a public burden from the moment of their arrival in America. The landlords of course knew that anyone unwanted and "surplus" in Ireland would be unwanted and resented in America. They were interested not in the future of the emigrants or the burden they would become in their adopted country but in getting rid of them.

"They are going! They are going! The Irish are going with a vengeance!" the London *Times* screamed with delight. "Soon a Celt will be as rare on the banks of the Liffey as a red man on the banks of the Manhattan [Hudson]." It was all for the advancement of civilization, the London *Times* assured the world: "Law has ridden through Ireland; it has taught with bayonets, and interpreted with ruin. Townships levelled with the ground, straggling columns of exiles, workhouses multiplied, and still crowded, express the determination of the legislature to rescue Ireland from its slovenly old barbarism, and to plant there the institutions of this more civilised land."[11]

When this effort "to rescue Ireland" became apparent even to those unwanted tenants who were not offered assistance to emigrate, they responded by buying passage tickets with the rent money they owed the landlord. In Limerick, this "knavery and fraud of run-away tenants" was denounced by the *Limerick Chronicle* when thirty of what the newspaper called "comfortable" farmers decamped to America with the fruit of their produce, leaving behind stacks of straw disguised as wheat. Other farmers secretly sold their herds and embarked for America at Cork before their creditors could catch up with them.[12]

With the entire country crumbling, every tenant, cottier, and landlord was out for himself, although the first two had more reason to be. They had become desperate enough to panic; the landlords had not. Suffering temporary financial loss was not to be compared with facing death from starvation and disease. Still, the landlords demanded that their tenants remain loyal and true right up to the moment when they were declared to be in the "surplus" category. This was justified, according to landowners like Mrs. Smith of Blessington, who in her diary wrote that one of her tenants, upon being refused a loan to enable his cousin to emigrate with him, quietly opened a secret drawer in her presence. Though he had paid no rent for two years, he took from the drawer seven pounds, more than the amount of the loan she'd refused. "Such a set," she wrote, " 'tis worth all they have cost to be rid of them."[13]

Her comment expressed the attitude of all landlords who expected their tenants to pay the rent through potato plenty and potato rot. This rot had started two years earlier, in 1845, and her tenant, with no pig and no produce to offer as rent, had held on to his life's savings rather than use it further to enrich Mrs. Smith during a famine when money was the only insurance against starvation. By showing her his precious seven pounds, he was both deliberately shocking her aristocratic sensibilities and declaring his independence of her. Had she lent him the money, he would not have shown her the contents of his secret drawer, but he would have honored the debt, as virtually every other Irish emigrant did after getting started in America. In his eyes, the seven pounds represented the means of getting started—his one and only cushion against hardship upon arrival. Mrs. Smith, having never known hardship, understood her problem but did not bother to try to understand his.

On the other hand, the farmers, artisans, and shopkeepers who decided for themselves to emigrate, who had the desire and the wherewithal to start a new life in a strange land, outnumbered those being "shoveled out" by landlords pruning their estates of excess humans. So many newspapers lamented this departure of the best of the country's stock that every boatload was said to have a potential world champion on board. If this was less than the truth, as indeed it was, the Irish accepted it as a witty expression of genuine sorrow. For the ships at anchor in Ireland's harbors were being filled with a cross section of Irish society—the one exception being the landlords, who had no reason to leave, knowing as they did how close they were to London and Paris, where most of them lived, and on which side their bread was buttered.

The idea that the peasantry had become superfluous in Ireland, that more attention should henceforth be given to ridding the land of people and stocking it with cattle, gained more and more adherents among Ireland's landlords as the famine's ravages continued. It was an idea set forth repeatedly by Lord Carlisle during his visits to Ireland, in words like these: "Here we find, in the soil and climate, the condition best suited for pasture; hence it appears that cattle, above all things, seem to be the most appropriate stock for Ireland. . . . Corn . . . can be brought from one country to another from a great distance, at rather small freights. It is not so with cattle, hence the great hives of industry in England and Scotland can draw their shiploads of corn from more southern climates, but they must have a constant dependence on Ireland for an abundant supply of meat."[14]

Great Britain wanted a pastoral country nearby to produce meat for its industrial workers, and since a pastoral country could not be a populous one if its flocks and herds were not to be eaten at home, the Irish people were being told, by way of evictions and the pulling down of cabins, to clear out of Ireland. An undetermined number, of course, would remain, that number being necessary to take care of the cattle destined to supply food to England and Scotland's industrial workers.

So readily did the landlords accept Lord Carlisle's "solution" to Ireland's ills that notices began appearing in newspapers in the spring of 1847, at the very height of the famine, that referred to the people as though *they* were cattle ready to be shipped. "A favorable opportunity presents itself . . . to gentlemen . . . who wish to send out . . . the overstock tenantry belonging to their estates," wrote one emigration agent named McMullen in a Londonderry newspaper, "as a moderate rate of passage will be taken and six months credit given for a lump sum to any gentleman requiring such accommodations."[15]

This contempt for the indigenous population of a starving country incensed Dublin's Irish intellectuals, who had only their pens to help stem the tide of degradation. One of them, John Mitchel, wrote in *The Nation* the following Swiftian advice "To the Surplus Population of Ireland":

Most of you are not aware of the very gross nature of the mistake . . . committed by Divine Providence in bringing you and me (say two million of us Irishmen) into the world. . . . This is a question which . . . the most enlightened philanthropists of the day are striving to solve . . . and you would be flattered if you but knew the variety of plans they have devised to better your condition, all in some distant quarter of the globe. One gentleman knows a tract of land in South Australia, and also a district in Africa, where you could be very happy. . . . Another suggests that two million of you should be sent to Canada, and he offers you the consolations of religion there. And a third has taken pains to show you that you are not suited to this country, that you are exotics here, and would feel yourselves much more at home in the back-woods of America. . . .

Any of the schemes would cost money; the spirit of the age is against putting you to death in cold blood; and in short you are the "greatest difficulty" of every statesman who undertakes to govern the country.

Now, my dear surplus brethren, I have a simple, a sublime, a patriotic project to suggest. It must be plain to you that you *are* surplus, and must somehow be got rid of. Do not wait ingloriously for the famine to sweep you off—if you must die, die gloriously; serve your country by your death, and shed around your names the halo of a patriot's fame. Go; choose out in all the island two million trees, and thereupon *go and hang yourselves*.

I remain your true friend, and (as I hope I may now subscribe myself), An Ex-Member of the "Surplus Population."[16]

Members of the Anglo-Saxon gentry in Ireland had already launched a gigantic scheme (ridiculed in the above by John Mitchel) whereby two million Irish Catholics and a proportionate number of priests were to be transferred over a three-year period to Canada. One of the distinctive features of the scheme was that none but Catholics would be sent to this new Irish Catholic colony, where everything Celtic would be retained and perpetuated. In short, it was a scheme as attractive-sounding as it would be effective in ridding Ireland of the Irish, nine-tenths of whom were Catholic. A memorial on the subject was drawn up, signed by leading peers, members of Parliament, and Irish landowners, and presented to Prime Minister Lord John Russell with a short explanatory note expressing hope that the government would support and sanction the scheme. The eighty signers, including one archbishop, four marquises, seven earls, three viscounts, thirteen barons, nine baronets, eighteen members of Parliament, several deputy-lieutenants, and other honorables, went so far as to send a copy of the memorial to the Right Reverend Dr. Maginn, the Roman Catholic Bishop of Derry, who replied with scathing indignation:

In sober earnestness, gentlemen, why send your circular to a Catholic bishop? Why have the barefaced impudence to ask me to consent to the expatriation of millions of my co-religionists and fellow countrymen? You, the hereditary oppressors of my race and my religion,—you, who reduced one of the noblest peoples under heaven to live in the most fertile island on earth on the worst species of a miserable [potato], which no humane man, having anything better, would constantly give to his swine or his horses;—you, who have made the most beautiful island under the sun a land of skulls, or of

ghastly spectres;—you are anxious, I presume, to get a Catholic
bishop to abet your wholesale system of extermination—to head in
pontificals the convoy of your exiles, and thereby give the sanction
of religion to your atrocious scheme. You never, gentlemen, laboured
under a more egregious mistake. . . .

Is not the quarter-acre clause test for relief your creation?
Were not the most conspicuous names on your committee the abet-
tors of an amendment as inequitous as it was selfish—viz., to remove
the poor-rates from their own shoulders to that of their pauper
tenantry? Are not they the same members who recently advocated,
in the House of Commons, the continuation of the fag-end of the
bloody penal code of the English statute book, by which [Catholics
in England] could be transported or hanged for professing the creed
of their conscience . . . ? What good could we expect from such a
Nazareth?[17]

Great Britain's prime minister declined on behalf of the
government to take up the great colonization scheme. The
government, he said, was of the opinion that emigration, left to
itself, would transfer the starving people to the United States
and Canada as quickly as those countries could absorb them.
This shrewd calculation that the people would be starved out
of their own country, despite the British government's efforts
"to mitigate present suffering," turned out to be correct. For
with the number of surplus, evicted cottiers increasing daily,
with the roads leading to every port clogged with the homeless, the impatience to escape was universal. No longer did the
length and danger of the voyage matter; the fleeing emigrants
were prepared to undergo any horror save that of remaining in
Ireland. What had formerly been a last resort was now a first
necessity for survival. Brokers in Dublin declared that a hundred vessels would not satisfy the demand of those seeking
passage to America.[18]

It must be remembered that there was still enough wheat,
oats, barley, butter, eggs, beef, pork, and lamb in Ireland, even
in this famine year of 1847, to feed for a year four times as
many people as were leaving the country. But all this produce
was still being sent to Liverpool on the very same ships that

carried the emigrants, whom the English lawmakers claimed could not be fed, were redundant in their native land, and therefore had to go somewhere else. On one ship alone, the steamer *Ajax*, which sailed from Cork in 1847 for England, the cargo consisted of 1,514 firkins of butter, 102 casks of pork, 44 hogsheads of whiskey, 844 sacks of oats, 247 sacks of wheat, 106 bales of bacon, 13 casks of hams, 145 casks of porter, 12 sacks of fodder, 28 bales of feathers, 8 sacks of lard, 296 boxes of eggs, 30 head of cattle, 90 pigs, 220 lambs, 34 calves, and 69 miscellaneous packages.[19]

"You draw away our resources to your own country," one writer in *The Nation* said to England. "You feed your soldiers plentifully among us, while the native people of the land starve; you have us pensioners on the alms of a foreign country [the United States], your enemy and conqueror; you scoff at our wants, our hopes, our ancient nation—by God's eternal justice, this must end *now*! . . . One more effort, then, for dear Ireland . . . that we, too, may not be flung into coffinless graves, amid the bitter scorn and contemptuous laughter of mankind."[20]

But nothing happened. The same journal reported a short time later that "twenty vessels sailed out of the Shannon this week with grain and provisions for London, Liverpool, Bristol, Gloucester and Glasgow."[21] Counting all Irish ports, about twenty such vessels sailed every day from Ireland with the same general cargo: the country's prime produce and, on the same vessels, the unwanted produce—the "surplus" humans on their way to Liverpool to board ships for America.

Like some species of animal whose value was far below that of cattle, pigs, and sheep, the Irish were being ferried over standing room only, on the upper deck, where they were subjected to dreadful exposure during the thirty- to thirty-six-hour crossing to Liverpool. Sometimes as many as a thousand emigrants, with a full cargo of pigs between decks, were taken aboard steamers weighing only eight hundred tons. These steamers were so heavily laden that the seas washed over the upper deck, completely drenching the standing emigrants, who were packed so tightly together that it was impossible, except for those already at the rail, to vomit over the side. No attempt was made to limit the number of those boarding or to increase the number of lifeboats, though there were enough to carry no more than three of every hundred passengers jammed on the upper deck. Nor did this persuade the British steamship companies to lower the fare; they still demanded ten shillings for the ferry crossing to Liverpool.

"They do not get half that money for the pigs," a compassionate Englishman named John Besnard testified before a parliamentary committee, "and yet the pigs are comfortably lodged between decks, because they are of value to somebody, while these poor people are not looked after at all."

Besnard, a port inspector at Cork, went on to say that "I have gone to Liverpool expressly to await the arrival of the Irish steamers, and no language at my command can describe the scenes I have witnessed there; the people were positively prostrated . . . from the inclemency of the weather . . . seasick all the way . . . drenched from the sea and rain . . . suffering from cold at night . . . debilitated . . . scarcely able to walk after they got out of the steamers. . . . In fact, I consider the manner in which passengers are conveyed from Irish to English ports disgraceful, dangerous, and inhuman. . . ."[22]

No one contradicted Besnard, and all the other witnesses corroborated his testimony, but nothing was done. The Irish continued to crowd into the ports, all saying in effect the same things, that they were "glad to leave their wretched country." "All we want is to get out of Ireland . . . we must be better off anywhere than here." "Bad legislation, careless legislation, criminal legislation, has been the cause of all the disasters we are now deploring."[23]

These sentiments, which the emigrants took with them if they took nothing else, were soon to coalesce into a profound loathing, a savage hatred, of Great Britain. In time this hatred would give life and impetus to Irish societies on both sides of the Atlantic, and it would be handed down from generation to generation. As early as 1845, one of England's great future prime ministers, William Gladstone, had prophetically called Ireland, in a letter to his wife, "that cloud in the west, the coming storm, the minister of God's retribution upon cruel and inveterate and but half-atoned injustice."[24]

Now, with the exodus destined to continue into the next century, Irishmen in New York, Boston, Philadelphia, Baltimore, New Orleans, Chicago, and points west, all with ancestors who had survived the famine, would agree with John Mitchel that the British Empire was a "ferocious monster," a "diabolical power," "the most base and horrible tyranny that has ever scandalised the face of the earth." When they remembered Ireland and the wrongs done her by England, they would remember too, with Mitchel, the terrible hope of the Psalmists, and repeat it on behalf of Ireland: "that thy foot may be dipped in the blood of thine enemies, and that the tongue of thy dogs may be red with the same."[25]

Even the London *Times*, which celebrated the famed emigration of '47 with the gleeful declaration that the Irish were "gone with a vengeance," would in a later editorial express fear of the hatred the Irish were taking with them: "If this [exodus] goes on, as it is likely to go on . . . the United States will become very Irish. . . . So an Ireland there will still be, but on a colossal scale, and in a new world. We shall only have pushed the Celt westwards. Then, no longer cooped up between the Liffey and the Shannon, he will spread from New York to San Francisco, and keep up the ancient feud at an unforeseen advantage."

At this point, the London *Times* tells the truth: "We must gird our loins to encounter the Nemesis of seven centuries' misgovernment. To the end of time a hundred million spread over the largest habitable area in the world, and, confronting us everywhere by sea and land, will remember that their forefathers paid tithe to the Protestant clergy, rent to absentee landlords, and a forced obedience to the laws which these had made."[26]

The writer of these lines might well have taken one of the Liverpool steamers over to Ireland to observe firsthand what was going on there. Or perhaps he received some shocking dispatches from reporters at the scene. In any event, the myriad claims of British malfeasance in the Irish crisis, based on the overwhelming evidence of eyewitnesses, finally began to find expression in the editorial pages of the London *Times*. Placing the blame on the Irish had at last become untenable.

Chapter Thirteen

... Historians and politicians will some day sift
and weigh the conflicting narrations and
documents in this lamentable year, and pronounce
with or without affection, how much is due to
the inclemency of heaven, and how much to the
cruelty, heartlessness or improvidence of man.
The boasted institutions and spirit of the empire
are on trial. They are weighed in the balance.

> —*The Times*,
>   quoted in *The Ocean Plague*,
>   by Robert Whyte

NEVER before in Ireland's history had there been anything like this outpouring of people. Like the Israelites "seeking to escape the Egyptian bondage," as one observer put it,[1]
emigrants from all walks of life were crowding into embarkation points from every corner of Ireland, leaving whole
stretches of deserted countryside and the smell of the grave
behind them. Some ports along the Irish coast, where the evils
encountered were often worse than the evils fled, bulged with
three to four times their normal populations. Wagons and carts
loaded with both inanimate and living freight kept coming in,
some drawn by beasts whose owners would now sell them to
the highest bidder, others pushed or pulled by men from
whom the miles had taken a heavy payment. Although the
worldly possessions of the majority consisted of nothing more
than a mind troubled and embittered in a body weak from
starvation and disease, there were farmers with the grass of
thirty cows who brought with them furniture, curtains, carpets,
pewter plates and dishes, brass candlesticks, bed and table
linen, blankets, and an abundance of pots and pans.

Some small farmers, unable for sentimental reasons to part with their tools and equipment—some of it medieval in design —drove wagons loaded with harnesses, spades, shovels, sickles, hoes, ploughs, axes, picks, hay knives, door hinges, hammers, and an assortment of nails. When they reached Boston, New York, Philadelphia, Baltimore, or New Orleans, the cost of transporting hardware of such weight and unwieldiness to the north or west would far exceed its value. They had been told to sell all such heavy equipment before departing, that it would be cheaper to buy in America, but they brought it any-way, almost as if they were bringing the best part of Ireland with them. Luckier were the mechanics and carpenters with their compact boxes of tools, like survival kits—all they would need when they reached America and set out in search of a job. Luckier still, or smarter, were those with books, which could be read during the voyage and then sold in America for double what they cost in Ireland.

In every street, emigrants who had never seen a city, a wharf, or a body of water larger than a lake tried to anchor their minds against the rush of impressions. Warehouses, counting rooms, shipping offices, courts, jails, taverns, and tall buildings of unknown function hemmed in streets through which rattled carts, cars, jingles, and mounted horses. There was everywhere man-made noise rather than natural sound, an intense, jabbering business activity rather than quiet labor. Everything seemed out of tune with the rhythms of working the soil—and out of tune, too, with the famine horrors from which they were fleeing. No town, no fair, no marketplace in the interior, even in normal times, had been anything like this. To the exhausted emigrants, it was an animated, bewildering, frightening scene. They were being jostled and jarred into a miniature of the urban existence awaiting them in America, and they fit the part perfectly, their village wonder and village costume of frieze making them immediately recognizable, their perplexity and famine-induced humility inviting swin-dlers of every variety and degree of deceit to impose on them.

There were the agents selling passage on ships with delayed sailing dates, ships in need of repairs, ships headed for ports other than those contracted for. Some emigrants who had bought passage tickets in their hometowns thought they were embarking from the Irish port to which they had been told to report. But in the majority of cases they were forced to take a preliminary voyage eastward across the Irish Sea to Liverpool, the great port of embarkation.

Worse than the agents were the tavern and lodging-house runners, who urged, directed, drove, and dragged emigrants to establishments where board and bunk would be available at exorbitant rates until the ships were ready to sail. Hawkers in the street, as widespread as gutter pigeons ready to pluck up whatever was left to go around, urged them to buy tents, camp beds, fishing tackle, and water cans for the voyage. Slabs of cheese as tough as boot soles were up for sale, along with cans of used tea, sugar laced with sand and sawdust, and meal so old and mildewed it was growing in the bag.

Since the emigrants' average stay in Cork before the sailing was a week to ten days, the runners, sharks, and lodging-house keepers had ample time to ply their trade on the country people, who kept pouring into the city seven days a week. They lodged in the lowest, filthiest houses on the north side of the lee, the sick and the well sleeping together several to a room, on the floor, for threepence a night. So ruthless were the keepers that they claimed carrying and storage charges for bags and boxes of belongings, served contaminated food, and encouraged the kind of excessive drinking that insured extravagance on the one hand and gullibility on the other. Men who had taken Father Mathew's pledge to avoid liquor lost their money by being persuaded that the pledge was no longer binding because whiskey was the best preventive of seasickness.

These taverns and lodging houses were neither regulated, inspected, nor licensed, and given the slimy, lice-ridden rooms and the way they were endlessly occupied and reoccupied by people, some of whom were already infected, it was not long before typhus broke out and alarm spread among the city's inhabitants, especially among those who were themselves not leaving Ireland and resented their city's being jammed with diseased people who were. Many emigrants were thus turned out of the taverns and lodging houses into the streets, where they were forced to buy food until their funds were nearly exhausted while awaiting passage. Some died in the alleys and cellars; others barely survived long enough to board their ship. And all the while the influx from the interior continued, so that by the spring of 1847 the streets were clogged with people, their children, their belongings, and the lice carried by all three.

"No tongue can describe, no understanding can conceive, the misery and wretchedness that flowed into Cork," declared Father Mathew, who then publicly castigated the "rogues called brokers," who added two shillings to the cost of every pound of sea stock and sold to credulous emigrants packets of chicory worth threepence as coffee for two shillings, sevenpence.[2] Along one of the quays, a sleight-of-hand thimble rigger drew crowds of incoming emigrants, whose eyes were not fast enough to see him palm the pellet while appearing to cover it with one of the three thimblelike cups. They watched with the utmost concentration while he moved each cup in between, around, and beside the other two, and when, with the pellet still in the palm of his hand, he offered to bet that no one could tell under which cup the pellet lay, he always had two or three takers.

Some unscrupulous agents, after selling steerage tickets to five or six emigrants for the same price that more-demanding travelers paid for second-class cabin passage, warned them that they would not be allowed on board without liquor, pistols, telescopes, bowie knives, fishing tackle, and whatever else their accomplices, standing conveniently a short distance away, had to sell. Another fraud was "dollaring," whereby worthless foreign coins or bank notes were exchanged for the emigrant's little stock of gold. The more gullible the emigrant, the more precious valuables he parted with before sailing and the fewer he would have in New York or Boston, where he would need them most.[3]

These swindlers were sometimes themselves Irish, and in

normal times they would have been denounced, ostracized, probably murdered. But with displacement and upheaval everywhere, they came into being like excrescent social sores, feeding off misery and helplessness without fear of reprisal. That fear, ordinarily in Ireland a more effective restraint than fear of the law, had been removed. They knew that the emigrants had lived too long with harassment and abuse to demand fair treatment now, let alone to retaliate. Besides, they were leaving Ireland for good. The time to fleece them was now.

In a few rare cases, the emigrant answered in kind by cheating anyone he could before he left. Every Irish port had examples of this fifth-column kind of fraud, when the art of Irish beggary suddenly blossomed among departing emigrants who did not have to beg and had never begged before. Some, with their valuable luggage and gold concealed, put on rags and wooed for bread or for anything else that would add to what they were taking with them. Begging as much to avoid being begged upon as to realize a profit, they solicited aid especially from the swindlers, who often committed the swindler's sacrilege of giving them something—but on condition they moved on and stopped interrupting business.

One Limerick farmer posing as a begger had in his pocket 160 pounds, a small fortune in those days;[4] another went to a broker's office in Cork on the pretext that the deposit he had paid weeks earlier covered the entire cost of his passage ticket. Gibbering and vociferating that he was entitled to passage without additional payment, he used the whine of the mendicant, tears, blasphemy, obscenity, distorted facial expressions tricked up with scraps of jocularity and humor—the repertoire of an experienced Dublin beggar. Every variety of flattery was expended so long as the slightest chance remained that, whether from compassion or contempt, the clerk would relent. When he stood fast, adamant and unmoved, the quaint, wheedling foulness of the emigrant's language turned to the most scurrilous and outrageous abuse. Still the clerk waited, arms folded, eyes cold, Irish himself and an expert judge of his sly countrymen, until the emigrant smiled, dug into his rags, and coolly produced a five-pound note.[5]

Informed at last that boarding time had come, the emigrants carted their belongings from alley or lodging house to the side of the ship, the *Mersey*, named after the famous river leading from Liverpool to the Irish Sea.* Peddlers were everywhere amongst those anxious to board, trying to make last-minute sales of licorice, nuts, taffy, tobacco, or additional provisions for a voyage whose duration they correctly claimed was unpredictable. One peddler pleaded with the emigrants to buy him out of his supply of chamber pots for when the calls of nature came on. "It's the mercy of God that I'm here to sell them to you," he cried, holding one up in each hand. "Ladies! *Modest* ladies! It's yourselves will be blessing me every day of the voyage!"[6]

In the crush toward the gangplank, friends and members of families shoved and shouted in attempts not to be separated; teen-agers clambered up the ship's dangling ropes in their impatience to get aboard; women in rags chatted as happily as if they had shoes on their feet. Some emigrants going in a party from the same village had made arrangements to take a pig or two with them, to be fed aboard with the leavings of the group and eventually killed and butchered during passage to provide a most agreeable fresh food. These pigs, with wisps of hay attached to their fore and hind legs to check their propensity to roam, joined the crush at the gangway with the decorum of trained, overweight basset hounds, to no one's dismay or disgust. Cackling in protest, ducks and geese, which also did well at sea, were brought aboard for the same reason.

---

* For the sake of both brevity and focus, the *Mersey* was made a composite of several British ships taking Irish emigrants to America in 1847. The conditions and mortality aboard these ships were far worse than those aboard the *Mersey*. In short, the voyage of the *Mersey* understates, rather than exaggerates, the voyages of the other ships, as will be borne out by the mortality figures of the other ships mentioned in the text.

The shelves of bakers' shops were emptied by passengers adding bread to their sea stock of dried codfish, pigsheads, suet for dumplings, eggs packed in salt, carrots, turnips, onions, flour, oatmeal, rice, sugar, tea, coffee, castor oil, rhubarb pills, epsom salts, vinegar to smother as much as possible the taste and smell of the water on shipboard, and, last and most miraculously in this worst of all famine years, sacks of old but still sound potatoes with which the peasants refused to part. No fewer than seventeen tons of them were put aboard one vessel embarking from Cork in the spring of 1847. The Irish had been warned to bring along their own supply of food and not depend on what was called the "parliamentary diet," and, having tasted Soyer's soup, they heeded the warning as far as their pocketbooks allowed.[7]

The emigrants had left their homes and villages for the last time; now, for the first time, they were boarding a ship, an ocean-going ship taking them forever from the only land they knew to a land they could only try to imagine. In many ways the boarding itself was more disturbing than the leaving; the imminence of departure was suddenly as shocking as the ship was strange; the beautiful green rug of Ireland was being pulled from under them. Never before had they been on anything afloat, anything so alive to the rise and fall of water. The dialogue between ship and sea, even in this comparatively calm harbor, was never ending; it on the one hand engrossed them and on the other reminded them of the momentous move they were making. What would the dialogue be like during the crossing—in a storm?

For one eloping couple, a boy and girl running away to America, the pressure and suspense leading up to departure created a crisis that unalterably changed their lives. They had been driven to their embarkation point by a young man named Micky Quinn. The forty-mile trip had carried them through quiet farming country to this noisy, overcrowded seaport, where everything different and strange excited the young girl but confused and frightened the young man.

"Sure enough," he said, "the more I see of this, the less I want to see."

"It's not thinking of going back home you are, is it?" asked Dolores Kinsella, the girl eloping with him.

When the young man hesitated, Micky Quinn tried to urge him on with a bit of encouragement and hope. "God save you from temptation, Terry, and may you never button an empty pocket."

But with his imagination full of exaggerated visions of New York, Terry reneged and said he could not leave Ireland. Dolores and Micky looked at him, astonishment giving way to embarrassment and pain on both their faces. They were standing near a shoemaker's shop, whose dangling sign resembled those of other shops in that it was written in letters that started large, quickly grew smaller and smaller, and finally ran down into a corner in search of the necessary space. If anything symbolized Ireland and the Irish at this time, it was these homemade signs that began with expansiveness and hope and ended with a downward slide to almost nothing.

"By Him that made me, I'll go alone if I must," said Dolores, a black-haired teen-ager with Spanish in her blood and steel in her gray-green eyes.

Something like agony twisted and distorted the young man's face; he moved his arms and legs in odd, unnatural ways, while Dolores and Micky, friends since childhood, watched and waited. Nearby a woman was selling buttermilk; another, bullocks' hearts, liver, and other scrappy organ meats; another had dried mackerel on a board next to some cockles she claimed had been caught that day. Here and there a hound or two went stalking by.

Several seconds passed, until Micky Quinn, whether to end the torture or take advantage of an unusual opportunity, found a solution. He suggested that he take the ticket and give the young man the horse and cart to return to the Glen, from which they had come.

Micky, an illiterate dressed only in a homespun jersey,

knickers, and his dead father's old shoes, boarded the ship with
Dolores. On arrival in New York, she would join her married
sister in the city's infamous Five Points section around Mulberry Street on the Lower East Side, and he would gravitate to
Greenpoint, Brooklyn, to land a job in a saloon and learn to
read and write. But they would keep in touch with each other,
off and on at first, then more often the more he learned to
write. In two years they would be married in St. Patrick's
Cathedral on Mott Street in lower Manhattan—the first St.
Patrick's in New York City (replaced thirty years later by the
Gothic building now standing at Fifth Avenue between Fifti-
eth and Fifty-first streets). Micky and Dolores would have six
children, each one as real and delightful as their boarding the
ship together had been unforeseen. Eventually, Micky would
come to own the saloon and send home to Ireland for a footing
of turf. When it arrived he would place it, by itself and without
a word of explanation, in the middle of the saloon's window.

"No Irishman ever passed without going in," a friend
would recall many years later. "That piece of the old sod did it.
Sure, Micky had whips of money after being away twenty
years. When he returned with his lovely wife and children, he
built half the houses you see today in Cushendall—Steven-
son's, the Collam's, he built them all, a man who couldn't read
or write when he left. There was a saying in those days, and it's
as true today as it was then: 'the only part of Ireland where a
man can get ahead is in America.'"[8]

Another man named Diarmud Dempsey, boarding the
ship with a secretive air, had with another girl something like
the reverse of Micky Quinn's experience. In those days many
of the younger girls who went to America, especially the pretty
ones, could have married and remained in Ireland, only they
did not want to make "brock" of the family. Custom required
that the oldest girl of a family be married first, then the next
oldest, and so on to the youngest. It was thought very bad for
a girl to make brock of the family by marrying before an older
sister.[9]

This man Diarmud Dempsey, now aboard the *Mersey* with Micky Quinn, had two months earlier left his home in the Donegal mountains and made his way down to the Glen to ask a girl's hand in marriage. It was the second girl in the family he wanted, the pretty lissome one named Deirdre, and when she consented, the marriage was set for that day a month later. He had carefully observed her posture and gait before asking, for he had been warned repeatedly by a close friend: "See her walk, I tell you. See her walk before you say you'll have her. It was only last week that they very nearly had me married to a girl. If it hadn't been that they differed about the price of a cow, I'd have been married to her. They had her set out on a chair facing me, as nice a looking girl as you'd wish to see. It wasn't till the week after, when the marriage was off, that I found out she'd had only one leg on her."[10]

But Diarmud had secretly watched Deirdre dancing through the fields; he had even accidentally seen her milking her father's cows. She had two legs, two arms, and the feet and hands that went with them. So he knew he was getting someone as undamaged as she was beautiful.

At that time all the women went to chapel wearing heavy veils, and on the day of the marriage Deirdre was wearing a good thick one. After a memorable ceremony attended by both families and all the people in the Glen, the couple were married. Arm in arm they led the procession out into the sunlight, and when they passed through the gate and the girl lifted the veil, Diarmud Dempsey's heart became a stone in his chest. It was not Deirdre but the older sister he had married—the sister who was even older than he, whose face had become hardened by disappointment and crabbed with worry.

Diarmud never said a word; he simply turned, like someone yielding to another in a fruitless argument that would never otherwise end, walked down the hillside leading from the chapel and went on to Carn. In Carn he got on one of Paddy Politics's cars going to Cork, where he used his dowry money to obtain steerage passage on the *Mersey*. Now, aboard and bound for America with a much luckier man named Micky

Quinn, Diarmud Dempsey was never again to be seen by or heard from by Deirdre or anyone else attending his marriage to the older sister who had cheated him.[11]

On deck,' Micky Quinn, his wife-to-be, Diarmud Dempsey, and all the other passengers took in the features of their new home: the bulwarks, windlass, bowsprit, and, towering above them, the masts, yards, booms, rigging, and great folds of sail. Nimble sailors could be seen running up the shrouds, creeping along the stays, and lying out on the yardarms, where they managed to locate themselves with wonderful ingenuity, to check things in preparation to sailing.

The masts especially, spirelike pines from America, captured the imagination of the Irish headed for that country. At least fifty inches around at the base, they went up so high into the sky and became so slender and delicate at the top, above the yardarms where the sailors were working, that from deck it was easy to imagine them being broken by the fingers. How they could support such weight and how a ship so narrow could support *them* without turning over, especially in heavy weather, mystified the emigrants and would continue to do so throughout the voyage.

Having had no sea experience, they had no way of knowing whether the ship was too deeply laden, too lightly loaded, or too crowded with passengers; whether the ventilation, lighting, and height between decks and the cooking facilities on deck would be adequate. How many privies—or water closets, as they were called—had been installed? Were they sturdy enough to withstand the pounding of the sea? The farmers and cottiers assembled on deck knew none of the answers and were offered none by anyone among the ship's officers.

All the same, no one aboard asked to be let ashore. On the contrary, the captain's main concern now was putting ashore everyone who did not belong aboard. The first step in this process, the roll call, was something like a last-minute inquisition, intensifying for every passenger the painful ordeal of leaving. For a paid-up ticket was not enough; you could be rejected for being sick with fever or for any number of other reasons. When your name was called, you came forward to be peered at and inspected as a slave up for sale might be, only you had neither the strength nor the value of a slave. Except for your ticket and the money you might spend on the captain's exorbitantly priced whiskey, you were looked upon as worthless. So you stood there, answered questions, opened your mouth to show your tongue and teeth, and, once accepted, moved to one side to relax, knowing you were at last on your way to the one country in the world that had freed itself of British rule.

The roll call was conducted in the presence of the captain by an Irish clerk, a young man usually, who broke down some of the tension by wending his way down the list with banter and raillery. If he came to a Patrick Boyle, he might shout out, "Paddy Bile, come here awhile," or order a William Jones to "show his bones." Unfortunately, most among the motley crowd on deck, from the infant to the feeble grandsire and shriveled crone, had little more than bones to show. Nothing was left of them but the lees of misfortune and the last remaining hope of something better in America. The really exhausted and decrepit among them should have been rejected and sent ashore with their passage money, either to recuperate or die in Ireland.

"All the Cork and Liverpool passengers are half dead from starvation and want before embarking, and the least bowel complaint, which is sure to come from change of food, finishes them without a struggle," declared one Dr. Douglas before a Parliamentary committee during the famine.[12]

Another observer wrote: "It would in my opinion have been more humane to have deprived them at once of life."[13]

Had the emigrants been given the dreadful choice of burial at sea or burial in Ireland, all would have chosen Ireland. But they had their passage tickets, they were standing on their own feet on deck, and they wanted to leave for America, however slim their chance of reaching it.

It was usually during the roll call that frauds were discovered, some of them as desperate as they were ludicrous, like one woman's attempt to pass off her eight-year-old son, who was required to pay half the adult fare, as an infant at the breast, who traveled free. "Captain, Sir," she said, making up the difference, "if there was falsehood in my words, there was none in my heart."[14]

Another involved a couple representing their strapping eighteen-year-old son as "under 12." When the captain, inches shorter than the couple's son, threatened to have him put ashore, the couple gave out with moans and wails that could not have been worse if the captain had shot the son dead. Having neither money nor anything to sell to make up the difference, they pleaded with the captain to allow the lad to work off the difference during the voyage, or at least to wait until their eldest son, already a year in America, made up the difference in cash on the ship's arrival in New York.

"May God deny my words, Sir, if our son will not be there on the dock with the necessary dollar bills, as they call them, and more besides," the father said. "And may God increase all ye have, Sir, after our safe arrival."

Only when a collection was taken among fellow passengers to the amount of ten shillings, and several others pledged security against the balance being paid by the other son in New York, was the young man allowed to remain on board.[15]

There was also the solitary man, trying by whatever means to get to America to make the fare money for the wife and children he was leaving behind. Hungry-looking and dressed in rags, the kind of man who, as they said in Ireland, "would wrastle a ghost for a ha' penny," he answered roll call with a half-paid ticket and begged the captain to take him at what he had the audacity to call the half-price rate. Like the man who had tried to deceive the clerk in the broker's office, he was as full of tricks as a monkey, putting as much energy, effort, and imagination into his harangue as he would have put into a job paying a decent wage. America had both the job and the decent wage, but he had to get there first, and to get there, with as much money to spare as possible, he was willing to lie, cheat, beg.

"Before I tell a lie, Sir, let me say that I didn't believe it either," he said to the captain. "T'was ashore that I heard it, Sir, the welcome news that your fine ship had a half-price rate for all those with more brawn than money and the willingness to spend it on honest labour."

To please the captain he would have sworn in one breath that there was no God and in the next that the Blessed Virgin Mary was His mother. Half-pagan, half-Christian, trying desperately to compete in a materialistic world with hand-me-down mysticisms, he spoke with the kind of sincerity and conviction that truthful men envy.

"Cut my tongue out if that's a lie, Sir." He held his tongue out with the thumb and forefinger of one hand and pretended to cut it out with the forefinger of the other. "Out! But for the love of God, let me go for the half-price rate."

Not until two crewmen took him by the arms and were about to escort him by force off the ship did he, with the vacant face of a pickpocket, find in his threadbare trousers the other half of the fare—that precious five pounds five shillings he had hoped to have in New York to get himself started. He would gladly have starved for a week aboard ship rather than produce it, and if, somewhere else in his rags, there were more five- and ten-shilling notes, no one aboard would ever see them. He was Paddy with a mission—shrewd, incorrigible, dedicated, as impervious to the scorn of the passengers as he would be during the voyage to the abuse of the crew, the kind of man who, to help his wife and children, would auction off his body for dissection on his way to the gallows. In New York he would become lost in the crowd; no one aboard ship would care or remember. When he changed clothes and went in search of a job, no employer would know, or have to know, that he had come over in steerage.

So great was the desire to get out of Ireland that a person

without passage money would hide, bare_y
an overstuffed mattress or packed up to the
barrel punctured with only the smallest of air hole.
perate stowaway named Martin Dooley hid himself so su
fully with provisions down in the bilge of the ship *South Caro
lina* that on arrival in Boston, Dr. Moriarty, the port physician,
had to amputate his mortified legs.[16]

The captain of the *Mersey*, aware of most of the decep-
tions used, had the passengers roped off on deck while crewmen penetrated every corner and recess of the ship with lan-
terns, candles, and long, pronged poles. They hammered,
lifted, and tested the passengers' baggage, bedding, and barrels; they checked folded sails and searched the ship's belly
right down to the lowest level of her inner hull.

"It's myself you've found!" cried one young man in rebuke
to the two seamen who had discovered him down in the filthy
bilge of the ship and brought him up on deck to be put ashore.
"And you couldn't have tried harder if I'd been made of gold!"
He was reprimanding them, two workmen as lowly as he, for
not searching the bilge *without* finding him. Who would have
known? What difference would it have made to them?

When seamen on deck hit upon something suspicious, like
an especially heavy barrel, instead of breaking it open they
stood it on end, thus doing the same to its occupant, if there
was one, until he cried to be released. On the *Mersey* this trip,
one stowaway, suffocating in an upside-down barrel with the
salt pouring down around his head, kicked open the end of it
and, legs flailing, climbed out. With salt clinging to his hair,
eyebrows, eyelashes, whiskers, and the hair on his arms, he
stood on deck before his dismayed co-conspirators among the
roped-off passengers, the three or four among them who had
vowed to feed and support him during the voyage. Dismayed
too were the others in steerage, who would never have informed on him or resented his traveling for nothing.[17]

"If you put six stowaways on a scale, and their total
weight has little or no effect on the buoyancy of the ship, no

one is hurt and six are helped," claimed one emigrant in 1847. "Sure, if God wanted it any other way, he would not have allowed hiding places for people in trouble."[18]

Suddenly this attitude was put to a test. The ship was boarded by a bailiff with a creditor's decree against one of the steerage passengers. With the usual official fanfare, he asked to see the captain, the one man aboard with the power to force the emigrant to pay his arrears before departure or be put off the ship. But the passengers had witnessed too many evictions and arrests in their own parishes not to know what was happening. They reacted as one, beating off first the bailiff, then the police. It was only when the British military arrived on the quay for a charge that the indebted emigrant asked the other passengers to resist no longer. He surrendered and was taken ashore, never to leave Ireland or learn what became of the passengers who had fought so unselfishly for him. By missing the ship he missed the frightening, unforgettable voyage awaiting the others, but also the chance of bringing life to account in America.[19]

III

The Voyage

Chapter Fourteen

... If any class deserves to be protected and
assisted by the government, it is that class who
are banished from their native land in search of
the bare means of subsistence. ... The law is
bound, at least on the English side ... to put an
end to that system by which a firm of traders in
emigrants purchase of the owners the whole
'tween decks of a ship, and send on board as
many wretched people as they can get hold of
on any terms they can get, without the smallest
reference to the convenience of the steerage ...
or anything but their own immediate profit. ...

—Charles Dickens,
American Notes

IT was not until after roll call and the search for stowaways had been completed that the already exhausted passengers were allowed to make their way down into steerage,
situated below the ship's main deck, to unpack and arrange
their belongings. If they had been awed, on boarding the ship,
by the height of the masts towering above the deck, they were
immediately dismayed and disheartened by the steerage hold
where they were to spend twenty to twenty-four hours a day
for the next eight to ten weeks.

"My soul from the devil," exclaimed one woman to her
husband, "this looks like his home."

"It begins ugly and will surely end with a smell," replied
her husband. "There'll be no living here with me if the day
comes when I run out of tobacco."

Just climbing down from the sunny deck into the dim,
unventilated, overcrowded quarters put everyone, but espe-

cially the weak and half-starved, under stress to the point of collapse. The mazelike bulkheads and partitions, the complete lack of privacy despite the intricate network of passages alongside and between the bunks, and the inability of all but the shortest to stand upright without hitting the underside of the main deck above would have been bad enough even in an airy, well-lighted place. But it was dark and there was no circulation. The endless bumping into strangers in a strange place; the family and female groups trying to seize, claim, and get settled in the compartment that they hoped would be theirs during the voyage; the jouncing and shouting of children, some lost and crying for their mothers, others expressing joy in the new world of a ship; the different smells of the other packed-in people, their foods, their breaths, the used and re-used air; and the claustrophobic strain of being enclosed in a dungeonlike place from which not even the sea would be visible during the voyage—all created a totally new kind of confusion for the Irish peasant, whose horrid hovel in Ireland had at least been surrounded by green and often wild open country, who had always given himself time to think and a good deal more time than that to act. All the sights, sounds, and colors of nature as he knew them were gone. For him steerage was like a foretaste of purgatory if not of hell itself.

The law required that every four adult passengers be allotted a space of six feet by six feet, which was to contain not only the two tiers of berths on which they were to sit, sleep, and eat, but also their clothing, bundles, chests, and sea store of provisions. These allotted spaces, resembling horses' stalls or cattle pens, were small enough to create in anyone a dread of tight, enclosed places. But any ship carrying a "Royal Mail" was exempt from the legal space requirements. With even one post-office bag on board, a captain could give his passengers even less space.[1]

The berth was nothing more than a sort of shelf made of unpainted fir or pine and fastened to a bulkhead or wall, with a strip of the same wood nailed to the outer edge to prevent the occupant from rolling out during the voyage. The width of each berth was an unbelievable eighteen inches, three to four inches less than the average width of the back of a man's coat.[2]

"Sure, they must have meant us to sleep on our sides," said one tall, gawky farmer. He was what they call in Ireland "a great gazebo of a man," a good twelve inches taller and broader than his wife. "Even for your wee back, Kit," he went on, "there isn't room on that board."

One official's description of these steerage berths was more brutal, if no less accurate: "The passengers have not much more than their coffins."[3]

Mattresses were not supplied by the ship, so each steerage passenger had to bring one aboard or sleep on the raw wood of the berth itself. Hair mattresses, being harder than most, were not recommended because the person sleeping on one could too easily roll off it during stormy weather. Feather mattresses, on the other hand, although light and receptive to the contour and weight of a person's body, became worthless once wet—a condition almost impossible to avoid when heavy seas splashed down into steerage from the main deck above. The mattress considered the most serviceable for the voyage was one made of coarse ticking well filled with fresh straw. It was the cheapest and could be thrown away on arrival at quarantine by all those whose "nice habits" would preclude their wanting to use ashore a bed used in the steerage at sea.[4]

But whichever bedding was used, it was seldom of the same width, nor were the chests, boxes, and bags of the same size and shape. This created strife almost immediately over distribution of space, encroachment into another's territory, which chest or bag to put where in the incredibly tight six-by-six-foot space, and, most important of all, sex separation. For when the bedding was laid out down both sides of the steerage deck, it raised each tier of berths to a common level, so that men, women, and children were sitting or lying in one promiscuous heap on what appeared to be, and almost was, the same platform.

Women and girls had to undress and sleep without any

assurance that decency would be respected. Single men had complete and uninterrupted communication with other passengers, including single women, who, being both Roman Catholic and from a country where illegitimacy was virtually unknown, were virgins.

"I have known cases of females who had had to sit up all night upon their boxes in the steerage," said one eyewitness, "because they could not think of going into bed with a strange man."[5]

Most parents kept their single daughters in their berths with them, sleeping with them if necessary, rather than exposing them to the dangers of bunks so inadequately divided. Some young girls never before exposed to even the rudiments of sex became hysterical when caressed in the middle of the night by men who did not have to reach far to touch them. The girls often jumped screaming from bed, racing and tripping through the crazy aisles to some other part of the ship, where they soon found themselves within arm's reach of other men.[6]

Even when the separation of sexes was attempted, as it was on the *Mersey's* previous voyage, it was usually undermined by officers who did not concern themselves with propriety in steerage. On that earlier trip, several men in steerage who had received no berths were told by the captain to take their mattresses and belongings to the women's quarters and sleep there.[7]

When all in steerage on the *Mersey* had settled in and the rattling noise subsided, mothers gave biscuits to children who said they wanted to get off and go home, fathers made sure their families' chests of provisions were locked, young men with pretty females nearby were as reserved and shy as they would have been in their own parishes in Ireland. Had these young men and women remained in Ireland, where marriage was arranged and conjugal infidelity virtually unknown, they would have had the Irish custom to follow. But aboard ship no pattern prevailed; habits and manners became as unstable as the bunks on which they slept; there were no rules to control either the awakening of passion or the gratification of it. So the young looked at one another, as full of potential as they were worried over what to do with it.

Meanwhile, the middle-aged and old wept while jogging their memories in an effort to find in their past experience some meaning to what was happening to them. They wondered where in America they would live, whether this move, one of such finality, would be worth the effort. All they really knew was that in America they had not the smallest hut they could call home, not a patch of land on which they could build, not even a definite place they could think of as a destination. They would have to begin at the very beginning again, with nothing, as they and their fathers and mothers had done at home so many times before. Only vaguely did they think of living off the earth in America, as they had so precariously lived off it in Ireland. Indeed, how they would earn their daily bread had long since become secondary to their earning it daily. The kind of job they would work at no longer mattered; the bread did, and in America there were supposed to be more jobs than people.

So they sat in steerage and waited, aware of the sea beneath them, stretching their imaginations toward the land where they hoped to find food and watch their children grow. Something like the Irish peasant's traditional caution hardened around them as they watched and listened to the younger and more resilient among them play fiddles and melodeons for those who wanted to celebrate in jigs their escape from Ireland. A musical instrument was the very last thing an Irishman pawned, and now no one tried or had any desire to stop the irrepressible singing and dancing. This was their way out of stress and trouble, and it was as appropriate in the dismal shadows of steerage as at a parish wake. They were in fact holding a wake, this time not over a dead person but over what in their eyes had become a dead country. The tears, laughter, anguish, dancing, moaning, and music, all combined and became one; everyone was sad, resentful and happy, distressed and relieved, half dead but still alive.

Suddenly it was pandemonium as the ship weighed anchor and everybody tried to get to the main deck to say farewell to Ireland. None aboard hated—indeed, none aboard had ceased to love—the country they were leaving. What they hated were the catastrophe it had suffered and the government that had allowed the catastrophe to happen. For the famine they were trying to escape was not in the exact and truest sense a famine, and all aboard knew it. The only failure was the potato crop, their food, the food of the poor, the only food allowed them according to the horrid scheme called "political economy." After they died, and their children and grandchildren and great-grandchildren died, the belief would remain firm that God had sent the potato blight and England had created the famine.

There were moans and prayers as they jammed the main deck on the starboard side for one last look. "May I never set eyes on anything greener than that!"

"Sure," said another, "if for no other reason, it was never meant to last."

"Last, is it? Did you say last? That island will stand, the soil will be there, moist and fertile, long after we're gone. Overrun with England-bound cattle it will be—and a few leftover Celts!"

Their belief that the spiritual and material worlds were very near each other came through in such sayings as "It's the mercy of God that kept us alive long enough to board this ship," or "With the help of God, we'll reach America before our food runs out."

Aboard were men who had left behind their wives and children, their aged mothers and fathers, affectionate brothers and sisters, and friends to whom they were bound by the strongest ties. They were exiling themselves from everything near and dear to them in their native country, and as the tears ran down their cheeks, it was with fists clenched in anger that they wiped them away.

"Lord John Russell, may you end in hell!" a man about fifty cried out in hatred of the British prime minister. He must have thought he was talking to himself, for when people looked around he regained control over both his sorrow and his anger, as though they were one and the same.

Nearby an old woman expressed a fear everyone was feeling. Earlier that day she had heard a blond seaman tell a young man his own age, a passenger who had expressed shock at the mockery of accommodations called "steerage," "Be patient, lad. There'll be more room in the hold the farther out we get."

What could he have meant except that people were going to die during the voyage and be buried at sea, leaving more and more room for the living the longer the voyage lasted?

"God save me," she said. "Old as I am, I should never have left Ireland. Who knows where I'll be buried now?"

All those around her listened in silence, their dread and ignorance of the sea summoning up the same thoughts of death and burial. Already removed from their parish registers in Ireland, and still not recorded in some parish in America, they too were homeless travelers without even a churchyard plot they could call their own. All their lives they had wanted and expected to be put in consecrated ground, and now for the next two months they would be surrounded by an ocean heaving and rolling and slapping against the sides of the ship with a heedlessness that seemed to exclude anything and everything afloat from the great but unknowable scheme of things. Deep and dark, bellying all around them, it was a vast, watery limbo, a mysterious place they prayed would not be their final resting place.

Everyone on deck grew silent, as though taking part in a funeral procession, as the ship began sliding silently through the water. Watching the *Mersey*'s movement against the shoreline, straining their eyes to see for as long as possible some headland they knew they would never see again, was like witnessing the premature and unnecessary death of a loved one. Need and oppression stared from their eyes; ragged misery hung from their backs. The world was not their friend; their country had been taken from them.

"Poor dear Ireland," exclaimed one aged female, "I shall never see you any more."

Another cried, "The poor ould country is destroyed t-totally."

For some, with thoughts fixed on the dead they were leaving behind, on the evictions, the pulled-down cabins, and the horrifying slow starvation of whole families, the land of their birth seemed to have become the land of their abhorrence. Their love for Ireland would flower again only after the wounds had begun to heal.

"When I was born," another man at the rail said, almost to himself, "if I had known this would happen, I would have asked God to take me before ever my eyes opened."

Chapter Fifteen

The emigrant should consider that no important
benefits can be had without toil, trouble and
trial. If he would find a better home beyond the
sea, he must encounter the difficulties of the
passage, and the pangs of regret at turning his
steps away from the places he has so long known.
. . . The richest man in the United States at this
time is an emigrant: Mr. John Jacob Astor, of
New York.

—Wiley and Putnam,
*The Emigrant's True Guide to
the United States*

FOR a while, everyone tried to turn a happy face to the
voyage and put old cares to flight. They were on their way
at last; the sailors high above them were putting out more
sail; the breeze was steady, the sea mild, the ship tight. They
could almost feel her bound forward, like something alive, as
the wind caught additional sails hoisted to the highest yards.
Spray rained over them from the foamy bows; tremors and
vibrations descended the masts to the deck supporting them;
the sea around them, itself alive, rose and fell in cascades of
sunlit waves from which an infinite variety of lacy eddies lingered.

Nothing now was to be seen but water and the very last
trace of Ireland, their lost country. It was this last trace, coupled with the boundless blue water, that turned their minds to
the land toward which they were headed. With their passage
paid and their destination set, they thought and talked of New
York Harbor and the teeming city it served, where there was
reportedly more wealth between Battery Park and Chambers
Street than in all of Ireland.

"If it's true," one man said, "that the land to the west is still almost empty, the farming will be too lonesome for us. We'll not have enough of society. I wonder, are there jobs enough for us in New York? Or will we be tracing ourselves back to Ireland?"

"God, look to your wit," the man next to him said. "Never again will you cross this ocean."

Some had relatives already in New York, brothers and sisters who had promised to check the ship-arrival notices in the *New York Packet* and other newspapers and be there to take them in hand when the ship hauled to a wharf down around the tip of Manhattan. Of all people in the world in the year 1847, the Irish, with the awful phantom of hunger still fresh in their minds, had the least reason to be hopeful. But being still religious, they were still hopeful too.

The beginning of disenchantment came on the first day as the ship's routine set in, when land passed out of sight and the sea around them accentuated their close confinement. The size of the vessels used during the famine (four hundred to six hundred tons), and the number of emigrants each carried (three hundred to five hundred), precluded the kind of space that would have made the voyage, if not pleasant, at least bearable.

On the five-hundred-ton *Mersey*, there was no possibility of movement; the area allotted to them on deck was limited to the waist of the ship, just above and forward of their living quarters. They could not go aft where the captain and cabin passengers lived, they were forbidden on the quarter-deck (the only completely open space on the ship), and were warned against using any facility except those built expressly for them up forward. The simple exercise of walking was impossible, there being so many of them jammed in amongst the lifeboats, casks, spars, ropes, and extra sails in a small area where much of the ship's work was done and where they were cursed by seamen and cuffed by officers for getting in the way.[1]

So covetous were the cabin passengers of their superior

accommodations and their separation from the poor Irish in steerage that they persuaded the captain to have a rope strung athwartships just aft of the mainmast to define the boundary line between those who had paid the minimum fare (three pounds ten) and those who had paid the maximum (fifteen to twenty guineas). The cabin passengers had no reason or desire to cross the boundary line and go forward toward steerage; the steerage passengers dared not cross it and go aft toward the "other house," as the quarter-deck structure was called. On a clear day, though, two or three young men among the cabin passengers would stand on the quarter-deck and quiz with binoculars the raggedly pretty Irish girls up forward.

Sometimes in fair weather the captain would allow clothes-lines to be strung between the masts for the drying of clothes washed in sea water—the only laundry water available to those in steerage. The soap gave no suds when the women tried washing their things, but by rubbing the soap in and then slapping and beating the garment over and over again against the deck, as they had done against the rocks along the rivers of Ireland, they at least got it clean. When it dried, they would shake out most of the salt so as not to itch and burn the skin.[2]

Then one day a heavy rain fell, and they watched as seamen stretched out a sail on deck to catch the fresh water. Laughing and talking amongst themselves, the seamen drank it, scooped it up in pots for later use, washed themselves and their clothes as well with it. From then on, whenever it rained, the steerage passengers came up with pots, pans, petticoats— anything that would catch and hold what one among them called the *Mersey*'s "lucky water."[3]

One man named Samuel Sullivan, with the black dirt of Ireland caked in his ears, clinging to his hair and beard, and embedded in the barky skin covering his face, neck, and arms, refused to wash his clothes or himself, or even to wet his skin with sea, rain, or cooking water, in the belief that washing not only gave him a cold but removed the very dirt that protected him from disease. When someone close enough to smell him on deck suggested that he too had better wash himself, he became genuinely alarmed: "Ga! Is it my death from catarrh you're after?"

He came to be known as "Sam Sweep," the one man on the *Mersey* who was carrying to America more dirt on himself than he could have in a bucket.

In fair weather the steerage passengers played cards on deck, told stories, sang songs, and, despite *Punch*'s notion that "every Irishman would rather own a race horse than a library,"[4] read books. The women shared notes on their remaining sea stock and discussed the merits of certain blends of "tay." "Oh, I found a super-excellent blend," one would say to another. "It takes such a fine grip of the second relay of water."[5]

It was these wonderfully impromptu expressions, coming as if from a natural spring of intelligence and wit, that sent glints of pleasure through the long hours of the day. Tea was scarce and the length of the trip uncertain, so a "second relay of water" was often necessary—but perhaps no more so than the charming way the people expressed themselves.

The women also sewed and knitted; tradesmen made money repairing shoes and clothes; boys and girls copied the characteristic rolling gait of the sailors or danced to the tune of the diminutive Irish fiddler, who played as indefatigably as a dummy cranked up after every song. During these few hours when gaiety surmounted the underlying sadness, anxiety, and fear, the crowded foredeck was like a bit of Ireland revisited.

Nearby, the sailors and apprentices, listening to the infectious music and shouts of joy, swabbed decks, mended sails, tarred ropes, spun yarns, and chopped broken spars into firewood. To the surprise of the Irish women on deck, the sailors did not sit and sew as tailors did on land. Instead of folding their legs beneath their haunches, they stretched them out straight before them on deck to give themselves more leverage against the movement of the ship. Their thimble too was peculiar, being worn not on the top of the finger but on the ball of the thumb, to which it was fastened by a leather strap buckled around the wrist. All the same, the Irish women ad-

mired their speed and neatness, the tight, even stitches they
made with their long threads and coarse needles.[6]

The many risks and variables of an ocean voyage led to
another diversion among the steerage passengers. They began
placing bets on the daily progress of the ship, on what day
another ship would be sighted, on whether that ship would be
coming from or going to America. There were also bets on the
day and even the hour when the pilot would board the ship at
Sandy Hook, with side bets on how long it would take him to
bring the ship to her anchorage.

Betting on the ship's daily mileage, though, which was
determined in those days by "heaving the log," remained the
most popular if only because each day's betting was decided
that day. A log or block of wood, fastened to a line run out
through a reel, was heaved over the stern of the ship, and the
rate of the ship's motion through the water measured by how
much of the line was let out in an hour. From the number of
miles she made in an hour, a rough estimate of the mileage for
that twenty-four-hour period was made and posted for the
benefit of both cabin and steerage passengers. The bets were
paid in cash, rum, flour, meal, salted fish, meat, lemonade, or
anything else anyone needed or was willing to risk in a bet.[7]

Then there was a lottery in which almost everyone bought
a chance. It was to be decided by the day and hour when land
was first sighted, with the understanding that the holder of the
winning ticket would receive the entire amount collected. To
prevent fraud, each ticket carried the signature of the man
running the lottery, that man being a huge blacksmith named
William Gilhooley, whose uniquely flamboyant signature virtually precluded forgery.

"Big Gil," as he came to be called, became well known for
another reason. He had brought aboard a small case of odd-
looking tools, and throughout the trip he built miniature sailing ships in bottles with a finesse that delighted and amazed
his fellow passengers. One day, after a week's work building a
perfect replica of the *Mersey* in a magnum, he presented it to
the captain, whereupon he was given, despite his steerage

status, run of the entire ship. He became special in everyone's
eyes except his own, if his behavior was any indication. Like
many big, powerful men, he was not one to use his size and
strength to his own advantage. He simply wanted to be like
everyone else, no more and no less.

There were also those among the steerage passengers
who frittered away their time drinking rum, which the
captain sold illegally at enormous profit to himself. Another
activity engaged in below was love-making, an inevitable result of the sleeping arrangements, which permitted the most
unrestricted intercourse between the sexes, placed modesty
and decency at a discount, and ended with many young
women on their way to becoming mothers before they were
wives.[8]

Sometimes the mate, as though slumming, would try to
strike up an acquaintance with a pretty Irish girl on deck.
Dolores Kinsella, Micky Quinn's wife-to-be, was once approached in this way by the mate, who said to her, "If the
devil were to board this ship and show himself now, which of
us do you think he'd take, you or me?"

"He'd take me," Dolores said, her mind as swift as her
glance.

"Why do you think so?" asked the mate.

"Because he'd be sure of you anytime," said Dolores, stroll-
ing back to Micky, who had heard with astonishment and love
her every word.

The voyage was only beginning, as was their serendipitous
relationship.

Chapter Sixteen

What ordinance makes it obligatory upon the
captain of a ship to . . . place the galley, or
steerage passengers' stove, in a dry place of
shelter, where the emigrants can do their cooking
during a storm, or wet weather? What ordinance
obliges him to give them more room on deck,
and let them have an occasional run fore and aft?
—There is no law concerning these things. And
if there was, who but some Howard in office
would see it enforced? And how seldom is there
a Howard in office!

—Herman Melville,
Redburn

FOOD is more ritualized and enjoyed at sea, even by
those with no fear of deep water and no past encounter with
hunger. But for the *Mersey*'s steerage passengers, who had
never been in water over their heads and who with the sea
around them instinctively turned to things that had become
habitual for them on land, the food ritual was infinitely more
important. Finding the sea alien and treacherous and having
known and experienced hunger on land, they linked the two
and turned to food, the cooking and the eating of it, as a way
out of the hour-to-hour and day-to-day anxiety and ennui. But
even here they were frustrated by the hopeless inadequacy of
the cooking facilities furnished by the British shipping companies.

Although most of the Irish in steerage had brought their
own food aboard as insurance against the "parliamentary diet"
supplied by the ship, every man, woman, and child lined up
for his or her share whenever the "parliamentary bell" sounded.
The cook, steward, or mate distributed the rations daily or

every second or third day from barrels hauled up on deck or lowered into steerage by the crew. The Irish crowded round with crocks, pots, pans, and jars in which to carry away their portions. Others without containers carried away their share in towels, aprons, shawls, turned-up petticoats, or in their bare hands.[1]

On the *Mersey*, as on most British vessels in 1847, each adult received a pound of bread or meal daily; children under fourteen received a half-pound, and those under seven, one-third. Bread could be eaten as is but was almost never served; meal, which required cooking and was almost always moldy, was distributed five times a week, biscuits being given out the other two. One hungry youth aboard the *Mersey* who broke a front tooth on a biscuit as "hard as a stone chip," thereafter crushed them against the deck and then ate the small pieces after thoroughly wetting them in his mouth.[2]

Captains often evaded the law by putting on board both good and bad provisions and issuing the latter during the voyage. Since penalties were imposed only if the inferior food-stuffs were aboard while the ship was being cleared, the captain had only to wait for clearance before taking on food in midstream. Then, even if inferior or moldering food was discovered or reported before the sailing took place, nothing could be done about it because the ship had already been cleared. The offending captain could not be punished, the inferior food could not be removed, and the passengers could not refuse to eat it if they wanted to eat at all once their own food ran out. During inspection in port, some captains even went so far as to represent the passengers' own sea stock as part of the ship's provisions.[3]

Another fraud practiced with the connivance of the captain was the use of false measures for the rationing of water and dry food like meal, flour, and maize. The gallon-water measure, for example, contained but three quarts, and this was all each person received each day for cooking, drinking, and washing. The supply of water shipped on board in port was always abundant, but the ration for those in steerage was so scant, even in the rare case when it was an honest measure, that the emigrants were often obliged to throw overboard their rice and salted fish because they had insufficient water to cook these two most important foods and still have enough left over to satisfy their raging thirst afterward. With not enough water to cook with and drink, there was nothing left for personal hygiene. It was one or the other, and their choice was as anyone else's would have been.[4]

On the foredeck was a fireplace, called a caboose, round which the emigrants thronged with their supplies to do their cooking for the day. The hot coals were contained in a metal cage bordered on three sides by a large wooden case lined with bricks and shaped like an old-fashioned settee. The cooking grate itself, though, could accommodate only four or five pots or pans at a time, and there were days when food ready to be cooked never reached the grate.

"It's little will be left of us when we get to New York," commented one woman, "with this the only cooking place for all four hundred of us."

Every morning, as the gauzy light of dawn spread over the water, someone in steerage would crawl up from below and search the foredeck for kindling (some rope yarn, tarred canvas, discarded rags, wood splinters from a broken spar) and make a bed of it for the coals, which the cook scooped from a barrel and placed in the metal cage. Knowing how important the fire was to those in steerage, this so-called deck cook, who did no cooking himself but simply superintended the cooking of others, always lighted the kindling with a flourish, like someone on stage before a captive audience. For by the time he appeared on deck the caboose was surrounded by men, women, and children with their clattering pots, pannikins, and pans, all of them anxious to get their day's food cooked before the real madness started.

From the comparative comfort of the quarter-deck, beneath which bread was baked and food cooked in an enclosed galley for the captain and his cabin passengers, the sight of all these human beings surrounding a glowing fire up forward had a certain charm. The poor people and their children appeared busily engaged; the smoke from the cook's funnel mounted tranquilly up into the sea air as if from a chimney in some Irish city street; even the smell carried aft by the wind was redolent of something crustily edible.

A few of the quarter-deck onlookers, though, found the scene painful and embarrassing. For their own parents had once resembled the people they were now watching, and no one is more repelled by the scarecrow clothes, coarse expressions, and greedy gestures of extreme poverty than the children of parents who were born in it. Their parents had escaped the poverty and serfdom of a tenant farmer's life by "jumping" from Catholicism, with its stigma, to Protestantism, with its job opportunities. But they had no more escaped the memory and detritus of that serfdom than they had its effects.

Now the children of these "jumpers" were going cabin-class to America with the specter of their parents' sordid past up forward: the swallow-tailed coats full of holes and almost touching the ground, the shapeless breeches with their gaping kneebands sagging close to the ankles—the very emblems of the beggary and degradation their parents had escaped by becoming converts to the Church of England. It was enough to make them hate themselves, and especially the proselytizing hand of the Anglican Church, which had given their parents the extra food, the better jobs, and the social ladder on which to begin their climb. The real heroes were the ragged ones up forward, who had clung to their religion and were now trying with their battered pots and pans to get their food cooked.

Some around the fire baked oatmeal cakes on blackened, makeshift griddles; others used all kinds of vessels to make stirabout of meal, vegetables, and salted fish; and those lucky enough to have potatoes put what they were eating that day into a net, to separate them from the others, and boiled them in the same communal pot. The oatmeal cakes were about two inches thick and, when baked, though still raw in the center, were encased in a burnt crust coated with the smoky taste of the coals. The stirabout, because of all the struggling to get to the grate, was seldom cooked long enough to break down the meal, so some people got on line twice with the same pot, in the hope that a second turn on the coals would make the stirabout digestible. They had never before cooked on a rocking and swaying stove that made the kettles and pans slide and jump as if in a crazy dance. Sometimes a pot of porridge, to which molasses had been added, would slop over and not only kill the fire but send up that familiar acrid smell that only burnt molasses can create. Meanwhile, sailors aloft amongst the sails and rigging did what was wanted to the ship. The stove, the smoke, and the crowds of passengers trying to get their provisions cooked seemed not to concern them at all.

Given the steerage passengers' physical weakness, their craving for food, and their desire and responsibility to cook it, they had every right to expect from the deck cook the highest possible degree of impartiality. But as he saw it, his main duty was to determine arbitrarily every morning, as the passengers began to "pig together" around him, which of them had first rights to the grate. Since cooked food was seldom if ever distributed, his importance—and the way he threatened the unruly with a ladle of scalding water—made it necessary to curry his favor by flattery, bribery, or sexual inducement—the latter if you happened to be pretty and female. He had the cold, sneering, cowardly face of a man who takes delight in the discomfort of others, who could neither be kind nor suffer others' kindness.

"By my soul," whispered one old man near the end of the queue, "I'd crack the back of that cook if I had the strength."

The woman in front of him turned with a nod. "He's as great a rogue as ever escaped hanging."

"A worse man never faced the sun," said another.

Seeing the unfairness of the system and the absence of any discipline in the queuing for what should have been everyone's rightful turn, the passengers became embittered, contending with one another rather than with the cook whose job it was to see that places at the grate were apportioned fairly on a first-come, first-served basis. This only added to the cook's power over them and the willful partiality he imposed. Those with money to bribe him came first, by his order; those strong enough to muscle their way to the front came second; the rest, the majority, waited from morning until late in the afternoon for their turn, the weak and infirm among them often forced to the wall, where they were reduced to eating raw flour.[5]

One Irish tailor, whose shiny red cheeks brought out the blue and white of his eyes, had obviously made some sort of bribery arrangement for the entire voyage with the cook. Every day at the same time, this tailor's wife came to the caboose and with painstaking care made dishes in several pots as though working in her own kitchen. Even the bribed cook appeared awed by this woman's patience at the stove despite the thronging impatience behind her.

Another man with a very large fry pan had so little food to cook in it everyday that when his turn came at the fire he looked as if he were panning for gold. He created suspense every time he appeared on deck, for everyone expected him either to come up with a smaller pan or to add to the amount of food he cooked in the large one. In either case he would no doubt have been applauded, for though he could not have been more than twenty years old, his sores and famished body had long since robbed him of youth's resiliency, giving him instead that stolid, care-blunted look that comes from prolonged suffering and worn-out hope. Still, he never changed; it was always the same pan, always the same amount of food. One woman named O'Reilly, commenting on the phenomenon, got a little ahead of herself when she said to another: "If that young man doesn't get himself a smaller pan soon, he'll starve to death before ever we reach New York."

This propensity of the Irish to make fanciful or bizarre blunders in language is as prevalent today in rural Ireland as it was a century ago. A deep-seated national characteristic, it springs not from mental sluggishness or a paucity of ideas but from mental quickness and a profusion of ideas, all of them at the same time jostling the brain, which then gets them ludicrously mixed up in the course of expression. Like the woman in Limerick who, on seeing a tiny coffin displayed as a gruesome trade sign in an undertaker's window, exclaimed, "Oh! Is it possible that coffin is intended for a living creature?," the O'Reilly woman was partaking of a droll mental peculiarity of the Irish people.[6]

Big Gil, the blacksmith who initiated the lottery to be decided on the first sighting of land, was also at the caboose every day. A huge, muscular, kind, and considerate Irishman, he appeared every morning in a threadbare shirt of bed ticking that flared out like a tent but did not quite reach or cover his waist, around which a rope was tied to hold up a pair of knickers so old it was impossible to imagine them ever having been new. He always arrived on deck barefoot, carrying in his right hand his prize possession: a pair of shoes, which he put on before queuing up for his turn at the fire. The shoes were almost high enough to be called boots, and with the laces loose and the tongues and sides flapping outward, they looked like open mouths waiting for his surprisingly delicate, dirt-lined feet.

Big Gil—he liked the nickname and accepted it as a compliment—had no fear of the cook, always waited his rightful turn, and would allow no one to go ahead of him. One day he came up "with a drop in him," as they say in Ireland, and though he was as cordial and respectful as ever, one of his admirers, watching him slip into his shoes, whispered to another, "He's had a tayspoonful."

"A tayspoonful, is it?" said his friend. "And what good would a tayspoonful be, straying about in such a wilderness of a man?"

They and the others watched as he waited his turn, stepped to the grate, and, with his pot ready to use as a weapon, said to the cook, "You're a fool."

The ship lurched suddenly as she started on another tack, throwing bits of gravy from a few pans into the spitting fire. The sizzling sound and flare-up of flames only added to the tension as all eyes turned to the hated cook, who appeared as startled by the remark as everyone surrounding him.

"You must be drunk," he said.

"I may be," said Big Gil, "but I'll be sober tomorrow, whereas you'll be a fool then too."

And with that he placed his pot of salted fish and stir-about on the grate, folded his arms, and with his eyes dared the cook to retaliate. He had not yet presented the captain with his bottled model of the *Mersey* and was thus acting not on the basis of any special privilege but, rather, as one steerage passenger among many.

Appraising the huge man's strength, and realizing how close he was to being thrown overboard in one swoop, the cook said nothing until Big Gil left, whereupon he vented his cowardly rage on the next defenseless one in line. All the same, from then on he gave Big Gil a wide berth whenever the latter appeared on deck to do his cooking for the day.

The fire was kept going for hours because there was never enough room on deck for even a tenth of the passengers to line up. Some remained in their bunks below, others fought to get up to cook or to reach one of the two water closets up in the bow, while a few made their way surreptitiously into some dark corner below with a chamber pot. The quarreling and strife did not end until the fire was extinguished, at seven o'clock, when a seaman mounted the shrouds of the foremast and emptied a bucket of sea water on the coals, half blinding the tardy ones with steam as they snatched up their pots and pans and descended into the hold with half-cooked suppers.[7]

"The devil take that man," they'd mutter to themselves. "Look at the mess he's made of our supper, and we badly in need of it."

Without even half-cooked suppers, some hung around the forecastle, trying to cajole the sailors into giving them a mouthful "for the love of God." Like beggars in Dublin, working one or the other side of the street every day, they remained in the same spot, on the port or starboard side of the fore-castle, and never encroached on the "territory" of another beggar. It was this willingness on the part of the emigrants to share the luck of kindness that oiled and kept running the wheels of affairs aboard ship, at least among those in steerage.

Every day the sailors were each given a pound and a half of beef or pork, besides coffee, oatmeal, lime juice, and as much biscuit as they pleased, and in the evening they deposited the leftover fat and grease from the meat in what was called the "slush barrel."[8] From this and previous trips, they had become accustomed to the poor Irish on deck, dulled by the sight of them, by the sameness and surfeit of them. The more "famine crossings" these sailors made, the less they attended to the Irish in steerage, and the less they gave them in the way of leftover scraps of food.

Had the fat and grease, along with the bones the sailors threw overboard, been used as the base for a stirabout of vegetables and oatmeal for the steerage passengers, it would have been a great improvement on Soyer's soup. But custom decreed that the contents of the slush barrel belonged to the ship's head cook, who sold it on the ship's arrival in port or rendered it himself while the ship was still at sea.[9]

More than once during this voyage of the *Mersey*, the Irish beggars around the forecastle were caught digging into the slush barrel and avidly eating the fat and grease. They were that desperately in need of nourishment, but the captain, instead of breaking custom and using the slush as the basis for a common soup or stirabout for those in steerage, had the barrel guarded day and night so as not to offend the cook, whose rights to its contents had to be protected.[10]

At night, the many different working sounds of the ship, the creaks and strains whose mystery the darkness only heightened, absorbed those in steerage more than the familiar nightmare screams of children, the groans of the aged, the retching of the sick. Believing as they did that with every dip and roll the ship was drawing nearer to the United States, they listened in inspired silence until they became exhausted and fell asleep. For the insomniacs among them, it was a much more prolonged ordeal, with nothing to see but everything to hear. If anything did divert their attention and smooth over the rough edges of the night, it was the unexpectedly soft sounds that came from an arm's length away—the intense breathing and quiet rustlings of sex being consummated.

"Believe me, Kate, to lie awake here, as I did last night, is to lose all shame," a middle-aged man whispered to his wife one morning after sunlight had begun to angle down through the open hatch. "That young couple in the corner behind us? The blond lad with the money belt and box of tools? The one whose young lady calls herself his wife-to-be? They could be *heard*, I tell you. They did not even *try* to be quiet." With a suggestive smile that ended almost in a wink from both eyes, he added, "As sure as I'm here beside you, Kate, it was something to hear, if not to behold."

"Tell me this, Cornelius Cochran," whispered Kate, "why did you not put your fingers to your ears?"

"I wanted to, but I didn't. I tried, but I couldn't." He smiled again with his eyes. "I confess that to you, Kate, my love, knowing you've always been the first to forgive the sinner you married."

"Be off with you, Connie!" Kate said. "How could they manage? In so tight a space?"

"Himself asked that same question, Kate, over and over again in the dark. But if sound has meaning, manage they did."

"Get himself up on the cooking queue," Kate said. "I'll be up in a minute."

"Until tonight, then, right you are, Kate my love."

The ship was not long at sea and not far out of sight of land when she began to respond in earnest to the forces working on her. With wind in her sails and waves at her prow, her decks dipped and swayed as nothing ever did on an Irish farm. Some tried to ignore the movement by talking themselves into another state of mind, and these talked more rapidly the more their instability mounted. Others tried with their legs and

equilibrium to follow the rhythm of the ship, whose movements unfortunately were not that regular or recurrent. Still
others shut their eyes and locked their stomachs in the belief
that the pitching and rolling, the sliding of chests, and the
swinging from hooks of clothing would eventually stop. But in
the end, being down in steerage was for almost everyone like
being locked in a gymnasium in a nightmare.

"Just before I left Kilkenny, the cow died on me," one
man said. "And now this. I tell you, I'm not sure I want to go
on living."

Their land-based sense of balance failed them; they
watched as one by one those around them gave up the fight
and ran to retch, until the power of suggestion almost equaled
the power of the ship to dance with the sea. Those young or
agile enough climbed through the hatchway to the main deck
to vomit over the side; the very young and very old became
sick where they were—in their bunks or wherever on deck they
happened to be.

In some cases this seasickness lasted for days, during
which the victims grew weaker from dehydration and looser
with their baleful moans and unsavory contortions. Their faces
took on an almost holy, transcendent look that belied the profound regret they felt in being still alive. Though awake, they
reflected on nothing, cared for no one, longed for nothing but
relief. It was a kind of undifferentiated awareness of distorted
perception, sickening sensation, and a wheeling helplessness
exceeding anything ever before experienced. If they thought at
all, they thought the world should never have been made,
especially the watery part of it.

Relief came with the painfully slow readjustment of the
body and its equilibrium to the rhythm of a ship at sea. But
when it came, as it did except in the rare cases when the
victims wasted away with weakness and despair, even the
memory of what it was like to be seasick, like the memory of
summer's mosquitoes when winter's snow is on the ground,
was difficult to recapture and easy to forget. Those who had
been the sickest thought of food, water, and sleep; they were

delighted when something reaching their stomachs remained there to be digested.

Being seasick for a week, though, and unable to eat the food supplied by the ship did not mean that money was refunded. Whether you found the ship's food impossible to eat in your seasick state or in its moldy state, no adjustment was made. Such economic considerations were of course beyond the capacity of the seasick while their ailment held them in thrall. They could not think of food, let alone climb on deck to collect their share. It was only after they recovered and remembered all the meals they had missed, meals that their poverty led them to associate with the expenditure of money, that they wondered why a small refund or at least an increase in their current rations was not in order. Having traveled for a week or ten days on what today would be called a "no-frills" basis, they felt justified in approaching the ship's officers about it. Although they represented three-quarters of the passengers, all of whom had been too sick for over a week to collect or use their rations, they were refused, laughed at, or shouted down: "No one told you *not* to eat!"

Over two hundred passengers were thus denied the food they needed to regain their strength, and while they grew weaker, the conditions under which they were forced to live worsened to the point where it was almost impossible to go on living.

Chapter Seventeen

"You have stated that, after getting to sea, the
two privies on deck were destroyed?"

"Yes . . . they were only put up temporarily
. . . the day before she sailed. . . ."

"And that there were none below?"

"Yes. None below."

"What was the remedy?"

"There was no remedy. . . ."

"In consequence of that there was a very
bad smell below?"

"You could not stand below."

— Testimony of Mr. Delany Finch,
Minutes of Evidence Taken
Before the Select Committee
on Emigrant Ships, 1854

BY far the greatest suffering and distress and the most
persistent and degrading embarrassment for those in steerage
centered around the privy, or water closet, that most necessary
of all facilities wherever people in great number congregate.
There were exactly two water closets for the use of all three
hundred and fifty steerage passengers aboard the *Mersey*. Situated up in the very bows of the ship where the bowsprit juts
out from the stem, they were so exposed to the wind and spray
that it was almost impossible to use one without getting
drenched.

Indeed, where and how steerage passengers on emigrant
ships were to answer the calls of nature during the eight- to
ten-week voyage created the most pressing problem facing parliamentary committees during the great famine exodus. One
group of experts said that the water closets should be situated
on the main deck, where the wind and sea would keep them

clean as they could never be kept clean below. Besides, these experts claimed, when the water closets were below, the working of the ship deranged them, threw the piping out of line, broke elbow connections that carried the flush water and waste matter into the sea around the ship. Even in the rare cases when the pipes did not break, they said, the passengers, unfamiliar with water closets, caused clogging and back-up by throwing bones and all sorts of things into them.

"It is almost impossible to prevent their leaking," said Emigration Commissioner Murdock. "The people do not understand the plugs, and they every now and then set the water going, and do not turn it off, and then they flood the decks. We have tried to get them self-acting, but a thing that acts very well on shore as self-acting will not act at sea. I confess that we are quite at wit's end on the subject of water closets."[1]

Captain Schomberg of the Royal Navy agreed with Murdock that the class of people in steerage was totally unacquainted with the mechanism of a water closet, and that having them below would make the ship "perfectly pestiferous. I have found them universally the greatest nuisance and difficulty we have to deal with. . . . It is impossible, because they are so overused, to keep them pure and sweet."

Schomberg was never asked, and did not on his own explain, why only two water closets were expected to meet the needs of three hundred and fifty people two to three times a day for eight to ten weeks. Even in the slums of London at that time, no building housing a hundred tenants had fewer than two water closets, and most had from four to eight. But the members of the House of Lords Select Committee on Emigrant Ships never concerned themselves with the question of how many water closets would be needed by three hundred and fifty passengers during a ten-week voyage; rather, they deliberated about where the two water closets allotted to them should be situated.

Schomberg was at least discreet, knowing as he did that each ship was limited to two water closets no matter how many people were jammed in steerage, when he concluded: "I positively give it as my opinion that if you put water closets between decks of ships carrying out a mass of the lower population, you will increase disease immensely."[2]

The other group of experts claimed just the opposite on the grounds that during stormy weather, when access to the water closets on deck would be impossible, a much greater amount of filth would accumulate below than any caused by water closets situated there. To have them below, claimed Samuel Redmond, a port inspector, "would be the very means of preventing filth, for when they [the steerage passengers] cannot get up [on deck], they must necessarily stay below, and I have seen the consequences of their not being able to get to those privies. I have seen a most tremendous quantity of filth even in the docks, before the ship went into the river at all . . . and . . . the smell was most intolerable."[3]

Another argument in favor of water closets below was the daily embarrassment women and girls had to endure when they went on deck and made their way along the fore part of the ship (where the sailors spent most of their working time) to use one or the other of the two miserable water closets up in the bows.

"It is quite distressing to see the women at sea trying to make use of the water closets usually provided," said one witness before the Select Committee, "at times getting drenched with the sea rather than be exposed to the crew. . . ."[4] Another witness agreed: "Women and girls do not like to go to such places before sailors."[5]

This led committee members to wonder why the water closets were not built aft, and it was agreed that to have them aft would be a great advantage, especially to the women. For one thing, the privies would then be away from both the seamen's work area and the open fire where the steerage passengers did their cooking. Back aft, the privies would also be more protected from the weather—and kept in strict working order if only because the captain and his living quarters were nearby. The proximity of the captain was in fact what nullified the whole idea: water closets were not built aft because "the captain would be obliged to have this annoyance under his nose or eyesight."[6]

The great demoralizing effect of having the two water closets up in the bows of the ship came with the first real storm, an event magnified tenfold in steerage, where the raging sea could not be seen and it was difficult in the darkness not to imagine the worst. "Never be alarmed until the captain is," was a seamen's proverb in the days of sailing ships. In steerage, no one ever saw the captain during a storm, but when a sudden heave of the ship abruptly dislodged the members of a whole family from their berths and sent them headlong into other passengers on the other side of the ship, then hurled them back again against the rough partitions, where they were bumped and bruised, the children almost crushed to death, they did not need the sight of alarm on the captain's face to become themselves alarmed.

The shrieks and screams of fellow passengers, all of them rolling and flopping about in confusion and disarray; the water plunging down from above, soaking their mattresses and rising high around their ankles despite the constant working of the pumps; the sound of sliding pots, basins, jars, utensils, and broken bottles; the smashing of casks, tinware, and dishes; the quivering of the ship, the creaking of her masts, the screeching of the gale through her blocks, and the hoarse roaring in her shrouds and rigging as she pitched and weaved in torrents of water and wind whose battering power and wild noises reached ever higher peaks that competed for attention with the captain's orders, shouted through a trumpet and answered in wails and chants from the sailors in the shrouds; everything convinced them that the ship was about to break up and, with all aboard, be swallowed in the great deep. Terror-stricken as they were in the black dungeon that had become their prison at sea, weak as they were with nothing warm to eat and only contaminated water to drink, unable as they were to use the privies on deck, they would remember for as long as they lived the horror, misery, and elemental fear of being locked like animals in steerage during a storm, when insanity was the only escape and sanity an almost unendurable burden.

When the storm subsided somewhat and they began to believe the ship would survive, they looked around and found the sight even harder to believe than the cuts and bruises they'd sustained. A hurricane might have swept through steerage: pots, basins, and pans of every description and provisions of all sorts were strewn over the sloshy deck; clothes, shoes, bonnets, shawls, blankets, and nightcaps were jammed in amongst the twisted or caved-in berths. A woman whose arm had been broken by a fallen berth was so weak she could only whisper for help; a child's ribcage has been crushed under a cask that had rolled against her and broken open.

While the injured were given aid by the most knowledgeable among those in steerage, the others tried to retrieve their belongings and set things right again. But the hatch leading to the main deck, which had been closed and battened down from the start of the storm, remained closed for hours and sometimes for days, until the sea and wind calmed sufficiently to allow it to be opened again. During this period there was no access to the main deck, where the steerage passengers' only two privies were situated.

It did not take long for the younger passengers and little children to solve the problem for themselves. When the calls of nature came on, they did not very much mind where they went, locked below as they were with no proper place to go. Their behavior gave notice of what lay ahead for everyone, and as time went on and the adults too were forced to relieve themselves wherever possible, some desperately modest women and girls made their way down in the darkness to the orlop deck below the steerage deck, where the cargo was stored, braving even the horrifying curiosity of rats in order to defecate in private.

The type of cargo the ship carried was of great importance to those in steerage, who were almost always situated just above it. Since most merchant ships with Irish bound for America carried either pig iron or hides or both, the steerage passengers suffered in one way if they were lucky, or in two ways if they were unlucky. A ship carrying only hides, for example, had a stench almost as sickening as that of a slaughterhouse, but at least the weight was fairly evenly distributed between cargo and passengers. A ship carrying only pig iron, on the other hand, created no smell and, with its enormous weight at the bottom of the hull, exerted in light weather a steadying influence on the ship. But in stormy weather this enormous weight exacerbated the pendulumlike roll from port to starboard, starboard to port, creating a kind of Chinese torture based on repetition of movement rather than sound. If the ship was carrying both hides and pig iron, as the *Mersey* was, the emigrants had to contend with both— in fair weather the smell only, in foul weather the smell and the violent roll too.

Sometimes, a woman forced to visit the orlop deck preferred the company of another woman in the same predicament to the prospect of being alone in the darkness with the reconnoitering rats that gathered around her. Together the women would climb down amidst the cargo and try to find some unused place, talking and making as much noise as possible in an effort to disperse both the rats and their fear of them. It was no secret among the passengers that the orlop deck was used for this purpose; in fact, in time, as the number of women and girls using it increased, it became a public toilet minus one essential: a flush to send into the ocean the fecal matter. The waste simply accumulated, and the putrefaction and miasma it created rose up through the uncaulked plank deck supporting the steerage passengers above. Of course, there was an accumulation of waste on the steerage deck as well, from the children, the men and women too old or sick to care, and those whose habits had never been otherwise. But even if these living quarters had been emptied of the filth, fumigated, and aired after every storm, the stench from the feces and hides on the orlop deck below would still have risen through the uncaulked steerage deck and permeated the clothes, food, and bedding of everyone living there.[7]

The chamber-pot peddler in Cork must have had some knowledge of conditions in steerage when he told the emigrant women boarding the ship, "It's yourselves will be blessing me every day of the voyage." Before the ship was five days out, a chamber pot became a prized possession, and the few who had one absolutely refused, out of fear of its being lost or stolen, to share it with anyone. Those with nice habits tied the end of a clothesline to the pot's handle, and when they went on deck to empty its contents over the side (at night if possible to avoid being seen), they dipped it, with the aid of the line, into the cleansing, phosphorescent waters of the ocean, then took the clean pot with them back down into steerage.

These "night women," as they came to be called, would always linger on deck by the side of the ship, sometimes for as long as an hour if not chased back down into steerage by some officer or seaman. For at night the sparkling water was such a fetching delight compared with the disgusting hold where they had to spend almost all their time. Especially on very dark nights, the ship seemed to be sliding through a bed of liquid diamonds, heaving up glittering waters at her bow and leaving in her wake a long line of living, dancing light. Some women actually tried to capture the liquid luminosity by drawing it up on deck in their scoured chamber pots. And for a moment some bright and beautiful secret of nature seemed to be theirs as they poured the water on deck and watched it trickle like a string of liquid jewels toward the scuppers. Being there on deck, aware of what awaited them below and at the same time enthralled by the gorgeous diamonds of light that the water and the movement of the ship created, was like seeing emigration through the eyes of God.

In view of the repeated admission, in the minutes of evidence taken in England before the House of Lords Select Committee on Emigrant Ships, that the water-closet problem presented ship captains and officers with a trying dilemma in a dreadful situation, it is difficult to understand why private places were not set aside between decks for individuals in need of using a chamber pot. Surrounded twenty-four hours a day by an ocean capable of accepting all the waste the ship and her passengers created, the ship captains and officers nonetheless remained baffled as to how to get the waste over the side.[8]

If every steerage passenger had been advised to bring or had been supplied with a chamber pot, and then had been told from the start that it was everyone's daily responsibility to empty his or her own waste over the lee side of the ship, the ten-week voyage might have been bearable. The chamber pot had been used in England for centuries, even by royalty before the advent of plumbing. Why was it not used on the ships carrying the Irish to America?

Over two hundred years before this Irish-famine exodus, the *Mayflower*, a ship of only 180 tons burden, brought 102 passengers to America without the use of water closets. One man died of old age aboard ship during the two-month voyage, but the others arrived clean and in good health. How did these crowded Pilgrims get their waste matter over the side without the use of water closets? Why did not the Select Committee research the success of these much earlier voyages? Since even queens used chamber pots, however bejeweled they may have been, in 1620, when the *Mayflower* sailed, the reason for the hygienic success of the voyage seems obvious. Perhaps the members of the committee did not look into the possibilities of the chamber pot at sea for the same prudish reasons that today's compilers of encyclopedias do not include it in their listings.

On the Irish emigrant ships, the chamber pot might very well have solved the problem during storms when the hatch had to be battened down. The waste matter could have been deposited below in a tightly covered barrel, of which there would have been many as the different foods brought aboard in barrels were consumed. When the weather cleared and access to the main deck was again allowed, the barrel's contents, or the barrel along with its contents, could have been thrown overboard. If steerage passengers could die of the filth they were forced to live with below, if their bodies could be thrown overboard, why could not the waste of those still trying to survive be thrown overboard? Such a system, however annoying and inconvenient, would have been far better than closing the hatch during bad weather, preventing the passengers from getting to the water closets on deck, and thereby forcing them to relieve themselves helter-skelter below.

Necessity in this case was not the mother of invention for a simple reason: the improvement needed to afford decent conditions in steerage was needed by people who did not count and who were considered subhuman anyway. Most members of the Select Committee agreed that the Irish emigrants were content to live between decks "like pigs," that the accumulated effluvia and filth, the foul atmosphere and disease were the result of their own lack of cleanliness.

What these committee members would have done down in steerage during foul weather, with the battened-down hatch depriving them of the use of the two miserable water closets on deck, was never explained. Perhaps, emulating Harriet Martineau and her belief in "control over the expression of emotions," they would have controlled the movement of their bowels until the return of fair weather and the reopening of the hatch, at which time they would have lined up in orderly fashion on deck, all three hundred and fifty of them, and with stiff upper lip awaited their turn at the two bare, by now unhoused water closets in the bows. What they would have done to keep clean when they were supplied barely enough water to cook with (you either washed or cooked, but not both) also remains to this day a mystery. The filthy habits alluded to by the Select Committee, said Samuel Redmond, an English eyewitness to the horrors of steerage, "are not the natural inclination of the people but arise from the way in which they are circumstanced."[9]

Mrs. Caroline Chisholm, another English eyewitness testifying before the same committee, was more specific. She said that "If the steerage passengers in a ship carrying from three to six hundred have no convenience for washing their hands, which they have not, or if there are no wash-houses or bath places where they can go to, it is impossible for them to be in a state of cleanliness. So that before emigrants are considered and classed as a filthy set, and the blame is all put on pauperism, it should not be so, but on the neglect of those who do not provide the emigrants with the proper accommodation."[10]

For the Irish emigrants aboard these British ships, the weather-imposed confinement in steerage created an atmosphere as disgusting, degrading, suffocating, and depressing as it was inescapable and laden with disease. Locked in with their miserable fellow exiles, limited to partly alive sea biscuit because they could not cook their own food on deck, prevented by their coffin-tight bunks from even relieving their restlessness by a change of position, vomiting from seasickness, and cut off from the only two water closets available to them when they were unable to control their bowels, they remembered Ireland with an earth-hunger that only added to their hatred of the ever-moving sea and to their desire to reach America.

Beneath all the lower berths were bones, rags, urine, feces, vomit, and the rotting remains of food, putrifying and covered with maggots. To breathe in order to go on living became almost insufferable, so horribly offensive and all-pervasive was the smell. Even when fair weather allowed the hatch to the main deck above to be opened and the scuttles along the side of the ship to be unlocked and pushed ajar, the hot, fetid air below had such pressure building up from the surrounding putrefaction that a boiling-kettle set of forces was created: the hot air with its greater pressure escaped, but precious little fresh cold air was allowed to enter, and what little did was soon turned into pressurized hot air again by the hungry lungs, sweating bodies, and endless effluvia from the waste of those who during the bad weather had had nowhere else but below to relieve themselves. One member of the House of Commons stated before his colleagues that a navy captain who had been engaged in suppressing the slave trade off Africa had declared that "the condition of many Irish emigrant vessels which he had seen . . . beggared all descriptions of the state of the captured slave ships."[11]

During these mid-century years, more was in fact done by the British to eliminate the inhumanity of the African slave trade than ever was done to alleviate the suffering of the Irish, who as tax-paying British subjects, with representatives in Parliament, were entitled to the same treatment as any Englishman living in England. Instead they were made to live under conditions aboard ship far worse than those suffered by African slaves.

On all American ships during this same period, though the Irish were not yet American citizens, the accommodations were vastly superior to those on ships flying the British flag. According to an Englishman named William Cobbett, a man with extensive shipping experience who wrote an emigrant's guide for his countrymen, American ships also carried more sail and were faster and better navigated than British vessels. They made eight to ten knots even at night, more than twice the speed of British ships, most of whose sails were taken in at sunset. American captains were more alert to both danger and any advantage the weather offered; for example, they would immediately take in their sails at the sight of an approaching squall, then let them out again the moment the squall passed to take advantage of the strong wind that always followed in a squall's wake.

"I never knew an American captain take off his clothes to go to bed, during the whole voyage," Cobbett said. "And I never knew any other who did not do it."[12]

But more important than the speed of the ship, the vigilance of the captain, and the navigational skills of the ship's officers, were the ship's construction and what accommodations it offered. In 1847 the ordinary emigrant ship had four decks: the quarter-deck, which rose like a house above the main deck at the stern of the ship; the main deck, which extended fore and aft the entire length of the ship; the steerage deck, which extended from roughly midships to the bow just below the main deck; and the orlop, or storage, deck, which extended fore and aft below the steerage deck.

Unlike United States vessels, which by law had to have

permanent decks, British ships were allowed by law to have temporary decks to accommodate and accelerate the welcome flight of the Irish from Ireland. On American ships, that is, the steerage deck was caulked to allow a regular hosing-down with lime and water to limit as much as possible the spread of disease. On British ships, the planks were simply laid between the beams, one next to the other, and never caulked. Some planks were unavoidably warped, often with spaces in between as wide as the flat of a man's hand. With the cargo stowed on the orlop deck just below this steerage deck, water could not be used to clean the steerage quarters for fear of damaging the cargo, which was more valued by the master of the ship than were the steerage passengers.

Again, on every American ship the water closets were built as component parts of the ship during the ship's construction; they were as capable as the ship herself was of withstanding stormy weather. On British ships like the *Mersey*, while the ship was calmly at rest in Liverpool, Dublin, or Cork, a couple of carpenters were hired to build two makeshift closets up in the bows. The carpenters no doubt did their best, and on land the closets might have withstood the wind and rain for years. But at sea these hurriedly constructed adjuncts were torn apart by the waves and wind during the first storm, leaving only the two bare toilet bowls where women and girls were expected to relieve themselves before the eyes of sailors.

Finally, the bedsteads on American ships were not only made of iron, but suspended from the beams as permanent fixtures to afford better ventilation, cleanliness, and security. A steerage passenger on an American ship might be thrown out of bed by the heaving of the ship, but at least when he struggled back to his bunk he would find it still there. On British ships the temporary wooden framework often collapsed, and when it did, it remained in that condition until the ship returned to Ireland or Liverpool, where makeshift bunks were again built for the next load of Irish emigrants.[13]

All these matters and many more were discussed before the House of Lords Select Committee on Emigrant Ships during this period, which Lord Clarendon called "a calamity without parallel in the annals of history," until reports of the horrendous conditions in steerage began to embarrass the British on both sides of the Atlantic. Even the London *Times*, whose incendiary anti-Irish editorials had contributed to the way the Irish were treated, had to admit that "the worst horrors of that slave trade which it is the boast or ambition of this empire to suppress, at any cost, have been reenacted in the flight of British subjects from their native shores. . . . The Blackhole of Calcutta was a mercy compared to the holds of these vessels. Yet simultaneously, as if in reproof of those on whom the blame of all this wretchedness must fall, foreigners, Germans from Hamburg and Bremen are daily arriving [in America], all healthy, robust, and cheerful. . . . Nor do we see any way to escape the opprobrium of a national inhumanity except by taking the earliest and most effectual means to rectify past errors and prevent their recurrence."[14]

The horrendous steerage conditions aboard British ships had finally become public knowledge not only in the United States and Canada, where these conditions were observed firsthand by doctors and inspectors boarding the ships as they arrived, but throughout the seafaring nations of Europe. With the famine still destroying the population of Ireland, and those trying to escape still being subjected aboard British ships to conditions that virtually precluded their survival, newspapers in Ireland, England, France, Germany, Scandinavia, Canada, and the United States began printing stories that could no longer be denied by the London *Times* or the government for which it mostly spoke.

Britain's "coffin ships" had become a scandal in the eyes of the world, and though this stirred to action some concerned members of Parliament, the body as a whole reacted as it usually did to matters concerning the "Irish Question"—so slowly that it was not until 1854, seven years later, when the famine exodus was thinning out, that anything of significance was done to correct the situation.

The Passenger Acts already in existence in 1847 were to-

tally inadequate as guidelines for what those forced to leave
Ireland might expect. Instead of hundreds, thousands were
entering ports in search of passage, with the result that even
small vessels, some of them scarcely able to cross the Irish Sea
to England, much less the Atlantic to America, were embarking with passengers from inlets and minor ports never before
used for emigration. It was felt among British lawmakers that
to have restrained these passengers from embarking or the
vessels from sailing would have led to a higher mortality rate
and more widespread suffering. However reasonable and
humane this may have sounded at the time, the fact remains
that many of these small, unregistered vessels were never
heard from again; no complete and accurate account of what
happened to them or to their passengers was ever made. Obviously, the overriding consideration was not what happened
to the Irish after they embarked but, rather, that they be allowed to embark regardless of the size and condition of the
vessel in which they were trying to escape.

Meanwhile, avaricious and unscrupulous British shippers
were able to ride roughshod over any proposed legislation that
curtailed their highly profitable operations. Even in 1849,
when improvements were written into the Passenger Acts, they
were either evaded through the loopholes provided or completely ignored because of lax enforcement. Between 1846 and
1854, when history's most tragic episodes on land and at sea
were taking place, when British shipping companies should
have been forced by law to equal or exceed American standards, no significant improvement was made on behalf of
steerage passengers on board British ships.

Consider just a few of these British ships making the
crossing in 1847: the brig *Larch*, from Sligo, buried at sea 108
of its 440 passengers, and 150 of the remainder were seriously
ill when she reached the quarantine station; the *Lord Ash-
burton*, from Liverpool with 475 passengers, buried 107 at sea,
and 60 were still sick with fever and dysentery on arrival at
Grosse Isle; the *Virginius*, with 596 aboard when she set sail,
buried 158 during the passage and arrived with 186 more very

sick and "the remainder so feeble and tottering" they could hardly disembark under their own power; the *Sir Henry Pottinger*, from Cork, reported 96 deaths and 112 still sick, out of 399 passengers.[15]

For every death on board an American ship, there were three on board a British; for every diseased person arriving in America aboard an American ship, there were five aboard a British. Since the majority of these diseased persons died shortly after arrival, in either Canada or the United States, the contrast in the mortality rate between British and American ships would be even greater if these port-arrival deaths were included. Of the 98,105 emigrants traveling on British ships to Canada alone in 1847, 5,293 died at sea, 8,072 shortly after arrival at Grosse Isle and Quebec, and 7,000 in and above Montreal. This appalling figure of 20,365 recorded deaths out of a total of 98,105 emigrants going to Canada in 1847 does not take into account those whose early deaths in the hinterlands were either never recorded or not included in the emigrant death toll. It would therefore be conservative to say that out of roughly 100,000 emigrants carried aboard British ships to Canada in 1847, 25,000, or one in every four, died en route or within six months after arrival.[16]

The primary concern as usual was not humane treatment but profit, not dealing with exigencies but turning away from them. How or whether the Irish emigrants survived the voyage was far down on the list of concerns. Select committees met, they heard the horror stories told by eyewitnesses, but what they did to prevent the horror was not more effective during the exodus than were Britain's efforts at the height of the famine to feed the starving.

Even if the Irish had been scoured in a public bath and their clothing and mattresses fumigated before they boarded the *Mersey* at Cork, disease would have been inevitable with such living conditions, cooking arrangements, and food deficiencies. Diarrhea, gastric disorders, scurvy, dysentery, and most of the intestinal diseases would have been generated long before the voyage ended. But with no bathing facilities available in Cork and no fumigation required before embarkation, steerage passengers boarded the *Mersey* with clothing and mattresses infested with lice. The entire ship, with a few thousand stowaway lice aboard, needed only one passenger ill with typhus and another with relapsing fever for both diseases to become epidemic during a two-month voyage.

The lice were carried aboard in the clothing salvaged by emigrants from persons who had died in the typhus-ridden villages from which the emigrants were escaping. The clothing was either used by surviving relatives or auctioned off to prospective emigrants who needed extra clothing for the voyage to America. This practice would be prohibited today, but in 1847 the louse had not yet been linked to the spread of typhus and relapsing fever, and since everyone poor in Ireland during the famine was louse-ridden, and clothing was clothing, with or without lice, it is easy now to see why emigrant ships leaving Liverpool, not to mention Cork, Dublin, and other Irish ports, were so subject to "ship fever" and the high mortality it caused. The overcrowded slums and alleys of these cities, where passengers lodged until they embarked, were the true seed beds of the tragedies of 1847.[17]

Aboard the *Mersey*, these tragedies followed closely upon what had happened in Ireland. While the typhus and relapsing-fever microorganisms were growing and expanding in the intestines and bodies of the stowaway lice, all the other ailments associated with filth, contamination, and malnutrition began to show themselves. First came the spongy gums, loose teeth, livid skin spots, and prostration of scurvy, a disease suffered initially by those who had brought few if any provisions aboard in the belief that the "parliamentary diet" would sustain them. After being seasick for a week and then refused the extra rations necessary to give them back their strength and replenish the vitamin C they so desperately needed, they deteriorated to the point where their ankles and legs swelled with body fluids and they began bleeding into their skin and mucous membranes. This created great pain and suffering and brought on moans that alarmed neighbors ignorant of the fact that scurvy was not infectious, as the diseases soon to follow would be.

The comparatively well fed in steerage (those who had brought provisions to supplement the "parliamentary diet") scratched and killed the ubiquitous lice, drank the foul, vinegar-spiked water because there was no other water to drink, and tried to remain as clean as possible in the quagmire of filth that yielded under their feet as they made their way about in steerage. But in time even these stronger people came down with gastric and intestinal disorders germinated by the contaminated food, infected feces, vomit, and diarrhea.

With no washing water supplied, it was impossible—no matter how "disciplined" the Irish peasantry aboard were, or should have been—to prevent the dysentery bacteria from spreading from one packed-in person to another. If their bodies were not being searched by lice in need of a blood meal, they were being invaded by dysentery bacteria via the uncooked food or the unwashed hands handling the food. After a few weeks of living in this worse-than-prison, with the carcasses of chickens and the backbones and skulls of pigs all over the place, with lack of ventilation causing the ever-increasing stench to become more and more a part of the ever-diminishing air supply, the great wonder is why there is no record of anyone climbing in desperation to the main deck and jumping overboard. There was no other escape, and as the many different diseases spread to more and more people, as the prostration and moaning proliferated, the people in steerage remembered the remark made by the blond-haired seaman to the young man on deck: "Be patient, lad. There'll be more room in the hold the farther out we get."

Four weeks had passed since then, and the voyage was still less than half completed. They would be aboard for five, perhaps even six, more weeks, during which there would be more storms, more battened-down hatches, more uncooked food and foul water, more daily accumulation of filth. The prospect brought on a kind of stupor of indifference to their own suffering, an apathy so deep that it closed in and immobilized them like a paralysis. If the elderly among them were required to move their legs to let someone pass through an aisle in steerage, or if someone trying to pass moved their legs for them, their legs would remain in the new position indefinitely, until some other force outside themselves brought about another change in position. Having come to the realization that there was nothing they could do anyway—nothing to make the ship faster, the food better, the drinking water more plentiful, or the two privies on deck more accessible—they lay in their bunks haunted by the words: "There'll be more room in the hold the farther out we get."

One Irish cottier aboard the *Mersey* put it this way: "We thought we couldn't be worse off than we war. But now to our sorrow we know the differ; for sure supposin we war dying of starvation, or if the sickness overtuk us. We had a chance of a doctor, and if he could do no good for our bodies, sure the priest could for our souls; and then we'd be buried along wid our people, in the ould churchyard, with the green sod over us, instead of lying like rotten sheep thrown in a pit, and the minit the breath is out of our bodies, flung into the sea to be eaten up by them horrid sharks."[18]

Chapter Eighteen

I spent a considerable part of the day watching a
shark that followed in our wake with great
constancy . . . the mate said it was a certain
forerunner of death.

—Robert Whyte,
The Ocean Plague

THE first death was discovered shortly after dawn on the
second day of the fifth week, while passengers were making
their way through the bilgy aisles toward the open hatch to get
their food cooked on deck. Sam "Sweep" Sullivan, the man who
had refused to wash himself in the belief that he would thereby
escape disease, was found in his bunk face up with his eyes
and mouth open, his black bristly nostrils like fangs ready to
strike, his skin as crusty and dirty as a rag used to swab the
deck. Some even speculated that since he had had such an
offensive odor while alive, he may have been dead for a day or
two before being discovered.

There being no doctor aboard, no attempt was made to
determine the cause of death or to question or caution nearby
steerage passengers. The captain would attribute the death in
the ship's log to the all-encompassing "ship fever," but Sam
Sweep had not been feverish, and no lice or other vermin were
found on either his body or in the insufferably filthy clothes he
wore. His often expounded theory that the accumulation of
dirt on his body and the smell it generated scared off disease-
carrying vermin may have been true in his case. But he died

anyway, perhaps from some olfactory rebellion that brought on a heart attack.

The mate was not interested in how or why he died; his only concern was in getting the body over the side and into the deep as quickly as possible. Climbing down into steerage to prepare the body for burial, he took with him an old piece of canvas sailcloth in which to wrap the body, along with stone weights to put at the feet to make certain the body would sink immediately on being slipped overboard. When Big Gil offered to help him, he stretched out the sailcloth beside Sam Sweep's bunk, closed his eyes and mouth, and was about to lift the body onto it, with Big Gil's help, when three women, seeing the deep crevices of dirt in Sam's face, neck, and ears, intervened. He looked even blacker and dirtier in death than he had in life, and they objected to his being buried in this way. At least his face should be washed before he was wrapped in his canvas coffin.

"Spotless clean he'll be, minutes after we slip him over," said the mate.

"But the funeral service. He won't be clean for the service. And sure, 'tis close to sacrilege to read the service over an unwashed corpse."

The more they spoke—about the awakening on the Day of Judgment and how the living owed the dead this one last favor—the more Big Gil tended to agree with them. Finally the mate, who was not as stern as he tried to appear, relented. He of all people knew how the Irish feared burial at sea, so perhaps Sam Sweep, the first on this trip to go, deserved special attention.

"In half an hour, then," he said.

Using their own drinking water, a bit of soap kindly supplied by the mate, and some rags from an old dress, the three women proceeded to wash Sam Sweep's hair, hands, neck, face, and feet. A small, silent audience gathered round, and the more dirt the women removed, the more interesting and better looking Sam Sweep became. It was as if they were cleaning and restoring, ever so carefully, an old portrait found covered with decades of dust. The lines and crevices embedded with dirt turned out to be, once cleaned, not only less noticeable but more integral a part of the face itself—a face much more delicate and intelligent than the dirt had allowed anyone to notice. The women fixed his hair; they straightened his eyebrows, combed his beard, and trimmed the black bristles extending from his nostrils and ears. And the moment they were finished, when in an open coffin he would have graced an Irish wake with his presence, he was lifted by the mate and Big Gil and wrapped up out of sight in the canvas sailcloth. At least thirty pounds of stone were tucked in with his body at the feet, and the canvas carefully cornered at each end so that one long set of stitches along the top, sewn with surprising speed and expertise by an old seaman, sealed the interlocking folds and enclosed the corpse mummylike in its casing.

Only the form of Sam Sweep could now be seen; the tender ablution seemed for a moment to have served no purpose. But the three women who had worked over him were weeping, as were the onlookers who had seen his features almost come to life after death. Everyone, even the mate who had reluctantly given the three women permission to prepare Sam Sweep for Judgment Day, now seemed to have a more benign vision of the man they could no longer see and were about to bury. They hesitated, as if in silent tribute to a man they had met too late.

Then came a snag in this otherwise orderly preparation for the *Mersey*'s first burial at sea. One of Sam's possessions— the ticket he had bought from Big Gil for the lottery to be decided on the day land was first sighted—became a point of contention among the three women who had prepared him for burial. The woman who found the ticket in Sam's pocket thought it belonged to her, but the other two did not accept that. All three agreed, though, with Big Gil's helpful mediation, to settle the matter by drawing lots. The mate, impatient but determined to be fair, plucked three straws from Sam's dilapidated mattress and turned his back for a moment to make one longer than the other two.

"The one drawing the longest is the winner, and that's final," he said, facing the women with the three straws sticking from his hand.

The circle of onlookers drew closer, forgetting for a moment the wrapped-up corpse on the deck beneath them. Having lived with chance all their lives, they were addicted to it—compulsive gamblers on an unbroken losing streak. There were "oh"s and "ah"s as the first woman drew what everyone agreed had to be the longest straw, then more of the same as the second one drew one slightly longer. But it was the third woman, the one who had cleaned Sam's filthy feet, who came up the winner, and no sooner was she given the ticket than she reacted in a way so typical of the famine Irish.

Turning to the two losers, she said, "Don't fret, my biddies. If I win, every farthing of the prize I'll share with you."

The mate did not bother to ask the winner why she had not suggested that solution to begin with; he was too experienced with Irish emigrants and the tricks they tried to play on fate, no doubt in return for all the tricks it had played on them.

But a dead body is both feared and detested aboard a ship at sea, and already the ship's bells were tolling the beginning of the funeral service. Four seamen acting as pallbearers, their heads bared, came to lift the weighted corpse through the hatch to the main deck, where it was draped in the Union Jack, the flag of Great Britain, whose colors had so proudly flown atop Soyer's soup kitchen in Dublin. All the deck hands, everyone in steerage who could stand on his or her own feet, and even the cabin passengers, with their mezzanine view from the quarter-deck, were in attendance. The rope that had been stretched athwart ships just aft of the main mast to separate the steerage passengers from those traveling cabin-class had to be temporarily removed to allow more space for the stragglers climbing up from the hold.

Finally, when the flag-draped body was lifted onto a hatch batten (one of the long planks used to close the hatch against the weather) and the batten was placed on the bulwarks of the ship, the captain, tidily uniformed, appeared. Having worn only the sloppiest attire until now—attire more befitting a dishwasher than a captain—he not only surprised his audience but grabbed its attention as well. Holding the Book of Common Prayer up close to his chest, he waited until the four pallbearers had the batten balanced seesaw fashion over the side of the ship, the weighted feet of the corpse at one end over the water and the head at the other end over the deck, then began reading in a booming voice the service of the Church of England. It was obviously not a new experience for him, and like a seasoned actor he made the most of it, using intonations that seemed to hold the body in balance as much as the pallbearers, whose job it was, did.

The irony of using the Church of England service for Sam Sweep, an Irish Catholic forced by English laws to leave his own land, was not lost on the Irish attending the service. "They drive us to the grave," whispered one man to another on deck, "then cap it by using their service to bury us."

But the dead man was being shown respect, the same respect as would have been shown a member of the Church of England—more respect, in fact, than he had been shown in life. For this the steerage passengers were thankful; they stood at attention and listened carefully to every word as the captain read through the impressive and beautiful text. As he read "O death, where is thy sting? O grave, where is thy victory? With the full hope of a glorious resurrection we commit this body to the deep," the pallbearers tilted the plank seaward with an expertise that could only have come from experience.

The body of Sam Sweep slid feetfirst off the plank, made a perfect arc as it descended, and entered the water almost without a splash. Had they tipped the plank too quickly, the body would have turned in midair and belly-flopped into the water; but it went in like a knife and disappeared that quickly. Those at the side of the ship leaned over as if in search of some evidence of the end of Sam Sweep. But except for a tantalizing glimpse of some bubbles rising to the surface in a small circular area where he may or may not have entered the water, there was nowhere the slightest sign that anything had happened to the sea. The waves were as usual capped with foam, which in its inimitable way spread like lace over the surface, only to disappear and then reappear again as the waves moved on. Unlike funerals they had attended in Ireland, where interment of one's deceased relatives involved family and community preparation and bestowed even on death a feeling of social interest, this one seemed already to have been blanked out. Sam Sweep was gone as though he had never existed.

Now the pallbearers were carefully folding the Union Jack, which they had held on to as Sam Sweep's body slid from under it into the water. It was as if they had taken part in a disappearing act and were now getting their props ready for the next performance. The steerage passengers were stunned, dismayed, frightened; they felt in a vague way cheated. All their lives they had linked the material and the spiritual world in odd and delightful ways that made one as attractive as the other in what amounted to a mutually dependent relationship. One of their supersititions about death, for example, was that the last person interred on any given day had to perform menial services for all the other dead in that graveyard until some other person was buried last, on a multiburial day, in the same graveyard. Not only was this superstition believed in Ireland, it often led to two bereaved families racing in unseemly haste to the same graveyard to get their loved one into the ground first, thereby protecting him against the degrading chore of waiting on the others until relief came in the form of another tardy soul.[1]

Another belief was that the dead of one parish graveyard competed with the dead of another parish graveyard in the old Irish game of hurling. Each parish team had a living man from its parish to keep the goal, and when the teams met, always under a full moon, at one or the other of the graveyards, the two live goalkeepers had to be, and always were, present. They had to do this for seven years, whereupon they were believed to have the power to cure diseases against which doctors were powerless. Each live goalkeeper had to keep the dread secret to himself, otherwise he would be shunned by his neighbors. Nor could he change his normal behavior or disposition in any way Any untoward behavior on his part, any sign of gloominess or eccentricity, would lead to community suspicion that he was the goalkeeper for the dead hurlers.[2]

Sam Sweep's burial at sea prevented the steerage passengers from putting these benign superstitions to any imaginative use. In the middle of the Atlantic, the idea of two graveyards competing with each other in the game of hurling became even in their eyes a meaningless museum piece. They could in no way relate his disappearance over the side with the reciprocal relationship they believed existed between this world and the next. Their lifelong orientation to burial in consecrated ground, beside generations of relatives, left them emotionally and psychologically defenseless against the no longer groundless fear that they too might be buried at sea before the ship reached New York. Though no one realized it at the time, Sam Sweep's burial marked the division between two phases of the voyage, the second of which was about to start.

Chapter Nineteen

> . . . It may be thought that the immolation of so
> many wretched starvelings was rather a benefit
> than a loss to the world. It may be so. Yet—
> untutored, degraded, famished and plague-
> stricken as they were; I assert that there was
> more true heroism, more faith, more forgiveness
> to their enemies, and submission to the Divine
> Will, exemplified in these victims, than could be
> found in ten times the number of their oppressors.
>
> —Robert Whyte,
> *The Ocean Plague*

UP to the moment when Sam Sweep disappeared over the side by what seemed sleight of hand on the part of the crew, the main preoccupation among steerage passengers had been the voyage itself—the day-by-day progress, the endless tacking to windward, the crowding around the caboose, the storms, the water-closet problem, and the foulness of steerage, which had become such a prolific medium of misery and disease that germs were now swallowed with every breath. Even the elderly and sick had clung to the belief that they would eventually arrive in New York, tired and weak, perhaps, but still able to move on to the new lives awaiting them.

But Sam's death and disappearance, the way his whole life seemed nullified by the sea engulfing him, diverted their thoughts from the voyage itself to their chances of surviving it. With the *Mersey* still in the middle of the Atlantic, barely halfway to her destination, they retrenched to a still-lower level of existence. How to remain alive became the main pre-occupation, as it had been in the country they had just fled, except that now there was no chance of flight or even of improving the conditions under which they were forced to live. In Ireland they had been able to abandon an infected cabin or devastated town; aboard the *Mersey* they were locked in with the disease itself, down in steerage where the darkness writhed with the vilest revelations.

Immediately following Sam's burial, when they were told to return to their quarters below, a painful agitation seized them. Some lay in their bunks with open stares as if preparing themselves for Sam Sweep's fate; others, anticipating danger, moved their bedding from the moaners in the belief that the fever was contagious. But even as these cautious few made the change, they took with them the infected lice they were unwittingly trying to avoid. The "ship fever" they so greatly feared was in fact the "road fever" they had brought with them from Ireland—the typhus and relapsing fever they had carried with the lice on their bodies from one parish to another, and then, at Cork, onto a ship whose steerage quarters and unsanitary conditions made it impossible to prevent the propagation of these blood-sucking parasites and the two devastating diseases they caused.[1]

A characteristic of lice is to latch on to people who do not have long to live, who are too weak and emaciated to put the necessary effort into ridding themselves of this last insult before death frees them. This is not to say that the young and vigorous aboard the *Mersey* were not bothered; they were, but their reaction was quite different. The young women and girls especially, acutely aware as they were of any change in their skin or clothing, were the first to discover the lice.[2] One of these was Dolores Kinsella, Micky Quinn's wife-to-be, who had brought an adequate supply of soap and used it every day in her determination to be as clean on entering New York as she had been on leaving Cork.

One day she was sitting with Micky on deck, mending his only shirt, when she noticed a whitish-yellow speck moving along the cuff. Shaking the cuff so that the speck fell into the palm of her hand, she stared at it, waiting for it to move, which it soon did, across her palm. Her heart filled with anger against Micky, for there was no doubt that she had a determined and active louse in her hand. She crushed it with her finger and was about to castigate Micky for not using the precious soap she'd given him when she remembered the "itchy feeling" she'd experienced on waking the last few mornings.

Leaving Micky on deck, she rushed down to her steerage bunk and stripped to the skin to examine herself. Her legs, shoulders, and abdomen down into her pubic hair were covered with red spots that could only have come from the bites of lice. She had scratched herself and felt some pricking sensations, but in the darkness in which she'd dressed every morning, she hadn't noticed the bloodsucking marks. Grabbing her clothing and taking it to an open porthole where there was light, she could see the tiny lice in every seam of the woolen jackets and coats she had so carefully accumulated for her first winter in New York; they were in the hems of her petticoats, the soft wool of her skirts, the armholes of her vests—in everything she owned, even her underwear.

She cried, realizing that she would have to soak everything in sea water and lime, then dry everything and hope the clothes would still fit her. What would she do with her mattress? Where would she sleep if her bunk and the whole wooden structure of the compartment were infested? She thought of Micky, the friend she had been so ready to blame, and was almost ashamed to rejoin him on deck.

It was during this fifth week of the voyage, shortly after Dolores was forced to throw her mattress overboard and sleep on the bare board of her bunk, that Ireland's "road fever" showed itself and became the *Mersey's* "ship fever." One young man named William Smith wrote a voyage memoir, which included a firsthand account of his own fever symptoms and a vivid description of conditions in steerage. Unlike other fairly well-educated men aboard, most of whom traveled cabin-class, he was a steerage passenger who did not need binoculars or opera glasses to observe what was happening up forward, much less down in the "pit," as steerage came to be known.

"My provisions were consumed," wrote Smith, "and I had nothing but ship allowance to subsist on, which was scarcely sufficient to keep us from perishing, being only a pound of sea-bisquit full of maggots and a pint of such water as [the ship provided]. I began to get so weak that if I walked on deck for a short time, I was compelled to sit down with fatigue."

Smith had washed himself on deck with sea or rain water whenever the opportunity arose; he had remained on deck as much as possible so that he might breathe the fresh air and escape the fumes of sickness and decay below. By helping the seamen do their daytime chores, by chatting at night with the man at the helm or with the man on the forecastle watch, he had satisfied his craving for fresh air and the salty spray of the sea. It was not until break of day that he went below to his bunk to sleep for a few hours, while those still ambulatory in steerage were emptying out and climbing on deck. He did everything anyone could have done to remain healthy and strong, but the lice got to his bunk and to him too.

"I now lost all spirit," Smith went on in his very short but moving memoir. "I felt as though I had no life in me. A listlessness came upon me, produced, no doubt, by suffering from extreme want. I had been in this state two days, when I was seized with the ship-fever; at first I was so dizzy that I could not walk without danger of falling. I was suffering much from a violent pain in my head, my brains felt as if they were on fire, my tongue clove to the roof of my mouth and my lips were parched with excessive thirst. Cheerfully would I have given the world, had I possessed it, for one draught of water."

In this state Smith managed, with the help of his seamen friends, to get past the rope barrier and up on the quarter-deck to see the captain. Hardly able to stand, fatigue and tension haunting his face like an incipient tic, he asked for a draught of water to help him get through the day.

"Water will make you worse," the captain said, taking him by the arm to steady him. "Your only chance for life is in taking some medicine."

"I still earnestly entreated him to give me a little water,"

Smith said, "but he replied that should he give to all appli-
cants, he would, in a few days, be entirely out, and that he
could not give to one unless he gave to all. I drank the medicine eagerly, as any fluid, however nauseous, was a boon not to
be despised, under existing circumstances."

Smith made his way back down into steerage, where he
became so sick that he could neither sit nor stand. He just lay
in his bunk, which was one of four arranged in two tiers in a
tight, stall-like compartment up forward. "One of my bed-
fellows . . . was sick with the diarrhea, and another . . . afraid
to come near us . . . stayed on deck most of the time. I do not
blame him for this, for, beside the fever, the stench in the
steerage was horried: the causes of which it is neither necessary nor proper to state. Every day I felt weaker, and became
exhausted upon the least exertion, and, as if to increase my
misery, another storm arose and continued three nights and
three days. I had to use all the little strength I had to prevent
being thrown out of bed by the heaving of the ship. My
strength failed me. I got two persons to put my bed in such a
position that I could remain in it without having to grasp the
boards of my berth; the hatchways were again closed upon us.
. . . To hear the groans of the sick, the despairing cries of their
kindred, the misery of all, and the dismal prospect of everything around me, conspired to fill my heart with gloomy fore-
bodings."[3]

Three days later, when the hatch was reopened, though
the water supply had been somewhat replenished by the rain,
the fever in steerage had spread and was manifesting itself in
as many different ways as there were people suffering from it.
Some had typhus, that is, and others relapsing fever, and all
were passing through different stages of the infection process.
One feverish man climbing on deck was so far gone that he
fancied himself a priest with the power to invoke divine help
for his flock. Raising both arms with apostolic fervor, he
warned the passengers that they would all die and go to hell if
they did not allow him to sprinkle holy water (his own drinking water) and make the sign of the cross over their heads.

Many of those around him, susceptible to the admonition because of their growing doubts about outliving the voyage, got on their knees and took part in the baptismal rite of purification, which seemed to pacify the man long enough for seamen to get him below.[4]

Another man, whose wife had taken their younger child with relatives on an earlier trip to New York, had the other child aboard with him. He had already shown signs of mental collapse due to high fever and was being watched over by a friend of the family, but while left alone for a moment he had climbed up from the darkness and stench below to the sunlight and fresh air. Weak and almost dying of thirst as he was, the sudden change in atmosphere must have been more than his overheated brain could assimilate. Acting as though the voyage were at last over and unable to wait another moment to rejoin his wife and younger child, he broke out with cries of joy and, before anyone could stop him, threw himself into the sea as if in an effort to be the first to reach land.

In the confusion and alarm that followed, the captain was not informed until the man was nearly out of sight, his thrashing in the water now as hard to discern as that of a pigeon. The captain spotted him through a telescope and saw that it was already too late to save him; he was going under and would disappear long before a boat could be lowered, much less rowed that distance. To many on deck the captain's decision to continue on course seemed cruel, but his judgment was correct, as one more look through the glass made clear: the man was gone.

"Oh, the poor child," recalled one eyewitness, "weeping for hours, asking for its father . . . How my heart bled."[5]

A third delirious man who attempted to stab his wife, had to be tied down to his berth. He had been the kindest and most affectionate husband, his wife said, until seized with the fever. She continued to care for him, and in three days he was able to walk about the steerage, leaning on his wife's arm, until he finally recovered.

After a number of similar incidents, the captain had every

delirious person who appeared capable of injuring himself or others tied down in his bunk. And to prevent more drownings, fights, and possibly dangerous fire accidents around the caboose, he stationed a guard at each hatchway with strict orders not to permit anyone who appeared to have become delirious during the night to come on deck.[6]

As necessary as these orders undoubtedly were, they only added to the dungeonlike confinement of steerage and the pervasive fear that the ship was doomed. Reports reaching those in cabin class grew ever more alarming; it was said that steerage had become a plague house, that emigrants whose fever had subsided were now relapsing, that others had contracted it and were passing it on. The moaning and raving ("Water, for God's sake, some water!") kept these cabin passengers awake nearly all the night, treasuring their separation from the disease and filth but at the same time beginning to wonder whether anyone would reach New York alive.

One patient in steerage, a woman expected at any moment to die, was being cared for by an aunt and two cousins who were distraught and inconsolable because they had persuaded her to leave her father and mother and come with them. Many passengers recalled the clearness of her complexion when they saw her in health, the picture of good humor and contentment, shortly after the ship had sailed. Now her head and face were swollen with excess fluid to a most unnatural size, the face especially as hideously deformed as a carnival mask. Her feet were double their natural size and covered with putrid black spots. And though her puffy cheeks retained their ruddy hue, she was otherwise leprously white and scaly. More than three weeks ill, she had suffered terrible pain from the moment the swelling set in, starting at her feet and creeping up her body to her head.

Cabin passenger Robert Whyte thought her death and burial would cause great consternation among the passengers, but her remains were slipped quietly over the side within an hour after she expired while he was still in his cabin back aft. "When I went on deck I heard the moans of her poor aunt, who continued to gaze upon the ocean as if she could mark the spot where the waters opened for their prey. The majority of the passengers who were not themselves ill were absorbed in grief for their relatives; but some of them, it astonished me to perceive, had no feeling whatever, either for their fellow creatures' woe, or in contemplation of being themselves overtaken by the dreadful disease."[7]

As a cabin passenger, Robert Whyte had reason to be shocked at this growing indifference toward death among those in steerage. Himself a humane man, with no experience of the famine horrors they had suffered, he had all the strength, mind, heart, will, kindness, and consideration to be appalled by both the way people were dying in steerage and the indifference their deaths evoked in those still living. What he failed to take into account in this black year of Irish emigration was that the steerage passengers had long been exposed to disease, death, and mass burial in the country they were fleeing. Was it any wonder, with the voyage already entering its sixth week and no end to it in sight, that some of them began awaiting death as impassively as their dead relatives had in Ireland? What he observed in the Irish character on the *Mersey* was what other contemporaries had observed among the starving in Ireland—a kind of quietism that enabled the people to annihilate their will and endure without protest their suffering. It did not require philosophical analysis on their part; the reality they faced made this almost stoic acceptance inevitable. By giving up thinking or caring about how or where they would be buried, they saved themselves hours and days of anguish that could not have changed their fate anyway.

But other elderly passengers aboard the *Mersey* still clung to the hope that they would live long enough to avoid being buried at sea, where their flesh would be devoured and their bones suspended in mid-ocean like so much debris. These held out, fighting death and the smell of it around them, until each day aboard became an achievement, another encouragement to carry on.

Still, there were burials now every day, at any and every

hour of the day depending upon when the death was discovered. On the third afternoon of the sixth week of the voyage,
the father of two children, whose mother had died in Ireland
before their departure on the *Mersey*, was found dead in his
bunk by a friend. The old sails being used up, his remains were
slipped into two meal sacks, one overlapping the other around
the man's midsection and quickly sewn together with basting
stitches to hold them temporarily in place. With weights
fastened at the feet, the body was balanced on a hatch batten
over the side of the ship while the mate offered a much shorter
funeral service than Sam Sweep had received. The burials
were in fact no longer attended by the captain, and were so
quickly performed that people who might have wanted to attend did not have time to get on deck.[8]

Of the two orphans the man left, one was a seven-year-old
boy, who later that afternoon was seen on deck wearing his
dead father's coat. It was one of those decrepit, swallow-tailed
coats that had become the very emblem of Ireland's beggary
and degradation, and by wearing it, with the tails dragging in
a train behind him, the boy was transformed into a vile trav-
esty of Paddy, that standing butt of every caricaturist on the
English stage. And yet, in a touching way that expressed as a
painting might have the Irish peasant's almost benign affinity
with poverty, the boy seemed to feel refurbished by the acqui-
sition. With his eyes still bloodshot from crying, he might have
been touching his father as he ran his hand along the ragged
lapel that reached far below his waistline.

The remainder of the man's clothing was put up for auction by the friend who had found him dead and was now
undertaking care of the two orphans. Such clothing as the man
possessed could not have been given away in England, but this
was an Irish auction—free theater for everyone attending.
Each garment, however ragged and worthless, was held up,
talked about, examined, appraised, argued over, and then,
after more shouted bids than a spool of thread deserved, sold
to the highest bidder, who triumphantly carried it back to his
place in the crowd, with its creases and crevices still alive with

the lice that had fatally infected its original owner. Like everyone in the crowd around him, he was as unaware of the danger
as he was in need of clothing.[9]

The still-healthy teen-agers and children, after attending the
methodical funerals of some of their playmates, kept asking
their parents where land was and when the voyage would end.
They had seen nothing but water for over seven weeks, and
now every dawn was like another deception, with far-off surface haze hailed and acclaimed as land until it disappeared
before their eyes in flight from the rising sun.

Meanwhile, the deaths and burials became so commonplace that they were unattended except by relatives and the
closest friends. As one steerage passenger put it: "One got
used to it—it was nothing but splash, splash, all day long—
first one, then another. There was one Martin on board, I
remember, with a wife and nine children. . . . Well, first his
wife died, and they threw *her* into the sea and then he died,
and they threw *him* into the sea, and then the children, one
after t'other, till only two were left alive; the eldest, a girl
about thirteen who had nursed them all, one after another, and
seen them die—well, *she* died, and then there was only the
little fellow left. . . . He went back, as I heard, in the same ship
with the captain."[10]

Of the three hundred and fifty steerage passengers who
boarded the *Mersey* at Cork, sixty-nine had by now died and
been buried at sea and one had drowned, which amounted to a
loss of one for every five. The betting on the progress of the
ship stopped, as did the music, singing, and dancing. The
diminutive fiddler who had played as indefatigably as a
cranked-up dummy had long since died, his fiddle willed and
given by him, on his deathbed, to the child who in his mind
had danced on deck with the most joy and abandon. That
child, himself now seriously ill, lay in his bunk clinging to the
fiddle, the prize of his life, praying that he would live to learn
to play it.

Among the still-living and conscious there was a growing bewilderment about the voyage, which had become a siege upon their senses, their resistance, their hope that it would some day end. Time, so easily spent in Ireland, so stubbornly slow in passing at sea, was so monotonous and wearing that the miles of unbroken water around them became one with the boredom to which they felt doomed. They had sailed from Cork on the tenth of May, and it was now the tenth of July. In all that time they had seen no other ship, no floating debris, no human life beyond the bulwarks of their own ship. Already jaded by the surfeit of sea around them, they regarded its endless variety of movement, appearance, and sound as nothing more than a camouflage for sameness. It was this sameness, coupled with the grim routine to which they were daily subjected, that made Ireland now as remote as the land they were seeking.

For the elderly, sleep became almost the only anodyne to the nothingness and pain of steerage—that and perhaps the filling of your pipe with tobacco, lighting it, cupping it in both hands close to your face, and slowly smoking it in your bunk down to the last ember. In those days the lucifer match, tipped with a compound that ignited by friction, was a fairly new invention, and crudely enough made to contain a superabundance of the necessary chemicals. When scratched against a bulkhead or a wooden berth in steerage, it burst into a blinding flame that attracted the attention of everyone nearby. All knew what it meant even before the welcome aroma of tobacco eased the stench in the air.

Sometimes, too, through the whole night, a group of men would play cards and smoke tobacco in the light of a candle stuck against the side of the ship or set up on a tin plate in their berth. If a ship's officer appeared, the lighted candle and pipes were barely snuffed out before they were thrust under the bedstraw or in amongst some old clothes, creating a fire hazard that kept many a woman wide awake until the game ended.

No one aboard, though, had an adequate supply of tobacco, and when it ran out, the men in steerage followed the example of the sailors in the forecastle. They saved their used tealeaves, dried them until the tiny leaves twisted into what looked like bits of tobacco, then stuffed them into their pipes and smoked them. If the aromatic result was not as satisfying as the real thing, it was still a kind of placebo, reminding them of a pleasure once enjoyed and soon to be enjoyed again. The practice became so common in steerage that one English cabin passenger aboard the *Mersey* attributed it to the ignorance of the Irish. Himself ignorant of the fact that the steerage passengers were imitating the ship's British sailors, he said of the Irish emigrants, "They are so primitive that instead of making tea to drink they put the leaves in their pipes and smoke it."[11]

Meanwhile, the Irish continued to ask themselves the same question: Will we ever reach New York? They discussed the inconceivable distance they had already covered, the erratic behavior of the wind and currents, how the pounding seas kept hindering their progress. At home, surrounded by land, and having listened to stories told by harvest laborers who had sailed to and from England, they had mistakenly equated crossing the Irish Sea to England with crossing the Atlantic Ocean to America. All knew now how wrong they had been. The voyage to America was not only twenty-five times longer; it was an altogether different experience.

Whatever fate awaited them in America, all agreed now that a return voyage to Ireland was beyond conception. This voyage was their last no matter how long they lived or how determined they later became to be buried with relatives in Irish soil. For the first and last time they were crossing this continent-wide expanse of water, which gave them the awesome feeling of being almost nonexistent in God's scheme of things—less important even than the fish below, who now and then burst into the air beside the ship as if in shock and derision that a world other than theirs existed. Meanwhile, there was the movement of the ship and the fickle power of the sea, over neither of which they had any control.

IV

Through
the
Golden Door

Chapter Twenty

I was called on deck to *smell the land*—and truly
the change was very sensible. . . . It was the
breath of youth and hope and love.

—Diary of Mary Gapper

IN the beginning of the ninth week, a teen-ager spotted
seaweed floating upon the surface of the water, little hooplike
patches of it turning in circles along the side of the moving
ship—reminders that somewhere, somehow, something other
than water existed. When the captain was informed, he assured the desperate passengers that this was a sure sign that
land was near. He went so far as to predict that a landfall
would be made before week's end, that the ship would be in
New York Harbor within ten days. Anyone wishing to wash his
or her clothes before arrival, he said, had his permission to dry
them from lines that would be hung, as in the past, weather
permitting, between the masts by the seamen on watch. This
created a great bustle both in steerage and on deck. Buckets of
water were hauled up from the sea and clothes washed in it,
sometimes with soap that appeared as mysteriously as money
did from the rags the Irish wore. Their rags, it seemed, were as
full of essentials as their minds were of bitter memories.

But if the nearness of land led to the washing of clothes, it
led even more to renewed interest and speculation in Big Gil's
lottery, which was to be decided by the hour of the day when

land was first sighted, each hour of each day being represented
by one of twenty-four numbered and dated tickets. People
whose tickets had already run out of time tried to buy "still-
alive" tickets from those who had them. Even tickets whose
target dates were only two or three days away found buyers if
the price was right. There were endless exchanges made, one
man exchanging his 6:00–7:00 A.M. ticket for an 8:00–9:00
A.M. ticket for the same day if a half-pint of rum or a pound of
meal was thrown into the bargain.

Tickets covering the dawn hours were by far the most
valuable because land was most likely to be sighted then, after
hours of darkness during which land lights would be difficult
to identify with sufficient accuracy to be recorded. But by far
the most valuable tickets, given the captain's landfall predic-
tion, were those with dates and hours covering the period a
week to ten days hence. All the holders of these tickets acted
as if they knew a wonderful secret that they were forbidden,
for the time being, to share. Close as they were to America,
where good luck and Divine Providence seemed to work hand
in hand, they could not restrain their belief that winning was
about to become a habit.

Then, not in the ninth week, as the captain had predicted,
but in the beginning of the tenth, the day came, without warning, when suddenly the steerage passengers felt caught up in
what seemed another beginning of the world. Staten Island
had been sighted, and there were too many shouts of joy coming from too many people on deck for it not to be true. Some
fell to their knees and thanked God for His mercy to them,
others wept and embraced whoever happened to be nearest,
while the young around them capered about with an extravagance that almost propelled them overboard.

"It's a beach, I tell you! With hills behind!"

"By the grace of God! Land at last!"

"On my mother's grave! A better sight my eyes will never
see."

"As green as Ireland it's not," said another.

"Mind your tongue, or risk being sent back," whispered a friend.

The bedridden in steerage, climbing up through the hatch with their tired hearts and constitutions hardly able to withstand the excitement, caught glimpses of the fabled land only days, in some cases only hours, before they were to be buried in its soil. One old man who had not left his bunk for a month reached the main deck alive enough only to make death possible. Leaning on the rail of the ship to support himself, a man with no time to waste, he kept looking at the southern tip of Staten Island until absolutely certain that his eyes were not deceiving him, that what he saw really was land, an identifiable place he could know existed. It was almost as if he were utilizing his frailty, which told him he was about to die, by making it one with this final joy of his life—the sight of America. For he knew that no one was buried at sea once land was sighted, that he need no longer struggle to remain alive, that he could struggle no longer anyway. Finally, freeing himself of all other wants and desires, or perhaps merely waiting for all other wants and desires to free themselves of him, he closed his eyes and slumped to the deck dead—the first casualty of the long-awaited sight of land. Even when laid beside the mast out of the way of traffic, he appeared as content and patient as someone who had been given too much to drink.

Only minutes later, another old man, bent on committing suicide ever since the beginning of the voyage but reluctantly resigned to prolonging his life to avoid being buried at sea, hung himself in steerage from a deck beam up forward near the bow. A tall man could not have managed it, but this short man did, with his dangling feet less than three inches above the steerage deck from which he had kicked away the cask he'd stood on to noose himself.

Meanwhile, on the main deck, passengers kept looking toward the southern shore of Staten Island, where a long neck of land was rimmed on the ocean side by a deserted beach struck by waves that sent lovely white signals to those approaching. There were still pockets of low clouds here and there, but as the ship drew closer, everyone could see more clearly, just beyond the beach, the green, mossy hillsides dotted with beautiful white cottages whose sides appeared laced with vines. Among the elderly on deck, though, were those who seemed affected in some ominous way by what had happened to the old man lying dead beside the mast. Whether his death had cued in them a similar response, or they were as close to death as he had been, the sight of land and the sense of uncertainty and change it evoked must have proved too much for them. Hopelessly exhausted, and knowing as they did that they could now die without being slipped over the side, they may have gravitated back to their past in Ireland, relinquished whatever vague hope for a future their dwindling strength allowed, and, like the old man, welcomed death.

Or perhaps they were overcome in the same way that their relatives had been in Ireland, when, starving and then suddenly given an ample amount of food, they died because their bodies could neither assimilate nor absorb so overwhelming an intake of the needed nutrients. The elderly aboard the *Mersey* may in a similar way have been unable to assimilate or absorb the sudden upsurge of hope that the sight of land created. Their shut-down dreams, suddenly put back into full production, might have precipitated more breakdowns than their hearts could stand.

Whatever the reasons, ten others aboard the *Mersey*, not counting the suicide, who was discovered later, died on this last day, within sight of the lower bay between Sea Gate and Staten Island, the first two inklings of the goal they had sacrificed so much to reach. Caught between their dismal past and their hoped-for future, like specimens pressed between pages of unrecorded history, they were destined for graves that no one would mark, visit, or remember.

"It would in my opinion have been more humane to have deprived them at once of life," the kind Englishman had said before their embarkation at Cork. Given the conditions under which they were forced to live in steerage, his solution would

indeed have been more humane—and for the British government more efficient as well.

Because Big Gil was determined to be fair in awarding the
lottery prize money, he asked the mate when land had first
been sighted according to the ship's official time. There had
been several false sightings by passengers, and now, dealing as
they were with the real thing, he wanted to be accurate. Luck-
ily, the official time was near the half-hour range of the winning hour—the thirty-fourth minute of the sixth hour of the
third day of the tenth week, to be exact—which precluded
the kind of argument that would no doubt have arisen had the
official time been close to the end of one hour and the beginning of the next.

"The person with ticket number six, dated July 21, 1847, is
the winner!" shouted Big Gil.

He had the money in a small canvas bag and was as
anxious to present it to the winner as he and everyone else was
to know the winner's identity. But no one came forward,
though the ticket, according to Big Gil's records, had definitely
been sold. Sixty-seven had been buried at sea up to this first
sighting of land, and down in steerage were fifty-five others
too sick with fever to be on deck for the awarding of the prize.
When the tickets of these fifty-five sick were checked, the winning ticket was still nowhere to be found, which led to the
conclusion that it had been buried at sea with the unlucky
winner, who had no doubt kept it as well hidden on his or her
person as everyone in Ireland did his or her burial money.

No one disagreed with Big Gil's suggestion that the two
tickets closest in time to the winning ticket—that is, the tickets
immediately preceding and immediately following the winning
ticket, should be declared runner-up tickets. The holders of
these two tickets, he said, should either share the prize money
or draw lots to determine the final winner.

There was great excitement and tension as everyone
awaited the appearance of the two contenders. People examined and reexamined their tickets, and a few came forward

with tickets that Big Gil had to point out were hours away from the winning ticket. He nevertheless advised them to hold on to their tickets in the event other tickets close to the winning ticket proved to be missing.

Finally, as if in awe of the crowd or in fear of being corrected, the first of the two winners came forward. It was the woman who had cleaned Sam Sweep's feet; she had the ticket immediately preceding the winning ticket, and with her were the two other women who had helped prepare Sam for burial and were to share her half of the prize money. They stood beside her, hoping as only the desperate can hope that no one would come forward with the other ticket—the ticket immediately following the winning ticket. Big Gil called out the date and the hour of the other winning ticket ("Last call! Last call!" he kept saying), until Dolores Kinsella could be seen making her way through the crowd.

Seasickness had paid her a visit, robbed her cheeks and lips of color, given her an almost devout look that at once sharpened and made more distant and detached the green beauty of her eyes. She might have been a nun wearing the dress she'd worn before taking her vows as she stepped up and handed Big Gil her winning ticket. She had hesitated not out of fear but because she'd been late in coming on deck and had not understood what was going on.

The stark difference in the appearance of the two contenders—the beautiful and young Dolores Kinsella on one side of Big Gil, and the wasted old woman, buttressed by her two equally wasted old friends, on the other—added poignancy and tension to the proceedings. The tension increased when someone standing just behind Big Gil speculated aloud that the real winner might still be aboard. A hurried and unseemly search was made of the old man who had dropped dead at the sight of Staten Island. This produced another worthless ticket and even greater interest in the outcome of the draw. Suddenly Dolores startled everyone by suggesting that she and the other winner forego the draw and share the prize equally.

"God bless that girl," someone said.

"God bless," others chimed in. "God bless!"

But the two old biddies who were to share their friend's prize money wanted no part of that—it was win or lose with them.

"Is it nothing at all you're after?" asked their friend. "Sure, this way we'll not go empty-handed."

"To share in the prize," her friends countered, "is to share in the decision."

This led Dolores to suggest that, since there were four of them altogether, they split the prize in four instead of two equal parts. That way, she said, no one would lose and all would win.

"May that girl's heart be light and her eyes gay into a late grave!" someone shouted. For she was giving up her chance for the full prize and settling for one-fourth of it. "God bless!" others chimed in.

The British sailors never ceased to be amazed at this harmlessly fierce competition among the famine Irish, who seemed as willing to gamble away their last farthing as they were baffled by what to do with their winnings. The sailors could not understand why the prize, once won, became so sharable. Nor could the Irish, whose attitude toward beggars was equally mysterious to the sailors, have explained. For them it was a mode of thinking never questioned or challenged, a folkway as twined with their pagan past as with the oppression they'd suffered for so long. With good reason they believed that good luck carried with it dangers as well as responsibilities: when it paid you a visit, you had to share that visit with someone or risk never being visited again.

"Agreed!" cried the woman who had cleaned Sam's feet. "God bless you, girl," she said to Dolores, then turned with vehemence to her two friends. "One more contrary word, and as sure as that's land ahead, I'll be contrary and give you nothing!"

In the canvas bag, all of it in different silver and copper denominations, were eight pounds, ten shillings, eight pence—a respectable sum of money in those days, almost enough for two adult passages in steerage to America. Everyone waited as Big Gil distributed it four ways, then watched as the coins were slipped with that Irish magician's skill into the folds of the winners' garments and disappeared behind the noncommittal gaze on the face of each winner. No one aboard the *Mersey* would ever see that money again or know where or in how many different places it was hidden. Henceforth it would never be discussed or alluded to again.

With the lottery finally settled and the ship still two hours away from the entrance to New York Harbor, an order came from the quarter-deck that every mattress, bolster, pillow, and blanket in steerage be thrown overboard. The Irish on deck were stunned; they had never discarded a rag, let alone a mattress, in Ireland. Why, they wanted to know, had they not been told about this on boarding the ship in Cork?

"You will otherwise be forced to spend weeks of detention in quarantine," the mate shouted through a megaphone. "In only a few hours a medical officer will be boarding the ship. If the bedding is still aboard, if anything at all capable of spreading disease is found, the ship and everyone in steerage will be quarantined. I speak from experience and urge you to heed my advice: if you want to get off this ship without delay, get the bedding over the side now."[1]

For the next hour, pallet, pillow, blanket, and mattress went overboard, followed by blackened pots and pans, bags of maggoty food, baskets jammed with leftover meat and vegetable soup makings, and bottles half filled with urine by those who had not wanted to add to the mess and smell below. The sea around the ship became a garbage dump on which floated straw-stuffed ticking, blankets with still enough air in their folds to remain alive for a while longer on the surface, baskets emptied of their contents and now too light to sink, and, here and there, one of those famous high-crowned Irish hats, looking as dilapidated and ready to go under as a ship battered by a storm.

The passengers were gazing over the side at this jetsam,

every miscellaneous piece of which vividly represented one or another aspect of their experience aboard the *Mersey*, when all able-bodied passengers in steerage were told by the mate to muster their forces for what he called the second prerequisite to their prompt release from the ship in New York: a thorough scouring of the steerage quarters. They were to shovel into buckets and throw overboard all muck and excrement that had accumulated during the ten-week voyage, after which they were to scrub, with sand and sea water, the entire steerage deck. The sick would then be carried up from below and the steerage quarters fumigated. There was no time to waste, the mate said, as medical officers were early or late in boarding an incoming ship, depending upon their schedule.[2]

This last-minute scrubdown was never necessary on an American ship, where weekly and sometimes even daily scourings, with the help and cooperation of the emigrants, were standard procedure. It was necessary on British ships like the *Mersey* because the emigrating Irish were looked upon as the dregs of an overpopulated country—a primitive people whose steerage conditions aboard British ships were no worse than the conditions they had created for themselves in their own country. This attitude had been induced and perpetuated by public comments made by members of Parliament and by editorials appearing in the London *Times*. In fact, it was not until the summer of 1847, with criticism of conditions aboard these floating "Black Holes of Calcutta" mounting, that English captains began giving last-minute orders that steerage passengers discard their bedding and get to work cleaning their quarters.

Instead of using their power as captains during the voyage, when it was theirs to use to enforce the kind of sanitary measures that would have prevented disease and saved lives, they waited until land was sighted. Then they used their power not to save lives but to protect the reputation of their ships. This helps explain why the death toll was so much higher on British ships than on those flying the American flag. The Irish brought disease aboard with them, but on American ships its spread was curtailed if not stopped altogether. On

British ships, disease spread as the filth in steerage accumulated, and the filth created additional disease, while the "parliamentary diet" continued to deplete everyone's strength to fight infection. It was no wonder that New York inspectors, even after these last-minute scourings aboard incoming British ships became common practice, looked upon each and every one of them as another charnel house.[3]

All the same, the *Mersey* was still afloat and at last within sight of her destination, loaded with passengers who could hardly wait to feel New York under their feet.

Chapter Twenty-one

It has sometimes been remarked of King
George III, that instead of fighting his American
subjects, he would have shewn somewhat more
prudence by removing family, court, and all, to
the States; and so leaving Great Britain, as the
lesser country, to shift for itself, as a colony. . . .

—William Chambers,
Things As They Are In America

THEY were approaching New York City as it was meant
to be approached, not by the back way from the north,
in some carriage, omnibus, or railway train, but by the front
way from the south, in an ocean-going vessel. Anxious and
afraid, their eyes chasing every illusory sign of life on the
water's surface and wherever land was visible, they crowded
the bulwarks with the intensity and suspense of spectators
awaiting the beginning of some momentous event. Above all
they did not want the land to disappear, as so many fog banks
had in the middle of the ocean. But no sound came from it,
and the beaches, if they really were beaches, were deserted.
Nowhere was there the slightest sign that America was alive
and ready to receive them, that their arrival would even be
noticed.

Then all at once America spoke: a small schooner appeared, tacking this way and that across the *Mersey*'s bow
with the alacrity of a lost umbrella playing tag with the wind.
The Irish on deck were excitedly sharing opinions as to what it

could be when the mate shouted, "Pilot boat heaving to off starboard bow!"

The schooner had by now lost headway and lowered her sails. Two of her seamen were launching a tiny craft with such ease that it might have been made of cork; a uniformed officer, the pilot designated by harbor patrol to bring the *Mersey* into port, was stepping into it to be brought to the *Mersey*'s side. A lean young man, he stood at something like attention in the swaying craft, deftly playing one leg against the other to keep his balance, until brought close enough to fling himself, without assistance, onto the *Mersey*'s deck.

For the first time in their lives, the Irish were standing face to face with a native of the land they were seeking—an American who in all probability had never been to Ireland and knew as little about their country as they did about his. This alone would have made him strange in their eyes, but he was so young, so clean, so immaculately dressed in his white uniform and peaked hat, that when he smiled there were irrepressible "ooh"s and "ah"s from the ragged Irish around him. Except for the Dubliners among them, they had never in their lives seen the likes of him, a fashion plate even at work, whose personality was so manifestly at one with his appearance and manner. If he represented the general population of New York City, if all the other natives were that clean, self-confident, and able, if their teeth were that white when they smiled, their mustaches that gleaming in the wind, and their knowledge of what they were about that sure and unassailable, where would *they* fit in, whatever would they do in the way of becoming American?

The impeccable pilot did indeed epitomize the native New Yorker at this time in American history. The privations of the revolution had taught his grandfather, who had taught his father, who in turn had taught him, to seize every opportunity to excel by making never-ending improvements in both his work and his way of doing it. Such a man develops in time the conviction that doing an acceptable job is not enough, that with vigor, dedication, and inventiveness he can surpass the achievements of others. While working with his hands, he thinks of ways to improve what he is doing; when his work for the day is done, he reads books by experts in his field, then experiments with their ideas until he comes up with new ideas of his own.

The way the pilot landed on the *Mersey*'s deck, like a gymnast leaving the high bar and landing, feet together, in the set position, expressed perfectly this irrepressible American desire to "go one better." These Irish emigrants, the worst-clad, worst-fed, and worst-lodged peasantry of Europe, who had lost to the British in every ill-conceived uprising and finally accepted squalor as their way of life, found it easier to believe he had come from another planet than from the American part of this one. He appeared too young to be in such command of himself, too self-confident and efficient to have been trained, educated, fed, and motivated as they might have been in Ireland, even if Ireland had been free. The yoke of oppression went back too far in their histories for them to imagine what they and their country might have been. Was he someone special or just another American? Addicted as they were to fantasy and superstition, they studied the length of his arms and legs and made sure he had only two of each; they looked at his hands and counted five fingers on each; they stared at his face and were relieved to find it handsomely fitted with two eyes, two ears, one nose, and one mouth.

All the same, if he had whistled rather than spoken when the captain came down from the quarter-deck to greet him, they would not have been surprised. But he spoke, and spoke English as well, though not the English they were used to hearing on the lips of their landlords in Ireland. There was a marked difference in emphasis and pronunciation, and this difference became another "something" about America, another worry to be attended to later. Right now there was land ahead, and they wanted to feel it under their feet and begin to believe in the reality of arrival. Some prayed, others rejoiced,

as the young American pilot gave orders to the *Mersey*'s crew
with such certainty and sense of command that every sailor
jumped to at once.

Just sailing through the Narrows, that well-named channel between Staten Island and Brooklyn, was like squeezing through
a bottleneck to freedom. For just beyond the channel's turbulent water was the spacious landlocked bay, with its magnificent vistas of land, greenery, and surrounding hills. Everyone,
including, perhaps, the impeccable pilot, felt relieved by the
sudden sense of safety and calm in the harbor. Ample and
deep, like an inland sea dotted with islands belonging by
some geographical miracle to the same country, it created
among the *Mersey*'s emigrants the feeling that America might
be the one place on earth where everything beneficial to mankind had been preordained. Here was a bay upon whose
waters the combined navies of the world could float in perfect
safety, a bay as easily defended against attack as the land surrounding it, as beautiful on all sides as it was enormous, as full
of fish as anyone living along its beaches and beyond would
ever need—all of it so mild in temperature that in the past
century it was only twice blockaded with ice. What a country!
What awe it inspired in the poor Irish on the *Mersey*'s deck
in this awful famine year.

Even wealthy visitors from Europe, sailing this way into
New York for the first time, were astonished by the sight of the
harbor and the land surrounding it, the way continent and
ocean had eons earlier become interlocked, with islands emerg-
ing here and there, their headlands and promontories reaching
out and upward like fingers to add to the marvelous intricacy
of it all.

"Nature has afforded no finer site for a great commercial
center than that upon which the Dutch established their 'New
Amsterdam', changed by the British to 'New York' when they
took possession of it," wrote one wealthy visitor. "A city so
favoured deserved a better name. By people in the neighborhood it is sometimes called York; poetically, Manhattan;

equivocally, in print, Gotham; politically, the Empire City; it is at the same time the least and most thoroughly characteristic of all American cities."[1]

For the *Mersey's* Irish, the whole panorama was made even more delightful and exciting, as they passed through the lower into the upper bay, by the smaller craft moving about in all directions like creations of the sea around the ship. Their oars working in unison, some looked like long-legged water bugs. Others had sails so tightly trimmed that they seemed to be daring the wind to knock them over. There were pilot boats shooting about in search of this or that anchored ship, doctors' boats with their medical flags flying, handsome six-oared gigs carrying immaculately dressed ship captains to shore. And running in between this to-and-fro traffic were longboats carrying dead steerage passengers to Staten Island for burial. It was a busy scene of life and death, with the ragged white linen and red petticoats of Ireland still hanging out to dry from the rigging of the ships, the straw mattresses and other debris, like telltales of the horror of steerage, following the ships into harbor with the incoming tide, smaller craft trying to dodge the mattresses. And there were the tears and excitement of the Irish, who kept trying to understand and encompass what was happening to them.

When the ship anchored off the quarantine station on Staten Island, a medical officer climbed aboard and immediately called to the captain on the quarter-deck: How many passengers? How many deaths at sea? Any sickness aboard? Its nature? How many patients at present?

The *Mersey's* death rate at sea, in the middle to high range, required that the medical officer inspect steerage, but given the wasted appearance of the emigrants on deck around him, he would no doubt have inspected it anyway. Climbing down through the open hatch, he held on to the ladder long enough to give his eyes time to adjust to the dimness. A solitary lamp suspended from the ceiling sent a glimmering light fore and aft between the stalls, where the last-minute scrub-

bing and fumigation had done little to dispel the odor of disease, death, and putrefaction. Besides, there was the orlop
deck below the steerage deck, still reeking like a stagnant
sewer clogged with the waste it was meant to disperse.

The harbor's medical officers hated to board incoming
British ships for this reason; many of them, indeed, wrote
scathing reports about the conditions under which the Irish
emigrants were forced to cross the ocean. These reports and
the official complaints they generated resulted in gradual improvements aboard British ships, but this was the summer of
1847, and the only improvement up until now was the last-
minute scouring and fumigation, which was no improvement
at all.[2]

Holding his nose to avoid vomiting from the smell, the
medical officer moved forward between the stalls, all of them
now without their filthy mattresses. The "patients," lying on
the eighteen-inch-wide wooden shelves, seemed to have lost all
interest in what the future had in store for them in the United
States, the target country that had long since become the
vaguest of objects in their dimming minds. Stopping beside the
first berth in which a patient lay, the doctor felt his pulse,
examined his tongue, squeezed his joints, and hurried back up
the hatch ladder to the main deck as if to protect himself from
contamination.

"There's fever here," he said, having already decided to
have all the sick passengers taken to Staten Island and kept at
the Quarantine Hospital until they either recovered or died.
Signaling to a steam launch flying a medical flag off the *Mersey*'s starboard bow, he waited until she sidled her way
through the water and tied up alongside the ship, then ordered
the British sailors to carry the sick up from steerage and put
them aboard the launch.

His was a decision that virtually every medical officer was
forced to make on British ships carrying emigrants to New
York—a painful decision because it cut through families, sep-
arating husband from wife, husband and wife from children,
husband from wife and children. By law, the infectious sick

had to be separated from the well, who were not allowed to remain with their sick loved ones even if they chose to do so. The long voyage had already so drained them that they needed one another more than ever, and now, on arrival, they were being forced to separate before they even knew where they would be living or how they would keep in touch and regroup.[3]

Robert Whyte described this dreadful process: "O God! May I never again witness such a scene as that which followed;—the husband,—the only support of an emaciated wife and helpless family,—torn away forcibly from them, in a strange land; the mother dragged from her orphan children, that clung to her until she was lifted over the bulwarks, rending the air with their shrieks; children snatched from their bereaved parents, who were perhaps ever to remain ignorant of their recovery, or death. The screams pierced my brain; and the excessive agony so rent my heart that I was obliged to retire to the cabin. . . ."[4]

After the dead aboard were transferred to another boat for burial in Staten Island, the *Mersey* weighed anchor and headed for Manhattan. One wretched husband, though, insisted upon accompanying his dead wife in the longboat to Staten Island, where she and all the other dead Irish from other ships were taken in 1847. He laid her in her pine coffin and helped dig her grave, which was on a hilltop overlooking the great harbor. After the coffin was lowered and the grave filled and covered with dirt, he took two shovels and placed them crosswise upon it.

"By that cross, Mary," he said, calling heaven to witness, "I swear to revenge your death. As soon as I earn the price of my passage home, I'll go back, and shoot the man that murdered you, and that's the landlord."[5]

In retrospect it would seem that conditions in British steerage were at least as much to blame.

When word came from the quarter-deck that the *Mersey* was to tie up at South Street, known the world over as "The Street

of Ships," the excitement could not have spread faster had it
been based on a rumor. The Irish kept looking as the ship
skirted the southernmost point of Manhattan Island, where
green lawns surrounded The Battery and promenading ladies
and gentlemen could be seen through the foliage. It was a
quiet, welcoming scene, in sharp contrast to what immediately
followed when the ship started up between Brooklyn and
Manhattan into the East River. For just north of Battery Park,
on the east side of Manhattan, came commercially alive South
Street and the many ships tied to her flank, their tangled
thicket of masts and rigging almost concealing the dingy warehouses behind them.

How could their ship slip in amongst all the others? It
seemed impossible, until there appeared a stall-like space of
water that the pilot and crew were apparently heading for—a
space between two ships whose size about equaled theirs. Sailors from these other ships helped guide them in by ropes
thrown to them from the *Mersey*. The ship was moving no
faster now than a man walking; there was a chorus of welcome, an almost coded exchange of questions and answers
between the sailors aboard the tied-up ships and those aboard
the incoming *Mersey*—a camaraderie shared by men who
spend their lives going round the world without going into it,
who use the wharves, the piers, and the immediately surrounding streets and buildings as extensions of the ships on which
they live. The perimeter of the land they touch is more than
enough to satisfy their needs on terra firma, and Manhattan
Island, with two rivers flowing down from the north into the
harbor, and the nearest groggery and brothel a stone's throw
away from the wharves along the shore, was no exception. As
wary of land as the emigrants were of water, they would wan-
der no more than a few blocks from "home"—the ships whose
sails they would soon be trimming for the next voyage.

The famine Irish had read in pamphlets and been advised
during discussions in steerage to beware of the fraudulent

practices they would be subjected to in New York, Boston, Philadelphia, Baltimore, New Orleans, and other American ports. Those aboard the *Mersey* were nevertheless unprepared for what actually happened once the ship was tied to her berth on this famous street of ships. For suddenly, over the bulwarks of adjoining ships, men began jumping like pirates onto the deck of the *Mersey*. Had they knives between their teeth and muskets in their hands, they could not have been more frightening. Most appeared to be Irish, except that they were both cheerful and grasping, eager and anxious, in a way unnatural to Ireland; and they spoke with a brogue at once accentuated by and tinged with a peculiar American difference to it.

These were the tavern and boardinghouse runners, working for both pay and commission to induce immigrants to the establishments employing them. The immigrants would be civilly treated in the teasing matter of boxes and trunks so long as they were willing to pay the exorbitant rates for being escorted off the ship to a tavern or boardinghouse where most of their remaining cash would be extorted from them.

After almost three months at sea, it was nerve-racking just to listen to the spiels of these runners, but the competition among them was such that they had with them back-up thugs both for protection and to help coerce potential customers into accepting their slanderous carting rates. The sudden appearance of these licensed plunderers, against whose extortions there was neither remedy nor appeal, the abusive way they hawked their services and establishments, and the piratical manner in which they seized a family's bags and boxes overwhelmed the immigrants, whose first and foremost concern was to disembark and find shelter somewhere. Whole groups were thus led off the ships by the runners to establishments ready and waiting to defraud them of their last farthing, while other passengers clung desperately to their belongings and insisted that they had relatives coming to meet the ship.[6]

A single immigrant carrying his or her belongings in one bag was less likely to be accosted by runners than someone loaded down with more than he or she could carry. The latter usually succumbed to the first runner who grabbed the luggage and almost always lived to regret it, though it would have made no difference anyway, one runner being as dishonest as the next. Sometimes, two competing runners would each grab half of the same immigrant's belongings and then argue interminably over who was to be given carting rights. The immigrant, anxious to get settled somewhere—anywhere—at least for the time being, would suggest that each runner carry half the luggage. This always led to concurrence on the part of the two competitors, and always with the same result: the immigrant was required to pay the same amount to each runner as would have been paid to one—that is to say, twice the going rate.[7]

Parents with children suffered even greater delay, disappointment, and expense, for most were too weak from the voyage to carry their belongings beyond the wharf at which their ship was tied up. They just stood there, beneath the jutting bowsprits and towering forest of masts, unaccustomed to moving about in a strange country, and having no fixed destination anyway.

"Ah! There you are!" a runner approaching them would say. "My specialty—an Irish family! For didn't I come from one myself?"

And with that he'd wheedle his way past the children, with a tender pat on the head for each, to the anxious and bewildered parents. "Lucky you are to be spotted first by me. For I can see that you need help and want to be treated fairly. And just as sure as my name is Jim Galloway, I've got just the place for you, a safe dwelling—mind you, I said safe—where you can ponder and decide your future. 'The Eagle's Haven' it's called, a respectable tavern within walking distance from here—no carriage charge—a place without pretension or fanfare, but *safe*, with good will and Irish smiles to share."

The father would ask about the going rate for room and board, whether the family could be together in the same "apartment," what kind of water-closet facilities were provided. He knew enough now, after ten weeks on the *Mersey*, to ask about such things.

"Ah! You've been schooled by your parish priest back home. And I say, God bless that priest, and you for asking. For at the *Eagle's Haven*, everything from A to Z is accounted for. Sure as the beautiful nose on your daughter's face, it will be heaven compared with steerage."

He answered not one of the questions put to him, but the bewildered parents had neither the heart nor the energy to ask for credentials to use to protect themselves. They felt even more entrapped than they had in Cork, where they at least had had a visible ship to board. Here in New York, they had no destination, no knowledge of how to move about, no way of knowing who was telling them the truth. The Irish swindlers who had erupted from the scum of society in the Irish ports from which the immigrants had fled were now erupting from an equally despised Irish society in the ports of America. The honest, willing-to-work Irishman, who had been cheated on departure and was now being cheated again on arrival, had little choice, given his ignorance of the city. How was he to know that within walking distance from South Street were many taverns and boardinghouses whose owners refused to hire runners to drag in trade off the ships or to charge the exorbitant rates that their hire made necessary? These places were for obvious reasons the least occupied and the most capable of satisfying the immediate needs of an incoming Irish family. But with all the fistfights and turmoil among the runners and their thugs at the waterfront, the father of such a family was given no time to investigate the alternatives, let alone learn where in the city they were located.

It was only when some member of the Irish-Immigrant Society was able to talk to and convince a frightened and bewildered immigrant that the latter was shepherded to a boardinghouse or tavern where the prices listed were the prices charged. These good people, trying to help their countrymen find a decent place to start their lives in America, were unfortunately as subject to abuse as the immigrants they were trying to help. The runners, as persuasive as they were deceitful, as willing to be obsequious as they were to enlist their bodyguards to gain their ends, bullied as well the members of the Irish-Immigrant Society, whose advice would have saved the immigrants time, trouble, and, most important on arrival, money.[8]

Chapter Twenty-two

New York is a very brilliant city. To give the best
idea of it I should describe it as something of a
fusion between Liverpool and Paris—crowded
quays, long perspectives of vessels and masts,
bustling streets, gay shops, tall white houses, and
a clear brilliant sky overhead.

—Earl of Carlisle,
Travels in America

IT was no doubt because of Big Gil's huge presence beside
them that Micky Quinn and Dolores Kinsella managed to
reach the wharf unmolested. Although Micky had picked up a
few extra pieces of clothing at auctions during the voyage, he
had no trouble carrying more than half of Dolores's luggage as
though it were his own. With Dolores carrying the remainder
of hers and Big Gil, like a shepherding relative, easily carrying
everything he owned, they were only temporarily detained by
the marauding runners, who were on the lookout for more
defenseless and encumbered immigrants. All the same, on
reaching the wharf they found themselves again surrounded,
this time by runners who had arrived too late to board the
Mersey but still determined to turn a profit for the day.

"Help in time is help rewarded," one of them said to
Dolores while trying to confiscate her luggage.

Big Gil intervened at once: "This young lady has an aunt
living less than a quarter of a mile from here. We know the
location and how to get there. She needs no help, no lodging—
nothing but the escort we'll be giving her."

"And where will his hulk be spending the night?" asked
another runner in an obvious effort to provoke an angry re-

sponse. His skin resembled the rough side of a colander; you could have grated potatoes against it. This may have been why there was as much whine as insolence in his voice.

Big Gil could see thugs moving into position behind their respective runners to assist if a brawl ensued. He had had his share of brawls in Ireland and was up and ready for this one if it could not be avoided.

"Thank you for your consideration and offer to help," he said to one and all, with the assurance and self-confidence of a dignitary arriving incognito. Ignoring the troublemaker, he turned to Dolores, who on his advice had tucked a small "pregnancy" pillow beneath the front of her skirt. "How is the little one doing?" he asked, with a downward glance.

He was counting on a well-known tendency among Irishmen to be both respectful and embarrassed in the presence of a pregnant woman. Even so, he would never have attempted such a dangerous ruse with anyone but Dolores, whose flair, wit, and presence had impressed everyone during the voyage.

"It's myself will be thanking God when I reach my aunt's," she said, with apprehension enough in her voice to suggest the need of a doctor's or midwife's help.

A way was grudgingly opened for her, and she passed through it, followed by Micky and Gil, to where the *Mersey*'s bowsprit came close to jutting into one of the warehouse windows fronting on the river.

"Come, this way," Gil said. "As though we know where we're going."

They started west through Maiden Lane toward Front Street, breathing easier, giggling with joy, patting and slapping one another with every step they took. It was as if they were escaping not only the treacherous New York runners but the *Mersey* herself and all the horrid memories of the voyage. At first they took no notice of the buildings on either side of Maiden Lane, they were too interested in their freedom, what it meant, how it felt, what to do with it. Then, suddenly, something happened that made New York comprehensible in their eyes, almost a part of the old country they had left. As they approached Front Street from the east, they saw a pig, a portly sow, roaming south, unconcerned and unattended, in the direction of Pine.

Accustomed as they were to the ubiquitous pig in Ireland, they burst out laughing at this sudden reminder of the old country in the city of New York. It was as if some Irishman had purposely sent the sow out as a welcome sign—"No famine here!"—to his newly arrived countrymen. But no, it wasn't that at all, for now, around the corner from Water Street and starting east along Maiden Lane, came two enormous hogs, their splotchy brown backs resembling overstuffed carpetbags worn to the cords. The ear of one had been mangled in what must have been a street fight with a dog; the tail of the other had been lost, perhaps to a slammed door or possibly a rat.

During the next ten minutes, Dolores and her friends saw pigs in every street, going like licensed city inspectors from one pile of garbage or offal to another. Showing no particular interest in passers-by, who gave them sufficient berth to avoid brushing against them, they turned up a turnip green here, some discarded potatoes or a stalk of cabbage there, then went waddling on to other heaps along the different streets, talking to themselves in a nonsyllabic language of grunts whose subtle distinctions and variations only they understood.

This use of the hog as the city sweep went back two hundred years to Peter Stuyvesant, who had herds of hogs led through every street in need of garbage removal. In those days, though, the streets did not offer more edible garbage than the hogs could consume, nor more trash and discarded clothing than the poor could retrieve and put to additional use. By 1847, the situation had worsened for the city and improved for the pigs, whose assignment, though the same, was now beyond even their capacity.[1]

Every morning these New York pigs took leave of their lodgings—the back of an Irish blacksmith's shop, the yard behind some groggery, a tenement cellar where an Irish mason and his family lived—and followed their calling as the city's

scavengers. Never fed or attended, they never went hungry.
Free to roam wherever they pleased, they always found their
way home again, eating their way to the last, as evening closed
in. Every day they gormandized at will, for all along the foot
pavements, standing like fixtures from morning till night and
often from one day to the next, were buckets of slop, boxes
loaded with refuse, lidless flour barrels, cans of ashes, baskets
overflowing with vegetable matter, decayed tea chests, worn-
out shoes, torn curtains, old hats without crowns, the unwanted bones and scraps from butchered animals, and every
other variety of household wreck.[2]

Even on Sunday, with church bells ringing and everybody
hurrying to or from service, the garbage was scattered about
beside doorsteps, spilling over into gutters, piled in cellar en-
trances, or knocked over and strewn, like a field of agreeable
inquiry for the pigs, who were perhaps more frowned upon on
the Sabbath but even then accepted as a necessary evil. Having been forced early in life to shift for themselves, in a city
whose garbage-laden streets offered a daily smorgasbord the
likes of which no other city in the world offered, they mingled
every day amongst the best of society with composure if not
decorum, neither proud nor ashamed of themselves, just being
what they were, pigs out on the town.

The lower part of the island, on which the city was then built,
is shaped like an acute angle, with great bays to the south and
deep rivers running along its sides. Steamboats going to and
from the interior or round to Boston and other seaports hauled
themselves to long wharves down by The Battery at the southern tip of the island. From there, running roughly northward
for three miles on either side of the angle-shaped city, were the
ocean-going ships of all nations, tied to docks to discharge or
receive cargo, their flags and pennants flying as if in tribute to
the ferry-steamers that kept running back and forth between
Manhattan and such satellite cities as Brooklyn, Williamsburg,
Jersey City, and Hoboken. These ferries were the finest of their
class in the world; resembling floating platforms, they were

capable of accommodating many carriages in the middle part and hundreds of foot passengers along the sides in long, weather-protected rooms from which the short crossing could be observed as well as enjoyed.[3]

With no bridges spanning the rivers at this time, these ferries were as numerous as they were essential. They came and went every five to ten minutes, and as the charge to Brooklyn was one cent, to New Jersey three cents, and to Staten Island, five miles away, only five cents, they handled an immense traffic from dawn to nightfall. Down at the foot of Peck's Slip, Dolores and her friends were stunned when a whole streetful of passengers, carriages, wagons, and carts moved forward on cue and boarded the Williamsburg Ferry. No sooner was she loaded and her gate closed than she steamed off on another trip, sliding through the water between the busily loading and unloading ships from all over the world.

The city was literally jammed with maritime traffic, with ships all but on the streets themselves on both sides of the island, their unloaded cargoes pressing day by day upon the business and residential sections in the middle. In this lower part of the city, with merchandise arriving from near and far, space at a premium, and trade and commerce expanding, there was a growing tendency for a particular kind of business activity to gravitate into the same street and concentrate itself there. The hardware dealers, for example, were located on Platt and nearby streets; the leather dealers on Ferry Street; the hat and fur dealers on Water Street, and the wholesale grocers on Front Street and intersecting crosstown streets like Beekman and Dover. Wall Street had the money, stock, and bond operations, and Pearl Street, the most irregular and most important business street in the city, had the lucrative importing and dry-goods businesses, which had already expanded into William, Pine, Cedar, Liberty, and other streets.

Dolores, Micky, and Big Gil, accustomed as they were to the "still life" of Ireland, where animals often appeared as stationary as the trees and carts moved at a pace slow enough to conceal their movement, hardly knew what to make of the

crowds, stores, excitement, and, most of all, combative urban
traffic, in which horse-drawn omnibuses, carriages, and hacks,
their warning bells keeping pace with their speed, competed
like warriors for every inch of passageway. With no stop signs,
no traffic cops, and no way of knowing whether a carriage was
about to veer around the nearest corner, they had good reason
to doubt their own judgment on this first day of their arrival.
They would soon learn how it was done, but right now they
lingered at intersections, trying to learn when to risk crossing,
when not to, and, given the manure and other debris that had
to be avoided during the flight to the other side, how much
time it required. Once they reached the offices of the Irish-
Immigrant Society and were able to check their bags and luggage *free of charge* they became more athletic and daring,
more like New Yorkers, in the way they crossed this or that
avenue or street.

Nearly half a million human beings now lived on this
island where two centuries earlier only a few hundred traders
lived. The end of the American Revolution had seen an influx
of people fired with ambition, enterprise, and a new spirit of
freedom. They had come from both the hinterlands and Europe, creating a population growth never equaled in the history of any city of the Old World—from approximately 22,000
in 1777 to almost 500,000 in 1847, an increase in seventy years
of over 2,200 percent.[4]

Buildings were springing into existence in one street after
another, while the city advanced northward into the adjoining
country and ascended story upon story into the air. The mix-
ture of poor wooden structures and splendid mansions was
giving way to a long series of high and handsome buildings of
brown sandstone and brick, with several of white marble and
granite. In the old sections below Prince Street, private homes,
long since vacated by the wealthy, were being replaced by six-
story and sometimes nine-story brick or stone buildings whose
main floors were rented by fashionable stores and shops.

The hoist, or elevator, a device used to provide vertical

transportation in buildings, made these higher structures possible. Though Elisha Graves Otis was yet to invent the safety
device (1853) that would prevent an elevator from falling in
the event a support cable broke, impetuous New York contractors couldn't wait: the buildings went up higher and higher
in the endless quest for more space in the same place and in
the belief, so strong then in America and especially in New
York, that if an improvement such as a safety device was necessary, it was also inevitable.

Dolores and her friends would come to realize that this
kind of hectic transition was characteristic of New York, a city
forever in the process of changing from one state or stage to
another. Unlike Paris and London, with their homogeneous
populations, their built-in resistance to change, and their appearance fundamentally unaltered year after year, New York
shocked even returning natives who had been gone only a year
or two.

But even more impressive than the upward-soaring buildings were the busy avenues and the streets between them. It
was anticipated by the city fathers, when they laid out the
plan for the streets of Manhattan, that the heaviest traffic
would be east and west between the rivers, the lighter traffic
north and south. They accordingly spaced the crosstown
streets close together and the longitudinal streets wide apart.
And though they did not envision the invention of the au-
tomobile and what it would do to the island's north-south
traffic, they wisely made the avenues running north and south
wider than all but a few of the crosstown streets.

All the same, in the tightly huddled business section
around the southern tip of the island, known as Tory New
York because under British rule the city was limited to that
area, the streets were the product of accident rather than design. The principal streets—Water, Queen, William, Nassau,
and Broadway—ran roughly parallel to the rivers but were
interlaced by crosstown streets that started, stopped, and
picked up again without any definite aim or direction, met

other streets at all sorts of angles, ended in churchyards, narrowed into lanes, or flowed into forks where they mysteriously lost their identity. Some ran into Broadway and then continued on the other side—though never exactly straight through —under a different name. Others were so narrow that sidewalks were forbidden on them. Still others were so packed with churches, taverns, cemeteries, tailors, grocers, hatters, haberdashers, and lawyers' and doctors' offices that it was hard to imagine a need that could not be satisfied within the distance of a few cobblestones.

These picturesque irregularities in the layout of the oldest city streets delighted some residents and annoyed others. In some sections, trees grew out of the middle of sidewalks, which were often no more than hard-packed dirt lanes, slightly raised, or planked with oak. Pump handles, hitching posts, bay windows, pitched roofs, stairs, stoops, and open gates obtruded into walking areas. Odd and even numbers were given to houses regardless of the side of the street they were on, and in some cases two houses bore the same number. The tailor at 62 Broad Street might or might not be next to the lawyer at 64. A grocer who happened to like the number 65 might be between them. The still-unpaved streets were seasonally so filled with puddles, mudholes, sheets of ice, or swirling pockets of dust that women "foot passengers" were carried by their husbands or friends from one side to the other, while their male counterparts gave the widest possible berth to carters, draymen, and fishmongers driving faster than a walk. Even the paved streets presented problems, though, for the cobblestones were laid in at such a slant from the curbs (to form a sunken and usually clogged gutter in the middle of the road) that New Yorkers were said to be identifiable by their gait alone.

But the classic thoroughfare was Broadway, which formed a kind of spinal column up through the middle of the island between the East and North rivers, with crosstown streets extending from it at right angles like ribs, each street running down to the water at each side. For beauty, fashion, the finest hotels, the most splendid retail stores, and the most prestigious churches, Broadway was the great promenade of New York City in 1847. Here could be seen the young, beautiful, slender, and elegant ladies of New York, dressed in the luckiest French bonnets, the handsomest cloaks, and the richest flounced dresses, with ribbons, tunics, and laces to match. That their costly silks and rich brocades swept Broadway's pavement with more effect than did the broom of the dustman only added to the shock of seeing them on their happy promenade.

Here, too, could be seen the rugs of Persia, the rich fabrics and cashmeres of India and Tibet, the fine silks of China, the paintings of Rembrandt, Goya, Stuart, and Gainsborough, and all the manufactured goods of Europe and North America. Precious jewelry, extravagantly fashioned hats, handmade boots "as soft as a maiden's hand," and dresses worth a laborer's yearly earnings dominated the glittering window displays. Onlookers without money could dream; those with money could hardly wait to enter and buy.

It was impossible to live in New York long without developing an eager interest in the news. Everybody from the shoeshine man to the doctor was aware of yesterday's murder or scandal, the number of casualties suffered in the most recent tenement fire, and the latest news from Europe, brought to town by the constant flow of incoming ships. "What's the news?" had already been shortened to "What's new?"

Unlike London, where everything taxable was taxed, New York had no duty imposed upon publishing or advertising, no tax levied on the manufacture of paper, no bond or security requirements at the custom house. The result was that a newspaper sold in New York for one-fourth what it did in London, where it was shared in every hotel lobby by the hotel's guests and then read the next day and the day after that by the hotel staff. In New York, newspapers were so plentiful and sold for so little (the high-circulation dailies sold for a penny) that they were to be seen in the hands of the laboring as well as the wealthy classes. On Broadway, at the doors of department stores, in railway cars and omnibuses, boys sold them until each day's edition ran out. At the Astor Hotel, every man sitting down for breakfast had his own *Herald, Post, Sun, Tribune,* or *Commercial Advertiser.* Over 120,000 newspapers were sold every day in New York in 1847, and read by the majority of its half-million residents. In Dublin, where the price of a newspaper was eight times that in New York, there were but five thousand copies published a day for its 300,000 inhabitants.[5]

Almost every idea about New York and how to improve it found voice in the daily press. Every officeholder, every legislative measure, was scrutinized with the most searching freedom. The press entered every home, office, and public place, generating and spreading ideas with epidemic speed among the families of charwomen, cartmen, merchants, lawyers, manufacturers, and public officials. The children of the poor were fed almost as many ideas a day as those of the wealthy; every garret, cellar, cottage, townhouse, and mansion became, in the evening at supper, a center of discussion about the day's events. With no radio, no television, and only the ringing of the bell in the cupola of City Hall to tell New Yorkers the approximate location of the latest fire, information came from letters received, visiting friends, incoming ships, and, most of all, because it was always on time and always anticipated, the daily press.

People knew that the newspapers lied, that the telegraph lied, that it was hard to get at the truth, and yet they wanted to hear or read about the latest talk, gossip, or rumor. They had to know what was said about this or that civic proposal or jury verdict, who was being talked about and by whom. Tomorrow would no doubt bring more contradictions and more lies, but for now they had to join the crowd and take in the strange fun and excitement. And if a controversy arose and two opposing sides developed, they would take one side or the other. There was no time to think, inquire, reason impartially, or wait for evidence and certainty. The great gregariousness of New York, the crowding in of ships from the world over, the telegraph, the public meetings, and the teeming press, all combined with the nervous temperament and tempo of the city to keep the people in a state of compulsively cooperative excitement.

To make matters even livelier, the stimulus to succeed in business seemed to have so intoxicated New Yorkers that they were indifferent even to failure. There was no time now to pause over a loss or to devise ways to avoid being cheated. Everyone, whether from a fortune rapidly made or a ruin suddenly suffered, moved on in the almost universal belief that activity and success were as closely related as the fore and hind legs of a racing horse.

The advertising expressed this infectious belief in New York's prosperity and the American way of doing things. Banners, billboards, placards, and posters, their blatant messages running the gamut from patent medicines promising cancer cures to underwear guaranteed to last a lifetime, lined the tight side streets like laundry hanging out to dry. All these advertisements could be seen by anyone looking upward or straight forward, to the left or to the right. For the foot passengers who with good reason, given the littered streets, walked with their eyes to the ground, the New York advertisers provided marble tablets set in the sidewalks, in back-to-back pairs, so that the inscribed message—the name and address of a mustard manufacturer, a whiskey distillery, a toolmaker—could be read by those, their attention focused downward, going in either direction. Law firms and brokerage houses were heralded by different-colored bricks spelling out their names on the sides of their buildings; hawkers with bright ribbons in their straw hats stood in intersections, selling dry goods, beads, hardware, tea, fish, fruit, and a great assortment of artifacts from the Orient.

In Pearl Street, Dolores and her friends passed two men carrying across their backs a board on which was written

GREAT SALE OF SEWING MACHINES
AT #56 BROADWAY, BETWEEN BARCLAY AND VESEY STREETS.
ONE FLIGHT UP.

No one passing the two locked-together men failed to look around, and chances are that even those who laughed told their wives later about the sale.

"Sure, if you're in a buying mood, this is the place to be," Gil said.

"The signs are free," Dolores said. "Read them, enjoy them, and don't buy a thing."

At the next intersection, at Broadway and Pine, they stopped as a horse fell from fatigue after dragging a heavily laden wagon down from the north. A crowd no sooner gathered than a boy sprang forward and stuck a bill in the harness of the stricken horse:

DOCTOR HORNSBY'S GARGLING OIL
GOOD FOR MAN AND BEAST.

Then there were the "sandwich men," who carried two huge signs hanging from their shoulders, the front sign usually advertising one product, the back sign another. The two products were often so totally unrelated that foot passengers got in the habit of looking around just to see what the rear sign advertised. Indeed, this may have been why sandwich men seldom wore the same sign front and back; it was much more effective to advertise with one sign a dentist specializing in "live teeth" and with the other a dressmaker offering three separate fittings for every garment ordered.

This crazy-quilt advertising and hawking of wares, inescapable except in the wealthy residential section to the north, may have started as a fad, as so many New York activities did in the middle of the last century. But it was to become so integral, and so effective, a part of New York life that even London and Paris would follow suit before the century ended. In London, Piccadilly Circus would rival Times Square in the number of its lights and signs; in Paris, the produce markets on the Left Bank would have as many hawkers as New York's fish market on Fulton Street.

As they walked along, going whichever way impulse took them, Dolores and her friends were struck by how often they passed a slaughterhouse—sometimes two in the same street.

"I say this without fear of rebuttal," Gil said. "More meat is eaten in this city in a week than in all of Ireland in a year."

There were in fact over one hundred slaughterhouses in the city at this time, many of them operating in the most densely populated tenement areas. With no reliable refrigeration to preserve the meat for any length of time (natural ice from commercial icehouses went mostly to restaurants and oyster cellars), droves of cattle, sheep, and hogs were driven six days a week to these establishments, through streets clogged first with their droppings and then, after they were slaughtered, with their blood and waste matter. In many cases the slaughtering could be seen by anyone passing along the street, and after school hours, the presence of children—twelve-year-old boys hired to clean the floors—was not uncommon. The Society for the Prevention of Cruelty to Children apparently did not consider this cruelty, for the practice continued for another forty years. On Eldridge Street, Dolores and her companions saw one woman with a four-year-old girl talking to a butcher in plain sight of the slaughtering. Judging from the look on the little girl's face, it was a sight she would never forget.

Not far away, in the same neighborhoods, were related trades, noisome places where entrails were cleaned, bones boiled, fats melted, hides cured, tripe treated, and swill prepared, all of them adding to the emanations from the manure heaps, uncleaned stables, and overflowing backyard privies. Without a brisk wind blowing, it was hard to breathe, let alone live, eat, sleep, and cook, in such a neighborhood, but live there the Irish did, along with a few ragpicking Germans and perhaps one or two of the early-arriving Russian Jews. It was a question not so much of choosing a suitable place to live but of finding a place you could afford, within walking distance, if possible, of where you earned your living.[6]

Most surprising to Dolores was the closeness of these foul neighborhoods to the charming streets where the wealthy lived in townhouses well attended by Irish servant girls, who every day, she would soon learn, brought good things to eat from the townhouse kitchens to their mothers and fathers in the adjoining slums. Dolores, unaware that this proximity of poverty and wealth had been a peculiarity of New York since early in the eighteenth century, was unable to imagine that it would continue through her century and on into the twentieth, when the highest and most sumptuous apartment buildings would rise next to and share the same shops and restaurants with the ugliest slums.

Even the wealthy, famous, and well-traveled found New York an extraordinary place in the middle of the last century. It did not and never would achieve the indefinable unity of atmosphere that characterized Paris, nor did its precious few landmark buildings compare with those strewn like gems all over London. With its constant influx of new people with different religions, languages, and backgrounds, its new buildings going up and old buildings coming down, its ever-changing banners, advertisements, and newspapers, New York seemed to be trying day in, day out to divest itself of the past. Yet it was this very feeling of transitoriness, that each new day, win or lose, was worth a wager, that made New York something like a vast and marvelous casino.

The famous department stores with their abundance and variety of merchandise only added to the excitement and diversity. Wealthy visitors wrote home about these stores and shops, the sumptuous hotels, the service, the food, and the beautiful women, whose delicacy and butterfly caution accentuated the filth of the streets on which they were seen. But they would remember New York primarily as a place whose power and alacrity to change far exceeded their own capacity to adjust.

In most European cities, the wealthy and the poor were separated not only socially but geographically as well—in fact, the one group seldom saw the other. The wealthy had no reason to visit the poor sections, and while the reverse was true of the poor, they did so only with good reason, when called upon to render some necessary service. The European visitor to New York was thus unprepared to find a charming neighborhood within walking distance of the underside of the city's life and its Pandora's box of evils—the obnoxious debris, night soil, vegetable refuse, and all the smells they created. It was not unusual for a judge to live only a block away from the chimney sweep who every six months cleaned his chimney. The judge lived with all the amenities in a beautifully kept house built to his specifications. The chimney sweep lived with no amenities at all in a room with his wife and six children. True, the wealthy were in the process of moving to the more exclusive sections to the north, where the streets were now being numbered instead of named, but the process took time, and meanwhile, the Europeans continued to write home about how their wealthy New York friends lived right next door to poverty. Not even their New York friends would have believed that such would always be the case, no matter where in the city they moved.

Chapter Twenty-three

A great problem was left for the first civilized
inhabitants of New York to determine. Nature
had made ample provision for the metropolis of
the western hemisphere. But two possibilities
were attached to its occupation by man—it could
be healthy or unhealthy, at the option of the
people. . . . From 1622 to 1866, a period of two
hundred and forty-four years, the people elected
that the city should be unhealthy.

—Stephen Smith,
The City That Was

AT one point during their walk through the city, Big
Gil and Micky asked Dolores to excuse them for a moment.
They had noticed two privies in amongst some buildings in a
backyard and, in the hope that no one would notice or mind,
started through a passageway between two frame houses to
where the privies stood. Next to the privies was another building, this one a six-story brick tenement, standing next to another of similar design in the center of what had been the
adjacent backyards of the two one-family frame houses in
front. This back area was surrounded by a picket fence, which
also enclosed a number of pigsties and some stables.

The two tenements were separated by an airway about
twenty feet wide. The sun shone brightly, yet in this space,
where thousands of worthless-looking rags and garments of
every description hung from clotheslines, it was twilight. A fire-
escape platform was attached to each of the windows, but
none had a ladder leading to ground level, and every platform
was choked anyway with boxes, coal scuttles, old tins, rags,
and vegetables on their way to becoming garbage. On the
ground, piled high against the picket fences, were rags mixed

with bones, bottles, and papers, and straw and other substances so metamorphosed that the stench was almost unbear-
able. To make matters worse, the passageway between the two
frame houses had become virtually impassable because of the
filth created by the privies, pigs, and horses; to remedy this,
planks had been laid. As Big Gil and Micky walked over these
planks, a thick, brownish fluid oozed up like molasses through
the spaces between them and completely covered the decaying
boards that gave under their weight. The sight of the oozing
fluid made even worse its smell, which reminded them of the
steerage quarters they had just left.[1]

No sooner did they start back from the privies to rejoin
Dolores than they were caught by the sub-landlord.

"Wait, now, wait! Do you live here, or are you poaching?
For as sure as I'm the landlord, the first is inside the law, the
second outside."

Big Gil and Micky could see at once that the man confronting them was Irish; he had the red hair, blue eyes, and
freckled cheeks to play Paddy on any English stage. He was
not, as he claimed, the landlord, but rather the sub-landlord,
carrying on for the real landlord, who had moved with his
family uptown to Twenty-third Street.

"As for calling the police," Big Gil said in an effort to
placate the man, "it's equal to me whether you do or not.
We're just off the ship *Mersey*, from Cork, looking as peace-
fully as anyone could wish for tenement accommodations." He
had been hoping the man would have none to offer, but the
man disappointed him.

"Accommodations, is it? Well, you've found them, then,"
the sub-landlord said, changing his tone and manner with the
speed of a charlatan. "My name is John Maguire, I manage
these premises, and I can assure you, your place is here, in the
very heart of old New York, well situated and as airy as can be
with the wind coming through the alleys off the water. Here,
come with me. Let me show you an apartment I've been sav-
ing. At the very top of the stairs. Just under the roof. As full of
air as a beach on Staten Island."

He was still Irish, but now separated from the old country by his knowledge of the Yankee's grasp of business, how it operated, and why it succeeded. Like so many others before him, he had arrived with that fatal Irish flaw: a willingness generated by a lifetime of oppression to do whatever was necessary to succeed in British-free America.

Big Gil and Micky had no choice but to pretend they were interested; they followed as Maguire, who also ran the saloon on the ground floor out front where Dolores was waiting, started through the tenement entrance into the hallway. Even Gil, a blacksmith long familiar with horses, was shocked to see that the only way the horses could enter or leave their stables in the yard was through the hallway of the tenement house, where the smell of manure permeated everything. John Maguire offered no explanation or apology for this as he led Big Gil and Micky up the stairs. If a pig could share the same hut with the family in Ireland, the horses could share the same tenement hallway with the tenants in New York.[2]

The stairway was all rickety and out of level, with only one or two of the balusters left on each flight to help keep the shaky handrail in place. Following the example of Maguire, who knew from experience how to steer clear of the dangers, they avoided the sagging middle of the stairs, worn from overuse to little more than a cardboard thickness. It was necessary to put your weight on either side of the stairs, where the upright board supporting each step offered the only secure footing.

"How do the tenants manage these stairs at night?" asked Big Gil.

"Ah, they do, going up or going down, with or without a drop in them, with no trouble worthy of mention."

He was not insulting their intelligence so much as assuming that they were used to such housing. Believing, as he obviously did, that the lodgings he had to offer in New York were no worse than those the Irish immigrants had left in Ireland, he spoke with the same equanimity as any landlord's agent would have in Ireland. Besides, he had the top-floor apartment to show them, and who in Ireland had ever lived six stories above the ground?

On the way up, they passed through hallways where the doors leading to the "apartments" were either ajar or wide open, giving every passer-by a view of the family living within. The families would of course have preferred privacy, but the doors had become so warped that they no longer fit the door-frames. The tenants would have had to shave either the edge of the door or the inside of the doorframe if they wanted privacy; none did, out of a fear instilled in them in Ireland that they would thus be destroying or altering someone else's prop-erty. What they did do, at night, was use rope to hold the doors as close to the doorframes as possible; during the day, with children coming and going, the rope proved to be more bother than help; the doors were allowed to remain open or ajar as their hinges dictated.[3]

On the fourth floor, when Maguire, without so much as a "May I?," led Big Gil and Micky through one of these open doors to introduce them to the family living there, the family was no more surprised than he was apologetic. In a close, foul-smelling room measuring about twelve by fifteen feet, with nearly all the plaster off the walls, the fixtures stained yellow with smoke, and the wooden floor so greasy with refuse as to make it dangerous to walk on, they encountered a mother, married daughter, unemployed stepson, and four children—eight in all, counting the father, who was out laying water pipes in the street. Here they lived, cooked, and slept, four stories above the ground-level privies, which were so overused and in such bad order that the calls of nature were attended to in the room and the vessels carried downstairs to be emptied.

The stove, set in a corner by the window, was capable of accommodating but one pot at a time. Big Gil and Micky, fresh off the *Mersey*, were therefore not at all surprised to see a big steaming pot jammed with everything from scrap meat and bones down to potatoes, kidney beans, carrots, onions, peppercorns, soup greens of every variety, and a surface scum still to be scooped up and removed. The inviting smell emanating directly from the pot unfortunately combined with, rather than dispelled, all the other smells that had lodged themselves like permanent boarders in the apartment. You ate there, sitting at a table, only if you were awfully hungry; otherwise you stood by the stove, away from the other smells, with the steam of the food you were eating reminding you that it did indeed have a smell similar to the one you were tasting. The sublandlord nevertheless continued to be proud—or at least not ashamed—of this property under his management as he led Big Gil and Micky to the "prize" he was offering them on the top floor.

These were the tenements awaiting the Irish in New York in 1847. Hurriedly built to accommodate the greatest number at the least expense, they had plumbing only on the ground level, where the crowding around spigots resembled the crowding around the ship's caboose on the way over. Not far from these spigots, on the same level or in the basement, were the tenants' privies, overflowing with what was then euphemistically called "night soil." This noxious substance was carted away twice a week—if the tenants were lucky—by street department personnel, themselves Irish immigrants, who shoveled it into horse-drawn wagons and dumped it into the river on either side of the island before even the milkman was up to make his rounds.[4]

It is true that people with dirty habits are likely to have dirty habitations and that a pauperized, intemperate people destroy the property they live in while making it the center of all kinds of vice and crime. But in 1847 it was a question not of which came first, the "dirty" Irish or the dirty tenements, but of how the tenements precluded any improvement in the way the Irish or any one else lived or wanted to live. The tenements not only led to dirty habits where none before existed; they choked off any nice habits the Irish might have brought with them or were likely to develop. To be dirty in these wretched, overcrowded tenements was easy; to be anything else was almost impossible.

Dedicated people like Dr. John H. Griscom, the city inspector of the Board of Health, found it shocking that most sub-landlords were once immigrants themselves. He and his staff were baffled that men who had started up the social ladder were the first to knock down, if they could, those just below them. These Irish sub-landlords were among the hardest bargainers, the most unprincipled cheats, to confront the newly arrived immigrant. By running the groggeries and groceries attached to the tenements from which they collected rents, they were able to keep a daily check on their tenants while pressing vice and other evils on them. The sub-landlords knew their bars would be well attended by tenants happy that their drinking companions were also Catholic. In such an establishment, dismal and cellar-damp though it might be, there would be no reason to mince matters with those of other religious persuasions or, worse, to disguise one's religious beliefs for fear of being unpopular. Rare was the Irishman who would do such a thing; indeed, whenever two or three Irishmen entered a tavern frequented by Protestant nativists, it did not take long for a violent brawl to erupt and spread into the street.

Had the Irish been members of one of the Protestant sects whose churches dotted the streets of New York, their brogue, their poverty, even their crazy hats and coats, would have been looked upon as quaint rather than disgusting; they would have been accepted and helped, ushered through the inevitable acculturation process. But their religion confirmed and perpetuated the stigma that their Gaelic language, brogue, and poverty made so obvious. Anyone wearing one of those decrepit swallow-tailed coats and ridiculously battered high hats was not simply another immigrant; he was another Irish Catholic immigrant.

In New York, this tenement-groggery arrangement developed from a pattern established long before the arrival of the famine Irish. The wealthy had built townhouses in all the nooks and corners of Manhattan's toe, on property owned by them, at a time when the vest-pocket size of New York made living there charming as well as convenient for both family life and business. The head of the family walked, rode a horse, or was taken in a carriage to his office, law firm, court building, or hospital, while his wife took the children to and from a nearby private school, shopped for clothes at Steward's on Broadway, visited friends, attended teas, and supervised the cook and maids at home.

But as the population grew and the incoming ships unloaded more and more merchandise from all over the world, this entire lower part of the island became dominated by business. Shops, fabric stores, oyster bars, and barrooms proliferated in every street; factories, tanneries, slaughterhouses, hotels, and tenements cropped up all over, until wealthy property owners began to leave their townhouses for the more respectable and less crowded areas stretching as far north as Forty-second Street.[5]

The wealthy knew better than to sell this valuable downtown property; they engaged, instead, sub-landlords to superintend it for them. The almost immediate result, given the low cost of labor and materials at the time, was the erection of six-story tenements where none had before existed—in the very backyards of the townhouses vacated by the wealthy. Now, instead of flower and vegetable gardens back to back, there were two six-story tenements facing each other, the distance between them so close that immigrants reaching out from one could, in some cases, touch fingers with those reaching out from the other.

The original townhouses remained and were themselves occupied from cellar to attic, the cellar by tenants or perhaps by an oyster bar, the next floor by the owner of the oyster bar, who was usually the sub-landlord as well, and all the floors above, into the highest attic recesses, by desperate and exhausted immigrants who had decided, in most cases correctly, that they had no other choice.[6]

Meanwhile, Dolores, still waiting for her friends out front, had become aware of the squinting windows on either side of the street, where the façades of these townhouses faced each other. She was being watched by already-settled Irish immigrants, just as she might have been back home in a city's Irish town, where the Catholic poor lived separate and apart from the Protestant well-to-do. When the Protestants rode through these Irish towns on horseback or in carriages, they were watched with hatred and envy from behind broken, half-boarded windows that looked like eyes damaged in drunken brawls. But this was New York, Dolores was obviously another Irish Catholic immigrant, and behind the windows now were mothers and grandmothers who should have remained in Ireland and died there rather than here. Too old to be left alone in Ireland and too weak to refuse passage, they had left and were now peering out in the hope that Dolores's appearance would add something extra to this particular day in their lives. Through what seemed a dim mist of time, they watched her standing there, the whites of their eyes, the cheekbones of their gaunt faces, and the tight knuckles of their hands flashing through the dark windows like flecks of dying hope.

When Big Gil and Micky rejoined her, she said in passing that she had seen several Irish women and children coming up from the cellars of the frame houses fronting on the street.

Big Gil nodded: "The 'cellar population,' the mate on the *Mersey* called them. They're even poorer, he said, than the tenement population in the rear."

"I've had my turn in the rear," Micky said. "And if ever it comes to that, I'll take the cellar over the tenement."

It was said that the steady influx of Irish immigrants from rural environments made sanitary laws unenforceable, but the streets of New York had always been used as a depository for garbage, rubbish, and offal. Wealthy New Yorkers had for years hired help to keep the streets clean in front of their townhouses. Some who could not afford this service refused to be seen sweeping side by side with the servants of their wealthy neighbors. The result was that even in the better neighborhoods, and long before the influx of the famine Irish, pedestrians had to be careful where they walked.

In the busier streets, the hawking of fish, vegetables, and joints of beef and pork added to the problem, since peddlers used the gutters as receptacles for fish heads, the viscera and trimmings of butchered animals, and the unedible husks, leaves, and greens from cauliflower, carrots, corn, beets, and lettuce. The ever-roaming swine of New York induced these peddlers to toss their refuse in the streets, and this in turn encouraged the Irish poor to acquire more pigs and piglets to roam the streets for food at no one's expense. Even when the piles of garbage, rubbish, dirt, blood, dead animals, and store and shop sweepings were removed in response to citizens' complaints, the offal wagon would no sooner turn the corner than the accumulation of decaying vegetable and animal matter would begin again, once more to be examined by the accommodating pigs.

Some streets in the tenement districts looked more like dunghills than thoroughfares in a civilized city. The gutters were loaded with, the sewer culverts obstructed by, everything from house slops to human excrement, the latter carried down in buckets from the tenements and emptied in the street because the night-soil man had failed to come by and empty the overflowing backyard privies. At irregular intervals, street cleaners with tarpaulin-covered carts would come round and rake out the black and decayed contents of these deep gutters on either side of the street. Nothing on earth smelled worse, especially during the summer months when the amount of waste matter increased along with the temperature needed to accelerate its decomposition. During interims when the street cleaner failed to appear for a week or more, the putrifying organic substances were ground together by the constantly passing horses and vehicles into a poisonous powder, clouds of which were raised by the endless traffic and carried by the wind in every direction.[7]

These nuisances alone would have been enough to tax the patience of visitors to the city, let alone of those living, working, and doing business every day within its limits. But the city's manure problem far exceeded even that of the garbage and offal. In 1847 there were in the city over six thousand public and private stables, accommodating over sixty thousand horses. The average manure production per horse per month being 0.43 tons, New York's total production per annum was well over 309,000 tons, almost all of it confined to the tightly packed area between The Battery and Canal Street.[8]

With the exception of the dirt cartmen and the fishmongers and greengrocers, who pushed their carts through the streets, horses provided the only motive power for the transportation of men and material. They pulled omnibuses and carriages that crisscrossed the city with passengers; they hauled away the garbage from doorways and the night soil from tenement-house privies; they delivered the milk and, in areas where the Croton Water Works pipes were still unlaid, the water as well; they brought into the city the furniture and hardware, the material needed for the never-ending construction of new buildings; they transported from manufacturer to shop or department store the dresses and haberdashery, coats, shoes, and hats that had already made New York City the great emporium of the United States.

They even drew incoming railroad cars down into the heart of the city after the locomotive had been detached uptown at what is now called Dyckman Street. Each car, still loaded with passengers, was drawn by a team of four horses on rails laid in the middle of East Broadway, a thoroughfare that terminated at the extremity of City Hall Park opposite the Astor Hotel.. Omnibus lines of rail—trolley lines—were also laid along several other prominent thoroughfares, all the cars traveling on them crowded with passengers and drawn by teams of horses running at a trot, their bells warning pedestrians of their approach. Horses were of necessity everywhere in the streets, as were the mounds of manure they produced.

For inland cities like Pittsburgh and Hartford, the transportation of manure from stable and street to surrounding farms was comparatively simple. The farmer wagoned in and paid for what he needed or had it delivered to his farm by the city stable of his choice. But New York City, surrounded by water, found it necessary from the start to use lighters, tugs, scows, barges, flatcars, and even sailing vessels for the regular removal of its enormous and ever-increasing manure production.[9]

City cartmen, most of them Irish immigrants, loaded tubs, boxes, and barrels of manure onto carts and transported them from the city's stables through the crowded streets to manure scows tied to docks on either side of the city. The tubs, boxes, and barrels were always too overloaded to be tightly covered, and the carts carrying them too old or poorly constructed to avoid spillage whenever a bump in the street was encountered or the traffic required a sudden switch or turn. It was by law the duty of the cartmen to shovel any spillage back onto his cart before proceeding, but the traffic of horses and carriages was such that when he tried to, he usually ended up with his cart capsized and his entire load of manure emptied in the street. Dolores and her friends saw this happen at the intersection of Grand and Mulberry streets. The cartman did his best to reload the spilled manure, but with the drivers of other vehicles speeding by in every direction, the manure was soon spread about and ground into the spaces between the cobblestones.

Whatever the spillage, the experienced cartman simply continued on his way, leaving behind him a trail of manure and an unavoidable smell, until he reached the waiting scow, unloaded, and washed his cart down with river water. Once a scow was fully loaded by manure cartmen from all over the city, it was towed along either the Jersey or Long Island shore, to be discharged within easy reach of farms.

The New Jersey and Long Island farmers, forced to pay for this extra transportation cost, bought the minimum of what they needed, and only when they needed it. This created a storage problem offensive to all New Yorkers except those in the manure business. Nevertheless, given the political corruption involving the Common Council in New York City at the time, it was decided that since manure was a marketable commodity subject to the farmers' vagaries of demand, it would be safer financially to store it not where it was needed but, rather, where it was produced, in the immediate vicinity of the city or in the city itself, from which point it could be shipped to farms on demand. Great heaps of manure were thus kept within the city, attracting huge swarms of flies and creating a sickening stench.[10]

People living anywhere near these dumps learned to weather what came to be known as "the four seasons of the manure year." From December to February there was a farmers' demand for manure, but the ice in the rivers and creeks prevented the barges and scows from reaching the small docks along the shore where the manure was stored. The heaps grew higher and higher during these months, but froze as well, which made the situation at least bearable. Then from February to May the manure was shipped without interruption, there being no ice to prevent the scows from supplying the still-existing demand. From May to August, though, the farmers were tending their crops and had no need for manure. And these were the hot, humid months, when every citizen received a sample of manure every time a fly alighted on his or her skin. From August to December there was again a demand among the farmers for manure, and the absence of ice made it possible to ship the daily production as it came in.

Twelve months of manure production were thus confined to six months of manure removal, the non-removal months being separated into two separate periods of two and four months when the manure had to be stored somewhere. Manure contractors, most of them pre-famine Irish immigrants who had started as dirt cartmen and saved enough to buy horses and manure wagons, continued to pick up and store on the docks the manure produced by the city's large livery and sales stables. This service went on without interruption throughout the year because the manure at such places, being generally free of hay and in greater demand by farmers, brought better prices.

But these same contractors had little incentive during the idle months to pick up manure at the privately owned stables in street after street throughout the city. The smallest of these stables, owned by professionals and businessmen with their own gigs and carriages, housed no more than four or five horses, whose manure production was not sufficient to interest the big contractors. The stablemen in charge, most of them Irish horseshoers as well, tried to make pick-up arrangements with small market gardeners in the outskirts of the city or with free-lance cartmen, but with little success. They remained dependent upon the established contractors, whose carts came round so irregularly that the manure overflowed in the vaults, losing half its value by becoming mixed with straw. Stables all over the city thus had piles of manure growing higher and more unmanageable every day.[11]

Meanwhile, the city kept growing, in the downtown section higher and higher, in the uptown section farther and farther northward. The only motive power making this growth possible was the horse; indeed, if anything distinguished water-locked New York City during these years, it was this problem of what to do with the manure produced by animals without whom the city could not and never would have survived.

Had the surrounding waters not been so productive of the finest shad and oysters in the world, the excessively straw-mixed manure might have been dumped into the rivers on either side of the island. No doubt a portion of it was disposed of in this way at night by small stable-owners, as was the night soil collected by Irish cartmen during the midnight hours when everyone was asleep. But manure being a salable commodity, needed as fertilizer by farmers nearby, it was not considered garbage and so accumulated within the city, never far from where the uncollected garbage lay.

Newspapers, civic leaders, politicians, prominent and ordinary citizens, all expressed anger and indignation at the condition of the streets, and many among them offered solutions. The use of street-cleaning machines and self-loading carts had been urged by the *Daily Tribune* as early as 1843. Even then the editor doubted whether the Common Council, always fearful of losing its patronage, would consider the idea, since the machine "*cannot vote*; and lacking this ability it may seem to the ruling powers to lack the only essential qualification."[12]

These same newspapers and public officials claimed that the revenue from the sale of manure was enough to cover the cost of cleaning the streets, and in early New York the revenue, on the one hand, and the cost, on the other, did in fact come close to matching each other; the manure was separated from the garbage and sold for a profit almost equal to the cost of collecting it and the garbage from the streets. Then came city growth, Irish immigration, and city graft, all of which threw the equation forever out of kilter. The amount of manure left in the streets increased every year, cost more to remove every year, but made less in sales every year.

Even the mayor, William V. Brady, had to agree with editorial writers in the spring of 1847 that there was an inverse ratio between the cost of cleaning the streets and the condition of the streets, that the first kept going up while the second kept getting worse. He called for an end to "this extravagant and wasteful expenditure," but the street-cleaning department, one of the most lucrative sources of political patronage, continued to be more concerned with clean profits than with clean streets, and every year the department cost more to run but accomplished less.[13]

When the police were accused of not arresting those who threw garbage and ashes in the streets, they replied that it was useless to bring the culprits before judges who invariably permitted them to go free. Later, when the chief of police was asked why these ordinances were not enforced, he said that since the offenders were mostly housewives, his officers could hardly be expected to drag them away from their children. Besides, he said, with more relevance to the matter in hand, the public did not support the authorities in this matter, believing as it did that the real culprit was the street-cleaning department.

It must indeed have been difficult in such a garbage-strewn city for a judge, who no doubt dropped his own cigar butts in the gutter, to punish someone for adding a mite to the ever-accumulating piles in street after street. What the city would have done during this period without the free-roaming pigs must have boggled the minds even of those who despised the sight of their snouts, bloated bodies, and little tails turning every corner. It was obviously a matter of either purging the street-cleaning department or allowing the unsightly pigs to continue serving the public in the only way they knew how.[14]

The Irish kept arriving by the thousands during this crucial period in New York City's history. And given their familiarity with animals, the piles of manure and garbage in the streets, and the problem created by both private and mass transportation, it did not take them long to fit together the horse, the pig, and the street-cleaning department in New York City's scheme of things. It was as if they had emigrated just in time to fill an urgent need. Not only did they add to and stimulate the city's growth during these years, they also made that growth possible by supplying the men needed to take charge of the city's increasing animal population and the manure that population created. The unpleasant job had to be done, and since native New Yorkers did not want to do it and were willing to pay to have it done for them, the Irish filled their own needs as well as the city's, at a time when continuing city growth made garbage and manure removal most urgent, and the graft that went with it more entrenched. Schooled as the Irish were in all the ramifications of British corruption in Ireland, they grabbed like children at the chance to be themselves corrupt in America. Democracy became something like an unrestricted playground—a place where they too were at last free to romp.

Dolores and her friends were quick to notice that almost all the street-department and manure men were Irish. Big Gil in fact spoke to one of them, a man in his late forties named Timothy Burke, with a worn and wrinkled Irish farmer's face and a brogue reminiscent of that in County Roscommon, up in the landlocked sector of Ireland where the ocean was seen only by those who traveled to the coast to emigrate.

" 'Tis true," Burke said, indicating his muck-laden rake in answer to Big Gil's query, "the Irish have a corner on this. We are not as offended by the smell as the people hereabouts who create it. They want nothing to do with it; they only want it removed. All right, then, we'll remove it, the Irish will remove it, but only at the price and pace we set."

Commentators during these years advised Irishmen to get out of New York and go west, north, or south to rural America where they belonged. But the Irish had seen their fathers and grandfathers in the old country work the land from youth to old age with nothing to show for it but a bent back. They were disenchanted with farming, and they liked the clannishness of the Irish in New York, the political corruption they perceived in the city, the easy access—not once but several times—to the polling booth. They all had witnessed the court system in Ireland, which the French writer Gustave de Beaumont had called "a lie of forms . . . a preparation for vengeance." Now the same kind of deceit, deception, and dishonesty might be theirs to channel through Tammany Hall for their own benefit.

Besides, the great city they had in so many ways feared turned out to be not so foreign and unaccommodating after all. The horses and pigs in the streets, the slaughterhouses and tanneries, the stables and blacksmiths' shops and all the rural smells they created, the hotels with their efficient Irish servant girls and slender young Irish waiters, the burly Irishmen laying the city's gas lines and Croton Water Works pipes in the streets—all these made staying in New York City more attractive than heading into the unknown countryside, where building canals, cutting through forests, laying railroad lines, or working the land presented almost the only ways to exist, all of them in lonely places bereft of the kind of "society" most Irishmen craved.

Then too, living in New York City, with the ocean beside them, made Ireland and their loved ones nearer, and what England had done to them easier to remember. This abiding hatred of the British delayed what would otherwise have been a speedy acculturation. The entrenched New Yorkers were, after all, of British or Dutch descent, and despite the Revolutionary War, British culture had no more been discarded by the wealthy than it was when King's College was renamed Columbia. Even the Gaelic-speaking Irish eventually acquired their inimitable version of the English tongue and were able to use it with the same dexterity that they had heard it used, minus the brogue and at their expense, in Ireland's courtrooms. Still, they became "American" very fast—except for their Catholicism, their distrust and misuse of government, and the alacrity with which they expressed, anywhere and in front of anybody, their hatred of the British Empire. Having lived so long with this cancer of hidden resentment, they could not wait in New York to expose it to anyone who would or could be forced to listen.

Nor did the Irish in the Midwest, surrounded by land whose fertility exceeded the wildest stories they had heard in Ireland, lose this hatred; they simply became too busy with and rooted in their new land to cling so tenaciously to the horrors and causes of the famine. They would go on being as faithful to Ireland and their loved ones as the easterners, but they would at the same time become more engulfed in America, in the entire continent surrounding them, in the work they had to put in on what they could at last call their own land, with no religious tithes attached and no pig needed for the absentee landlord's rent.

In the middle of the last century, as these Irish immigrants straggled off the incoming ships, mussed and frayed, many emaciated, others vacant and stupefied, they had no way of knowing that some of the worst features of the Old World had been carried over to the New, that no golden age existed on either side of the water, that vice and crime were as rampant in the New World as in the Old. It was almost as if the ships bringing the good people of Europe to America brought also the predators they were trying to escape.

Nor would the Irish realize, until much later, that they were on their way into an American society where all the fears expressed by the elderly at the American wakes back home would come to pass. Little by little, social, economic, and family pressure, the feeling of insecurity engendered by unfamiliar mores and surroundings, the scorn and ridicule directed at them by American nativists, would force them to lose or give up most of the uniquely lovable attributes that living in a tightly knit parish in Ireland had so benignly fostered. Irish and Catholic they would always be, but without the homogeneity of life in Ireland, where being Irish and "being" were one and the same.

In time, the folkways, stories, superstitions, fairies, and leprechauns would gradually thin out in their memories and cease to be believed. The tragic and glorious history of the Irish under British rule would be looked upon as an impediment to American respectability and so repressed if not forgotten. Irish-American lawyers, surgeons, judges, and politicians would shun dwelling on their ancestors' suffering in order not to jeopardize their place in American society. They would avoid at all cost any association with Paddy, that funny ragman who would haunt their nights whenever they reread the old letters of their emigrant ancestors or saw in a daguerreotype the similarity of facial structure in some long-gone aunt or uncle. "Belonging" would become uppermost among all but the unsuccessful lower-class Irish, who would dwell on past wrongs in lieu of anything better in the present. They would turn in self-defense to a kind of bigotry, still unknown in the land of their fathers, and give back what they'd received—a sour hatred of other ethnic groups and religions. By doing so, this ever-diminishing Irish minority would relinquish in America everything they had so desperately left Ireland to retain.

Different and apart from these unfortunate, doomed-to-fail immigrants, who did not live much longer in America than they would have in Ireland, but long enough to pass on their misbegotten bigotry to their children and grandchildren, were people like Dolores Kinsella, Micky Quinn, and William Gilhooley. Dolores and her friends had suffered through the same voyage and arrived with the same wonder at the sight of New York. But unlike the tired people, they still had the energy and adaptability to put the wonder of New York almost immediately to work. So eager were they to become Americans that in their hearts they already were.

These people and the thousands who arrived with them started their lives in New York at the lowest level, then very slowly worked their way upward against the grain of tenement poverty, Protestant prejudice, and a stereotype, created by a minority among them, of rude manners, boisterous behavior, alcoholic belligerence, and political trickery. Arriving mostly as unskilled laborers, they dug the Erie Canal, built the embankments for the Chesapeake railroad, laid the first railway line from Boston to Providence, extended the winding rails toward the anthracite regions in Pennsylvania, where many settled and went down into the mines. In the city itself many worked their way up from laborer and cartman to fireman, policeman, saloonkeeper, and from there, in some cases, to owner of some lucrative manure-removal company.[15]

It is also by now well known that the Irish make exemplary soldiers in the armies of other countries. In their own, though as brave and as willing to die in battle as elsewhere, they are mostly ineffective even as rebels. Perhaps the omnipresent British army, whose domination lasted for centuries, whose emasculating effects can still be seen—even today, in the eyes and faces of Dublin's beggars—made ludicrous the idea of an Irishman in an "Irish" army, fighting for his own country. After being as well trained in poverty and subservience by the British as dogs were in the conditioned reflex by Pavlov, the ordinary Irishman was not about to form an Irish army, complete with generals, colonels, captains, and so on down to private. It takes generations of freedom for a subjugated people to regain the ease, self-confidence, and grace of those who have for so long subjugated them. For Irish immigrants in the United States in the middle of the last century, this sloughing of the British yoke was destined to be much faster than it was to be for the Irish remaining in Ireland, where the custom of oppression would keep the memory and habit of it alive long after 1921, when freedom, at least in the south of Ireland, was finally won. The Irishman in 1847 had to go to a free country, like the United States, to show the world how well he might have fought for his own had his own been free.

There were also among them, given the Irish gift of speech and delivery, auctioneers, agents, salesmen, and newspaper reporters. But the great majority, limited in both experience and education, gravitated into whatever trades had jobs to offer. They became bartenders, butchers, brush makers, horseshoers, blacksmiths, brass fitters, bricklayers, coachmen, conductors, omnibus drivers, lumbermen, gardeners, ironworkers, janitors, junkmen, laundresses, leatherworkers, machinists, maids, masons, manure cartmen, oyster openers, pipe fitters, plumbers, roofers, ragpickers, seamstresses, servants, stewards, shoemakers, stonecutters, stablemen, street cleaners, telegraph operators, truckdrivers, varnishers, waiters, watchmen, wheelwrights, and weavers. Beneath the streets of New York they laid both the gas lines that lighted the streets at night and the pipes that carried Croton Aqueduct's pure water into the city's buildings. Above these subterranean pipes and lines they paved the streets with cobblestones, known then as "Belgian blocks"—stones naturally rounded and smooth on top and extending almost a foot down into the roadbed itself. It was over these solid stones that the city's horses clicked and hopped from one end of the day to the other, pulling behind them carriages and omnibuses whose iron-clad wheels added to the cacophony in every tightly packed street.

For a long time the Irish were thought to belong by nature to the servant and laboring classes. It was all right for them to save money and move to cleaner tenements, but when they tried to better themselves socially as well, they were looked upon with both scorn and amusement by the Protestant upper middle class. This would change as the more successful Irish grew wealthier and their children and grandchildren began to resemble in both education and dress, manner and speech, the wealthy Protestants whose snobbish attitude would only add impetus to the Irish family's drive toward what is now called "upward mobility." The wealthier they became, the easier it would be for them to pretend that they had always been wealthy. They would of course still be shunned by those with "old money," but these holdovers from Dutch and Tory New York would remain powerless against the Irish rise to elective office and the control and influence that went with it.

In time the Irish would produce dramatists, songwriters, and gifted actors whose art would help Americans understand and appreciate the Irishman's love for his homeland and his timeless struggles to defend it. Old ballads like "My Gentile Harp," " 'Twas Dying They Had Thought Her," and "The Wearing of the Green" reached from Boston, New York, Philadelphia, and Baltimore westward into the hinterlands. The great increase of Irish construction workers would produce such new songs as "Drill Ye Tarriers, Drill," "Paddy Works on the Erie," and others based on the hard life of the railman who each day worked his way farther and farther away from home.

The American theater would be graced by actors of Irish descent like John Drew, Effie Shannon, and James O'Neill. These would yield to the Barrymores, Helen Hayes, Walter Hampden, Margaret Sullavan, Spencer Tracy, Barry Fitzgerald, Victor McLaglen, Eddie Dowling, Tyrone Power, Bing Crosby, Nancy, Grace, and Gene Kelly, and then, on television, Art Carney and Jackie Gleason.

The Irish would produce playwrights Philip Barry, Marc Connelly, George Kelly, and the greatest of all American dramatists, Eugene O'Neill, whose father, actor James O'Neill, must have turned in his grave as the curtain went up on "Long Day's Journey Into Night." In the other arts, Georgia O'Keefe would become a renowned American painter; Irish-born Augustus Saint-Gaudens, one of our greatest sculptors. Padraic Colum, Joyce Kilmer, James T. Farrell, John O'Hara, and F. Scott Fitzgerald are just a few of the poets and novelists of Irish stock who gained world-wide recognition. In sports, politics, and the American labor movement, the names would be too many to list. In medical science, Dr. John Murphy was the first surgeon to remove an appendix; Dr. Joseph O'Dwyer saved the lives of tens of thousands of diphtheria victims with the intubation technique he devised; Dr. Roy Halloran was one of America's outstanding psychiatrists, along with the even more famous Harry Stack Sullivan.

These people and thousands of others, with their achievements in every field, would finally put Paddy to rest as a British creation—the scapegoat upon whose head the blame for centuries of misgovernment was placed. Fashioned in *Punch* and the London *Times* as the ragamuffin who could not be trusted, ridiculed in the streets of Dublin, Liverpool, and London, and made the butt throughout England of music-hall jokes, he might be called the funny bone in the structure of this now waning British Empire. But whatever name he goes by now—Al Smith or John F. Kennedy—he will forever, with his battered high hat, ragged swallow-tailed coat, dangling knee breeches, and bare feet, haunt not only Irish memory but also the halls and chambers of Westminster Palace, where Parliament tried for so long, without success, to do him in.

Notes

ABBREVIATIONS

IER: Irish Ecclesiastical Record.

NLI: National Library of Ireland.

IFD: Irish Folklore Department, University College, Dublin.

Alms House: Annual Reports of the Alms House Commissioner of the City of New York, 1847–50.

Documents: Documents of the Board of Alderman, New York City: 1845–60.

Evidence: Evidence Before the Select Committee on Colonization from Ireland, with appendix of letters, 1847.

Minutes: Minutes of Evidence Taken Before the Select Committee on Emigrant Ships, 1854.

New York Association: New York Association for Improving Conditions of the Poor, Annual Reports, 1847–92.

Papers: Papers Relative to Emigration to the British Province in North America.

Report: Report of the Select Committee to Investigate the Operation of the Passenger Acts, Parliamentary Proceedings, 1851.

Transactions: Transactions of the Central Relief Committee of the Society of Friends during the Famine in Ireland in 1846 and 1847, with appendices.

Chapter One

1. John O'Rourke, *The History of the Great Irish Famine of 1847* (Dublin, 1875), p. 153.
2. IFD, ms. 1,068, p. 68.
3. Redcliffe N. Salaman, *The History and Social Influence of the Potato* (Cambridge, 1949), p. 301.
4. Daily and weekly press, 1847, quoted in Census of Ireland 1851, p. 268.
5. Letter written by Father Mathew published in Parliamentary Papers, July 27, 1846, quoted in Census of Ireland 1851, p. 270.
6. IFD, ms. 1,069, p. 11.
7. IFD, ms. 1,069, p. 353.
8. IFD, ms. 1,068, p. 58.
9. Excerpts from letters from readers to Irish newspapers, August–September 1846.

Chapter Two

1. IFD, ms. 1,245, p. 3.
2. IFD, ms. 1,069, p. 144.
3. IFD, ms. 1,069, p. 70.
4. IFD, ms. 1,069, p. 370.
5. IFD, ms. 1,068, pp. 12–15.
6. IFD, ms. 1,069, p. 365.
7. IFD, ms. 1,068, p. 71.
8. IFD, ms. 1,411 (Conall O'Byrne), vol. 4, p. 21; ms. 1,407, p. 65.
9. Transactions, appendix 3, p. 202.
10. NLI, ms. 17,305 (Geraldine Henson).
11. IFD, ms. 1,245, pp. 70–71.
12. Lady Gregory, *The Kiltartan History Book* (London, 1926), p. 63.
13. Henry D. Ingles, *Ireland In 1834*, vol. 1 (London, 1835), p. 76.
14. James Hannay, *The Lighter Side of Irish Life* (New York, 1911), p. 147.
15. Thomas Carlyle, *Reminiscences of My Irish Journey in 1849* (London, 1850).
16. S. Godolphin Osbourne, *Gleanings in the West of Ireland* (London, 1850), p. 79.

Chapter Three

1. George Otto Trevelyan, *The Life and Letters of Lord Macaulay*, vol. 11 (London, 1881), p. 230.
2. Salaman, *History*, p. 254.
3. Arthur Young, *A Tour of Ireland*, vol. 2 (London, 1780), pp. 23–26.
4. NLI, ms. 17,305.
5. IFD, ms. 1,068, pp. 72–73.
6. IFD, ms. 1,068.
7. James H. Tuke, *A Visit to Connaught in the Autumn of 1847* (London, 1848), pp. 18–19.
8. Hugh Dorian, "Donegal 60 Years Ago. A True Historical Narrative," IFD, p. 16.
9. IFD, ms. 1,068, p. 53.
10. Alexis de Tocqueville, *Journeys in England and Ireland in 1835* (London, 1958).
11. IFD, ms. 1,068.
12. Osbourne, *Gleanings*, p. 50.
13. Hannay, *Lighter Side*, p. 179.
14. Osbourne, *Gleanings*, p. 92.

Chapter Four

1. (Dublin) *Evening Freeman*, January 5, 1847.
2. (Dublin) *Evening Freeman*, January 5, 1847.
3. *The Nation*, May 15, 1847.
4. IFD, ms. 1,069, pp. 371–72.
5. Transactions, appendix 3, p. 202.
6. (Dublin) *Evening Freeman*, January 14, 1847.
7. *Sligo Champion*, February 25, 1847.
8. Elihu Burritt, *A Journal of a Visit of Three Days to Skibbereen and its Neighborhood* (London, 1847), p. 14.
9. Osbourne, *Gleanings*, p. 17.
10. Burritt, *Journal*, pp. 12, 13.
11. F. F. Trench, Letter dealing with famine. Addressed to the Editor of *Saunder's News-Letter*, 1847. Pamphlets on Famine, Archives, NLI. MS. 13397(4).
12. *The Nation*, September 25, 1847.
13. Quoted in O'Rourke, *History*, pp. 301–02.

14. John Mitchel, *The Last Conquest of Ireland (Perhaps)* (Dublin, 1861), p. 32.
15. Quoted in O'Rourke, *History*, pp. 302–03.
16. Quoted in O'Rourke, *History*, pp. 263–64.
17. *The Nation*, December 26, 1846.

Chapter Five

1. *Freeman's Journal*, April 1, 1846.
2. *Freeman's Journal*, November, 1846.
3. Salaman, *History*, pp. 28–83, 293; *The Nation*, May 2, 1846; Mitchel, *Last Conquest*, p. 32; Tuke, *Visit*, pp. 10, 12, 24, 25, 61–70; Gustave de Beaumont, *Ireland: Social, Political, and Religious* (London, 1839), vol. 1. pp. 304–05; Osbourne, *Gleanings*, pp. 26–35, 43, 46–48.
4. Osbourne, *Gleanings*, p. 30.
5. Quoted in Giovanni Costigan, *A History of Modern Ireland* (New York, 1969), p. 181.
6. Interview conducted by John O'Rourke, quoted in O'Rourke, *History*, p. 389.
7. *Morning Chronicle*, December 15, 1846.
8. Tuke, *Visit*; Osbourne, *Gleanings*.
9. De Beaumont, *Ireland*, vol. 1, p. 282.
10. Osbourne, *Gleanings*, p. 52.
11. Ingles, *Ireland in 1834*, pp. 290–91.
12. De Beaumont, *Ireland*, vol. 1, pp. 327–29.
13. Michael MacDonagh, *Irish Life and Character* (New York, 1898), pp. 152–53.
14. MacDonagh, *Irish Life and Character*, p. 153.
15. Quoted in Costigan, *History*, pp. 137–38.
16. Quoted in Costigan, *History*, p. 134.
17. Quoted in Costigan, *History*, p. 138.

Chapter Six

1. Census of Ireland 1851, Tables of Death, p. 250.
2. Burritt, *Journal*, pp. 7, 10.
3. F. F. Trench, Letter to the Editor of *Saunder's News Letter*, March 22, 1847, pp. 2, 3.
4. William P. MacArthur, "The Medical History of the Famine," in *The Great Famine: Studies in Irish History*, ed. Dudley R. Edwards and Desmond T. Williams (Dublin, 1956), p. 265.

5. MacArthur, "Medical History," p. 272; Census of Ireland 1851, Tables of Deaths, p. 301.
6. MacArthur, "Medical History," p. 266.
7. MacArthur, "Medical History," p. 305; IFD, ms. 1,068, p. 29; IFD, ms. 1,069, pp. 35, 355. Many accounts of setting fire to infected homes appeared in Irish newspapers of the period.
8. Trench, Letter, p. 3.
9. MacArthur, "Medical History," pp. 278–81.
10. Census of Ireland 1851, Tables of Death, pp. 246–49.
11. Quoted in MacArthur, "Medical History," p. 296.
12. Quoted in MacArthur, "Medical History," p. 285.
13. Quoted in MacArthur, "Medical History," p. 285.
14. Quoted in MacArthur, "Medical History," p. 286.

Chapter Seven

1. *The Times*, March 26, 1847.
2. *Cork Examiner*, December 20, 1846.
3. *The Nation*, August 29, 1846.
4. *The Times*, March 31, 1847.
5. *Punch*, March 1848, p. 138.
6. Mitchel, *Last Conquest*, p. 257.
7. Census of Ireland 1851, Tables of Death, p. 243.
8. John Leslie Foster, Esq., M.P., an Irish landlord, before the Select Committee of the House of Lords in 1825, quoted in Tuke, *Visit*, p. 41.
9. Tuke, *Visit*, p. 13.
10. O'Rourke, *History*, p. 428.
11. Lord Cloncurry, public letter dated August 25, 1846, published the next day in several Irish newspapers.
12. O'Rourke, *History*, pp. 53, 105, 110, 111.
13. Quoted in O'Rourke, *History*, p. 103.
14. *Quarterly Review*, April 1847.
15. Tuke, *Visit*, p. 26.
16. *Cork Examiner*, January 28, 1847.
17. *Freeman's Journal*, January 23, 1847.

Chapter Eight

1. Edwards and Williams, eds., *The Great Famine*, p. viii.
2. Transactions, appendix 5, p. 219.

3. Transactions, p. 49, appendix 5, p. 267; appendix 8, p. 247; appendix 5, pp. 236, 250, 279; *Boston Advertiser*, February 25, 1847.

4. *The Times*, March 25, 1847.

5. Tuke, *Visit*; Osbourne, *Gleanings*; Burritt, *Journal*.

6. Quoted in *The Times*, March 25, 1847.

7. Transactions, appendix 3, p. 192.

8. Ingles, *Ireland in 1834*, vol. 1, pp. 106–07.

9. Ingles, *Ireland in 1834*, vol. 2, p. 102.

10. De Beaumont, *Ireland*, p. 35.

11. William Bennett, *Six Weeks in Ireland* (London, 1848), pp. 26–28.

12. Quoted in Costigan, *History*, p. 153.

13. Young, *Tour*, vol. 1, p. 181.

14. Quoted in Costigan, *History*, p. 228.

15. Costigan, *History*, p. 153.

16. Costigan, *History*, p. 154.

17. Nagatus, *The Connection between Famine and Pestilence, and The Great Apostacy*, Halliday Pamphlet, vol. 1,990 (Dublin, 1847), p. 49.

18. *The Achill Missionary Herald*, August, 1846, p. 88.

19. *The Achill Missionary Herald*, August, 1846, p. 88.

20. Hugh McNeill, "The Famine, a rod" (sermon privately published, Liverpool, 1847), pp. 23, 25, 26.

21. *The Packet*, February 4, 1847; *Tipperary Vindicator*, February 4, 1847.

22. Quoted in Costigan, *History*, p. 185.

23. Quoted in Costigan, *History*, p. 186.

24. Quoted in Costigan, *History*, p. 184.

25. Quoted in Costigan, *History*, p. 184.

26. Charles Gavin Duffy, *Four Years of Irish History 1845–49* (London, 1883), p. 128.

27. "The Antecedent Causes of the Irish Famine in 1847," lecture given at the Broadway Tabernacle, March 20, 1847 (New York, 1847), p. 21.

28. Bennett, *Six Weeks*, p. 138.

29. Quoted in Costigan, *History*, pp. 186–87.

30. *The Nation*, September 25, 1847.

31. IFD, ms. 1,409.

Chapter Nine

1. The Labour Rate Act, passed in September 1846, decreed that work must not be productive but, rather, the means by which workers would receive wages to buy food.

2. Quoted in *The Nation*, December 19, 1846.

3. NLI, Monteagle Papers, Wood to Monteagle, November 22, 1848.

4. Quoted in O'Rourke, *History*, pp. 333–34.

5. The Irish Relief Act, 10th Vic., C.7, framed in accordance with the views expressed by the prime minister in his speech of January 25, 1847. The act became law on February 26, 1847.

6. *Sunday Observer*, February 28, 1847.

7. *Sunday Observer*, February 28, 1847.

8. *Sunday Observer*, February 28, 1847.

9. *The Times*, quoted in O'Rourke, *History*, p. 429.

10. *The Times*, quoted in O'Rourke, *History*, p. 430.

11. *Illustrated London News*, April 17, 1847, p. 256.

12. *Dublin Evening Packet*, April 6, 1847.

13. *Freeman's Journal*, April 6, 1847.

14. *Dublin Evening Packet*, April 6, 1847.

15. *The Lancet*, April 1847.

16. Ten-page pamphlet, published by Sir Henry Marsh, April 1847, excerpted in many English morning and evening journals in April 1847.

17. Hannay, *Lighter Side*, p. 146.

18. *Punch*, April 1847, p. 111.

19. *Illustrated London News*, April 17, 1847, p. 256.

20. The Irish Relief Act, February 26, 1847.

21. IFD, ms. 1,069.

22. C. E. Trevelyan, *The Irish Crisis* (London, 1848), pp. 86–87.

23. The Irish Relief Act.

24. Trevelyan, *Crisis*, p. 87.

25. The Irish Relief Act.

26. *Evening Freeman*, February 12, 1847.

27. Burritt, *Journal*, p. 6.

28. Burritt, *Journal*, p. 11.

29. Transactions, appendix 3, p. 202.

30. Quoted in *The Times*, February 17, 1844.

Chapter Ten

1. IFD, ms. 1,068, p. 134.
2. Hans Hartmann, *Der Totenkult In Irland—Ein Beitrag zur Religion der Indogermanen* (Heidelberg, 1952), pp. 112–17, 151–72; IER, John Brady, "Funeral Customs of the Past," 5th series, vol. 78 (November 1952), p. 334.
3. IFD, ms. 1,068, p. 136.
4. IFD, ms. 1,069, p. 29.
5. *Saunder's News-Letter*, 1847, p. 1.
6. *The Nation*, April 24, 1847.
7. *The Nation*, May 20, 1847.
8. *Mayo Telegraph*, May 12, 1847.
9. *Mayo Telegraph*, May 12, 1847.
10. IFD, ms. 1,069, pp. 356–57.
11. IFD, ms. 1,068, p. 213.
12. IFD, ms. 1,068, p. 214.
13. IFD, Death & Burial: "Oral History" 28.
14. IFD, Death & Burial: "Oral History" 31.
15. *Illustrated London News*, March 20, 1847.
16. O'Rourke, *History*, pp. 278–79.
17. IFD, ms. 1,068, p. 110.
18. IFD, ms. 1,068, p. 140.
19. Trench letter to *Saunder's News-Letter*, 1847, p. 1.
20. *Cork Examiner*, March 19, 1847, quoted in Census of Ireland 1851, p. 310; *Freeman's Journal*, April 22, 1847; Tuke, *Visit*, pp. 18–19.

Chapter Eleven

1. Letter published in *Tipperary Vindicator*, January 5, 1848.
2. *Cork Examiner*, June 22, 1871.
3. IFD, ms. 1,411, pp. 412–13.
4. IFD, ms. 1,407, pp. 26–28.
5. IFD, mss. 1,407 and 1,411.
6. IFD, ms. 1,411, p. 226.
7. IFD, ms. 1,411.
8. IFD, ms. 1,407.
9. IFD, ms. 1,407.

10. IFD, ms. 1,411, p. 416.

11. IFD, ms. notebook of P. J. Gaynor.

12. Hannay, *Lighter Side*, p. 145.

13. Douglas Hyde, *Religious Songs of Connaught* (New York, 1893) vol. 2, p. 397.

14. Hyde, *Songs*, vol. 1, p. 169.

15. IFD, ms. 1,411, pp. 224–27; Hannay, *Lighter Side*, p. 181.

16. IFD, ms. 1,411, pp. 251–52.

17. *Limerick Reporter*, August 2, 1867.

18. *Irish People*, June 15, 1901.

19. IFD, ms. 1,411, pp. 330–31.

20. IFD, ms. 1,411, p. 224.

21. IFD, ms. 1,411, pp. 330–31.

22. Harriet Martineau, *Letters From Ireland* (London, 1852), p. 140.

23. IFD, ms. 1,411, pp. 119, 412; IFD, ms. 1,407, p. 11; Hannay, *Lighter Side*, p. 145.

Chapter Twelve

1. *Limerick Chronicle*, April 24, May 8, 19, 26, 1847.

2. *The Nation*, April 17, 1847.

3. IFD, ms. 1,411, p. 236.

4. Papers, 1847, pp. 11–15.

5. NLF, Monteagle Papers, Monteagle to Grey, October 9, 1846.

6. *Morning Chronicle*, March 2, 1847, pp. 5–7; *The Nation*, March 27, 1847, p. 389; *Galway Vindicator*, quoted by *The Nation*, April 24, 1847, p. 460; *Kerry Evening Post*, April 14, 1847; Papers, July 31, 1848, p. 39; Papers, July 29, 1847, p. 88; Report, pp. 618–20.

7. IFD, ms. 1,411, p. 224; *Waterford Mail*, February 27, 1847; Diary of Mrs. Smith of Blessington, April 6, 1847, quoted in Oliver MacDonagh, "Irish Emigration During the Great Famine, 1845–52," unpublished thesis, NLI, p. 175.

8. NLI, O'Hara Papers, ms. 20, p. 376.

9. *Armagh Guardian*, quoted in *Freeman's Journal*, May 14, 1849; *Morning Chronicle*, April 1, 1847.

10. Robert Whyte, *The Ocean Plague, or, A voyage to Quebec in an Irish Emigrant Vessel . . .* (Boston, 1848), p. 11.

11. *The Times,* quoted in Seumas MacManus, *The Story of the Irish Race* (New York, 1921), p. 610.

12. *Limerick Chronicle,* November 14, 1848.

13. Diary of Mrs. Smith of Blessington, April 8, 1847, quoted in Oliver MacDonagh, "Irish Emigration," NLI, p. 175.

14. NLI, Manuscript Room, Larcum File 7,600.

15. *Londonderry Sentinel,* March 22, 1847.

16. *The Nation,* August 21, 1847.

17. Public letter, April 9, 1847, widely circulated, quoted in O'Rourke, *History,* p. 494.

18. *Freeman's Journal,* March 25 and April 2, 1847.

19. *The Nation,* October 16, 1847, p. 851.

20. *The Nation,* October 9, 1847.

21. *The Nation,* quoted in *Limerick Chronicle,* October 9, 1847.

22. Report, pp. 712–14; Minutes, p. 92.

23. *Cork Constitution,* February 13, 1847; *Southern Reporter,* May 4, 1847; *Kerry Evening Post,* May 5, 1848.

24. *Gladstone to His Wife,* ed. A. Telney Bassett (London, 1936), p. 64.

25. John Mitchel, quoted in Costigan, *History,* p. 205.

26. *The Times,* quoted in *The Nation,* May 5, 1860.

Chapter Thirteen

1. *The Times,* March 1847, quoted in Whyte, *The Ocean Plague,* pp. 3, 4.

2. Evidence, question and answer 2,359, pp. 243–44.

3. *Morning Chronicle,* July 15, 1850, p. 6; *Liverpool Courier,* March 29, 1848, quoted by *Northern Whig,* April 4, 1948; circular of the Irish Emigration Society, quoted in *Limerick Chronicle,* May 13, 1948.

4. *Limerick Chronicle,* April 17, 1847.

5. *Limerick Chronicle,* April 15, 1850, p. 6.

6. IFD, ms. 1,408, p. 49.

7. *Cork Constitution,* March 5, 13, 18, 1847.

8. IFD, ms. 1,411, pp. 396–97.

9. IFD, ms. 1,411, pp. 217–18.

10. Hannay, *Lighter Side,* p. 156.

11. IFD, ms. 1,411, pp. 217–18.

12. Edwin C. Guillet, *The Great Migration* (New York, 1937), p. 64; Papers, 1847, pp. 30–31.

13. Papers, 1847, p. 33; Guillet, *Migration*, p. 91.

14. Guillet, *Migration*, p. 64.

15. Guillet, *Migration*, p. 64.

16. Guillet, *Migration*, p. 64.

17. Guillet, *Migration*, p. 64.

18. IFD, ms. 1,407.

19. *Galway Vindicator*, quoted in *Morning Chronicle*, March 24, 1847, p. 7.

Chapter Fourteen

1. Minutes, testimony of Captain T. W. C. Murdock, p. 21.

2. Minutes, testimony of Mr. Samuel Redmond, p. 81.

3. Papers, 1848, letters from Stephen E. DeVere to Earl Grey, pp. 13–17.

4. Wiley and Putnam, *The Emigrant's True Guide to the United States* . . . (London, 1845), p. 68.

5. Report, 1851, pp. 28–30.

6. Guillet, *Migration*, p. 86.

7. *Freeman's Journal*, August 15, 1850.

Chapter Fifteen

1. Minutes, 1854, testimony of Captain T. W. C. Murdock, p. 13.

2. Guillet, *Migration*, p. 71.

3. IFD, ms. 1,049, p. 96.

4. Quoted in James Hannay, *An Irishman Looks At His World* (New York, 1919), p. 118.

5. Hannay, *Lighter Side*, p. 190.

6. Whyte, *Ocean Plague*, pp. 2, 3.

7. Guillet, *Migration*, p. 102.

8. Report, 1851, evidence of Lietutenant Friend, pp. 489–90.

Chapter Sixteen

1. Guillet, *Migration*, p. 72.

2. IFD, ms. 1,409, p. 29.

3. Report, 1851, pp. 15–19.

4. Papers, 1848, Stephen E. DeVere to T. F. Elliot, pp. 12–17.

5. Report, 1851, pp. 23–25.

6. MacDonagh, *Irish Life and Character*, p. 93.

7. Whyte, *Ocean Plague*, pp. 25, 28, 40.

8. Whyte, *Ocean Plague*, p. 42.

9. William Smith, *An Emigrant's Narrative, or A Voice From The Steerage* (New York, 1850), p. 22.

10. Smith, *Narrative*, p. 22.

Chapter Seventeen

1. Minutes, testimony of Captain T. W. C. Murdock, p. 25.

2. Minutes, testimony of Captain Schomberg, p. 7.

3. Minutes, testimony of Mr. Samuel Redmond, p. 83.

4. Minutes, testimony of Captain Schomberg, R.N., p. 6.

5. Minutes, testimony of Mr. Samuel Redmond, p. 83.

6. Minutes, testimony of Captain Schomberg, p. 8.

7. Minutes, testimony of Mr. Samuel Redmond, p. 83.

8. Minutes, conclusion from testimony, pp. 6–105.

9. Minutes, testimony of Mr. Samuel Redmond, p. 84.

10. Minutes, testimony of Mrs. Caroline Chisholm, p. 90.

11. Hansard, 2nd Series XVIII (1828), p. 1,212.

12. William Cobbett, *The Emigrant's Guide—Containing Information Necessary to Persons about to Emigrate* (London, 1829), pp. 37, 102–05.

13. Minutes, testimony of several witnesses, pp. 6–105.

14. *The Times*, September 17, 1847.

15. Shipping reports in Quebec *Mercury*, August 10, 1847, et seq.; Report of Montreal Board of Health, August 12, 1847; *The Times*, September 17, 1847, quoted in Guillet, *Migration*, pp. 95–96.

16. Colonial Land and Emigration Commissioners' Annual Report, 1848.

17. Papers, 1847–48, Douglas Annual Report, pp. 8, 12–20; Papers, 1847–48, evidence of T. F. Elliot, pp. 43–44.

18. Whyte, *Ocean Plague*, p. 79.

Chapter Eighteen

1. MacDonagh, *Irish Life and Character*, p. 378.

2. MacDonagh, *Irish Life and Character*, p. 377.

Chapter Nineteen

1. Whyte, *Ocean Plague*, pp. 70–79; Smith, *Narrative*, pp. 14–19; Papers, 1847–48, pp. 138–40; Papers, 1849, pp. 38, 57–61.
2. Vilhelm Moberg, *The Emigrants* (New York, 1951), pp. 256–61.
3. Smith, *Narrative*, pp. 18, 19.
4. Smith, *Narrative*, p. 14.
5. Smith, *Narrative*, pp. 14–15.
6. Whyte, *Ocean Plague*, p. 16.
7. Smith, *Narrative*, p. 16.
8. Whyte, *Ocean Plague*, pp. 17–20.
9. Whyte, *Ocean Plague*, pp. 17–22; John Forbes, *Memorandums Made in Ireland in the Autumn of 1852*, 2 vols. (London, 1853), pp. 99–100.
10. Anna Jameson, *Winter Studies and Summer Rambles in Canada* (Toronto, 1838), vol. 2, pp. 161–66.
11. *Morning Chronicle*, July 15, 1850.

Chapter Twenty

1. Evidence, 1847, letter from DeVere to Elliot, pp. 45–48; Richard Weston, *A Visit to the United States & Canada in 1833* (New York, 1836), quoted in Guillet, *Migration*, p. 180.
2. Evidence Before a Parliamentary Committee on Emigration, 1844; Papers, 1847–48, November 30, 1847, p. 14; Report XI (198), pp. 3–6; Whyte, *Ocean Plague*, pp. 30–35.
3. *Freeman's Journal*, March 28, 1848; John F. Maguire, *The Irish In America* (London, 1868), p. 181; Papers, 1847, pp. 9–10, 26–27; Report, 1851, pp. 416–30, 486, 491–92; Friedrich Kapp, *Immigration and the Commissioners of Emigration of New York* (New York, 1870).

Chapter Twenty-one

1. D. W. Mitchell, *Ten Years In the United States* (London, 1862), p. 141.
2. Hansard, 2nd Series, XVIII, 1828, p. 1,212; *The Times*, quoted in Whyte, *Ocean Plague*, p. 3; Papers, 1848, letter from DeVere to Grey, pp. 13–17; Smith, *Narrative*, p. 8.
3. Whyte, *Ocean Plague*, pp. 77, 78; Evidence, 1847, pp. 45–48.

4. Whyte, *Ocean Plague*, p. 80.

5. Whyte, *Ocean Plague*, p. 86.

6. William Brown, *A Four Years' Residence in the United States & Canada* (New York, 1849), pp. 3, 4.

7. Quoted in Guillet, *Migration*, p. 186.

8. John O'Hanlon, *The Emigrants Guide to the United States* (Boston, 1851), pp. 45, 52, 57.

Chapter Twenty-two

1. John Duffy, *A History of Public Health in New York City: 1624–1866* (New York, 1968), pp. 376–79; *New York Daily Tribune*, September 17, 1842; *New York Sun*, June 28, 1844; Charles Dickens, *American Notes for General Circulation* (New York, 1868), pp. 290–92.

2. William Chambers, *Things As They Are In America* (London and Edinburgh, 1854), pp. 192–94; Duffy, *Public Health*, pp. 376–78; Alexander Marjoribanks, *Travels in South and North America* (New York, 1853), p. 133.

3. Chambers, *Things*, p. 35; E. Porter Belden, *Past, Present & Future* (New York, 1849), p. 35.

4. Belden, *Past, Present & Future*, p. 44.

5. Belden, *Past, Present & Future*, p. 117; Chambers, pp. 203–07.

6. J. Mooney, *Nine Years in America* (New York, 1850), pp. 144–45; Duffy, *Public Health*, pp. 180–84; *New York Evening Post*, June 12, 1832, March 18, 1839; New York Association, 41st Annual Report, 1844, pp. 21–24.

Chapter Twenty-three

1. John H. Griscom, *The Sanitary Condition of the Laboring Populations of New York* (New York, 1845), New York Association, 36th Annual Report, 1879, pp. 62–65; Stephen Smith, *The City That Was New York* (New York, 1911), pp. 19, 35–39, 59; Robert W. De Forest and Lawrence Veiller, eds., *The Tenement House Problem* (New York, 1903), pp. 70–79.

2. New York Association, 37th Annual Report, 1880, p. 19.

3. New York Association, 37th Annual Report, 1880, pp. 18–23, 38th Annual Report, 1881, pp. 18–21, 39th Annual Report, 1882, pp. 11–12; De Forest and Veiller, *Tenement House Problem*, pp. 70–79.

4. Documents, no. 18, IX, pp. 161–70, no. 16, XI, pp. 188–89; Duffy, *Public Health*, pp. 376–79; Allan Nevins and Milton Halsey Thomas, eds., *The Diary of George Templeton Strong* (New York, 1952), vol. 1, p. 110.

5. Belden, *Past, Present & Future*, p. 65. W. H. Graham, *The Stranger's Guide Around New York & Its Vicinity* (New York, 1853), pp. 53, 91.

6. Charles A. Dana, *The United States Illustrated* (New York, 1854), pp. 156–59; New York Association, 36th Annual Report, 1879, pp. 62–65.

7. *Daily Times*, June 8, 1853; Chambers, *Things*, pp. 192–94; Graham, *Guide*, p. 29; Duffy, *Public Health*, pp. 376–78, 384; New York Association, 42nd Annual Report, 1885, pp. 24–35; Documents, no. 60, XI, pp. 651–57, no. 6, XII, pp. 69–72.

8. New York Association, 42nd Annual Report, 1885, p. 25.

9. New York Association, 42nd Annual Report, 1885, pp. 24–30; Duffy, *Public Health*, pp. 363–64.

10. New York Association, 42nd Annual Report, 1885, pp. 24–25.

11. New York Association, 42nd Annual Report, 1885, p. 27.

12. *New York Daily Tribune*, June 7, 1843.

13. *New York Daily Tribune*, February 23, 1846; Documents, no. 1, XXVI, pt. 1, pp. 39–40, no. 19, XXIV, pp. 1–8.

14. Documents, no. 1, XIV, pp. 11–12, no. 1, XXI, pt. 1, pp. 5–8, no. 12, XXI, pt. 1, pp. 247–48.

15. Mooney, *Nine Years*, pp. 84–94, 138–43; Samuel P. Orth, *Our Foreigners: A Chronicle of Americans in The Making* (New Haven, 1920), pp. 113–14.

Bibliography

GOVERNMENT DOCUMENTS: AMERICAN

Aid to Ireland: Report of the General Relief Committee of the City of New York, 1848.

Annual Report of the City Inspector of the Number of Deaths and Interments in the City of New York, 1847–1848.

Annual Reports of the Postmaster General of the U.S., 1846–1850, 5 vols. Library of the Post Office Department, Washington, D.C.

Census of the State of New York for 1845, Albany, 1848.

Census of the State of New York for 1855, Albany, 1857.

Consular Despatches: Belfast, 11 vols., 1796–1906. Dublin, 11 vols., 1790–1906. Galway, 1 vol., 1834–63. Londonderry, 3 vols., 1835–78. Despatches to Counsuls: vols. 9 and 25. Diplomatic Despatches: Great Britain, 1850–60. All part of Record Group 59 in the National Archives, Washington, D.C.

New York Association For Improving the Conditions of the Poor, Annual Reports for the years 1845 through 1850.

New York City Alms House Board of Governors, Annual Reports, 1846–1849.

New York City Annual Reports of the Alms House Commissioners, Documents 44, 45, 46, 47, 48, 49, for the years 1847 through 1852.

New York City Inspector's Report, 1840s and 1850s.

Report of the Select Committee on Frauds upon Emigrants, New York City Documents, 1847. Assembly Doc. No. 46.

Statistical Review of Emigration, 1819–1910. Distribution of Immigrants, 1850–1900. Senate Doc. No. 756, 61st Cong. 3rd Sess.

GOVERNMENT DOCUMENTS: BRITISH

Census of Ireland: 1841 and 1851, General Reports and Tables of Death.

Colonial Land and Emigration Commissioners' Annual Report, 1847 and 1848.

Commissioners of Public Works to the Lords of the Treasury. Correspondence Relating to Measures Adopted for the Relief of the Distress in Ireland. Board of Works, Series 1, House of Commons 1847 (764), Vol. 1.

Constabulary Reports 1846 and 1847. Papers, Home Office, London.

Correspondence Explanatory of the Measures Adopted by Her Majesty's Government for the Relief of Distress Arising From the Failure of the Potato Crop in Ireland, H.C. 1846 (735), Vol. XXXVII.

Correspondence Relating to the Relief of the Distress in Ireland (Commissariat Series), H.C. 1847.

Devon Commission: Digest of Evidence Taken Before Her Majesty's Commissioners of Inquiry into the State of the Law and Practice in Respect to the Occupation of Land in Ireland. Parts I and II, Dublin 1847.

Evidence Before the Select Committee of the House of Lords on Colonization From Ireland (with Appendix of Letters To and From Settled Emigrants), H.L. 1847.

Extract from a Report of Commissioners of Inquiry into Matters Connected with the Potato Crop, H.S. 1846 (734), Vol. XXXVII.

Final Report; Board of Works, Ireland, H.C. Vol. XXIII, with Appendices.

First Report of Her Majesty's Commission of Inquiry Into the Condition of the Poor Classes in Ireland, 1835.

Minutes of Evidence Taken Before the Select Committee on Emigrant Ships, 1854.

Papers Relative to Emigration, 1847 and 1848.

Poor Inquiry (Ireland), H.C., 1836.

Private Letter Books, St. Anne's College, Oxford, 1846–47.

Report of the Select Committee of the House of Lords on Colonization from Ireland (with appendix of letters from Irish emigrants and others), H.L. 1847.

Report on the State of the Poor in Ireland, H.C. 1830.

Reports of the Poor Law Commissioners, H.C. 1845, 46, 47, 48.

Returns of Agricultural Produce in Ireland in the Year 1847, H.C. 1847–48 (923), Vol. VII.

Select Committee of the House of Lords on the Laws Relating to the

Relief of the Destitute Poor in Ireland, H.L. 1846 (24) Vol. XXIV.

War Office Files 1846–47.

GOVERNMENT DOCUMENTS: IRISH

Commission on Emigration and other Problems 1848–1954, Majority Report, Ministry of Social Welfare, 1954.

Correspondence relating to Kingwilliam Stown Quitrent Office Collection, Public Records Office, Dublin.

Department of Industry and Commerce, Agricultural Statistics 1847–1926, Report and Tables, Dublin, 1928.

Distress Papers, 1847, Carton 480, State Papers Office, Dublin.

Registered Papers, 1846, State Papers Office, Dublin.

Report of John Ball, Sept. 26, 1846, State Papers Office, Dublin.

NON-GOVERNMENT DOCUMENTS, LETTERS, ESSAYS, THESES, ETC.

National Library of Ireland, Dublin

Manuscript Room:

Buchanan Papers.

Emigrant Letters: manuscripts 13,875, 15,784, 18,236, 18,437.

Lalor Family Papers.

Letter of Rev. D. W. Cahill to Lord Palmerston, 1855, Pamphlet 719.

Letters from Missionaries in America.

Letters of Myles Walter Keogh.

Monteagle Papers.

O'Hara Papers.

William Smith O'Brien Papers.

Archives:

Distress in Ireland: Central Relief Committee of the Society of Friends, no. III.

Hughes, the Right Rev. John, Bishop of New York. "A Lecture on the Antecedent Causes of the Irish Famine in 1847," delivered at the Broadway Tabernacle, March 20, 1847, New York, 1847.

John, Earl of Shrewsbury. *Thoughts on the Poor-Relief Bill for Ireland*. Pamphlet, London, 1847.

MacDonagh, Oliver. "Irish Emigration During the Great Famine, 1845–52." Unpublished thesis.

MacDonnell, Eneas. *Irish Sufferers and Anti-Irish Philosophers, Their Pledges and Performances*. Pamphlet, London, 1847.

Scrope, G. Poulett. *Reply to Archbishop of Dublin on the Poor Relief (Ireland) Bill*. London, 1847.

Transactions of the Central Relief Committee of the Society of Friends during the Famine in Ireland in 1846 and 1847, with Appendices.

Transactions of the Royal Historical Society, 5th Series, Vol. V.

Irish Folklore Department, University College, Dublin

Dorian, Hugh. "Donegal 60 Years Ago. A True Historical Narrative." Handwritten, unpublished manuscript, Londonderry, 1896. A photostatic copy in author's possession.

Important data on the Irish reaction to the famine and emigration came from answers to a questionnaire formulated by Arnold Schrier, an American doing research in Ireland under fellowships from the Social Research Council and Northwestern University. This questionnaire was used by professional interviewers of the Irish Folklore Commission during the early months of 1955, when there were many Irish men and women old enough to remember their parents' stories of the famine and the exodus it caused.

The material returned by these interviewers is now bound, numbered, and catalogued according to subject matter in the Irish Folklore Department of University College, Dublin. Twenty-two interviewers, working in sixteen counties, submitted twenty-six handwritten notebooks, each one roughly one hundred pages long. The subject matter, name of interviewer, and county in which each worked are as follows:

Notebooks on Emigration, vols. 1,407–11
Notebooks on Famine, vols. 1,068–75, 1,136
Notebooks on Fatalism, vol. 1,245

INTERVIEWER	COUNTY
Ciaran Bairead	Galway (2 notebooks)
Frank Burke	Galway
Michael Corduff	Mayo
James G. Delaney	Wexford and Longford (2 notebooks)
P. J. Gaynor	Cavan
Michael MacEnri	Mayo
Thomas Moran	Mayo
Seamus Mulcahy	Tipperary
Michael J. Murphy	Antrim
Tadgh Murphy	Kerry
Lliam O'Brian	Leitrim
Conall O'Byrne	Donegal (3 notebooks)
Patrick O'Connor	Kildare
James J. O'Donnell	Roscommon
Sean O'Dubhda	Kerry
Sean O'Heochaidh	Donegal
Sean O'Keefe	Waterford
Mary O'Neill	Galway
Matthew O'Reilly	Meath
Dermot O'Sullivan	Kerry
Joseph Wade	Westmeath
Martin Walsh	Kilkenny

CONTEMPORANEOUS PRINTED SOURCES

ADAIR, A. SHAFTO. *The Winter of 1846–7 in Antrim*, with remarks on outdoor relief and colonization. London, 1847.

ALCOCK, ST. L. *Essay on a Poor Law Bill for Ireland*. Dublin, 1847.

AMICUS, POPULI. *Emigration and Superabundant Population Considered*. Dublin, 1848.

BELDEN, E. PORTER. *Past, Present & Future*. New York, 1849.

BENNETT, WILLIAM. *Six Weeks in Ireland*. London, 1848.

BENWELL, J. *An Englishman's Travels in America*. London, 1853.

BERKELEY, GEORGE. *The Querist*, 2 vols. London, 1735–37.

BROWN, WILLIAM. *A Four Years' Residence in the United States & Canada*. New York, 1849.

BROWNSON'S QUARTERLY REVIEW. *"The Know-Nothings,"* October, 1854, pp. 447–87.

BURRITT, ELIHU. *A Journal of a Visit of Three Days to Skibbereen and its Neighborhood*. London, 1847.

BUTT, ISAAC. *A Voice For Ireland. The Famine In The Land*. Dublin, 1847.

CARLETON, WILLIAM. *The Black Prophet*. London and Belfast, 1847.

CARLYLE, THOMAS. *Reminiscences of My Irish Journey in 1849*. London, 1850.

———. *Past and Present*. London, 1858.

CAVOUR, CAMILLO BENSODI. *Thoughts On Ireland*. London, 1844.

CHAMBERS, WILLIAM. *Things As They Are In America*. London and Edinburgh, 1854. Rep. ed. New York, 1968.

CROKER, THOMAS CROFTON. *Fairy Legends and Traditions of The South of Ireland*. London, 1870.

———. *The Keen of the South of Ireland*. London, 1844.

———. *Legends of the Lakes*, 2 vols. London, 1829.

DANA, CHARLES A. *The United States Illustrated*. New York, 1854.

DE BEAUMONT, GUSTAVE. *Ireland: Social, Political, and Religious*, 2 vols. London, 1839.

FORBES, JOHN. *Memorandums Made in Ireland in the Autumn of 1852*, 2 vols. London, 1853.

FOSTER, THOMAS CAMPBELL. *Letters on the People of Ireland*. London, 1847.

FRANCIS, JOHN W. *New York During the Last Half Century*. New York, 1857.

———. *Old New York*. New York, 1866.

GODLEY, J. R. *Letters From America*. Dublin, 1844.

GRAHAM, W. H. *The Stranger's Guide Around New York & Its Vicinity*. New York, 1853.

GREENLEAF, JONATHAN. *A History of the Churches . . . in the City of New York . . . to 1846*. New York, 1846.

GRISCOM, JOHN H. *The Sanitary Condition of the Laboring Populations of New York*. New York, 1845.

———. *The Uses and Abuses of Air*. New York, 1848.

HALL, BASIL. *Travels In North America*, 3 vols. Edinburgh, 1830.

HANCOCK, W. N. *The Tenant Rights of Ulster . . .* Dublin, 1845.

HENSON, GERALDINE. "Memories of The Irish Famine." Handwritten manuscript by a landlord's daughter, based on the reminiscences of her mother, Anna Selman Martin of Ross, Co. Galway. NLI, ms. 17,305.

HEYWOOD, ROBERT. *A Journey To America in 1834*. London, 1835.

HILL, LORD GEORGE. *Facts From Gweedore*, 5th ed. Dublin, 1887.

INGLIS, HENRY D. *Ireland In 1834*. London, 1835.

THE IRISH-IMMIGRANT SOCIETY OF NEW YORK. *Advice and Guide Book Middle 1800's*. New York, n.d.

JAMESON, ANNA. *Winter Studies and Summer Rambles in Canada*. Toronto, 1838.

KENNEDY, J. PITT. *Digest of evidence taken before HM's commissions of inquiry into the state of the law and practice in respect to the occupation of land in Ireland*. Dublin, 1847.

KING, CHARLES. *Progress of the City of New York During the Last Fifty Years*. New York, 1852.

KOHL, J. G. *Ireland 1843*. London, 1844.

MARRYAT, FREDERICK. *Diary In America*. London, 1839.

MARTINEAU, HARRIET. *Letters From Ireland*. London, 1852.

————. *Society in America*, 3 vols. London, 1830.

MCNEILL, HUGH. "The famine, a/rod" (sermon, privately published). Liverpool, 1847.

MELVILLE, HERMAN. *Redburn, His First Voyage*. New York, 1849.

MITCHEL, J. *The History of Ireland from the Treaty of Limerick to the Present Time*. Dublin, 1869.

MOONEY, J. *Nine Years In America*. New York, 1850.

NAGATUS. *The Connection between Famine and Pestilence, and the Great Apostacy*. Halliday Pamphlet, vol. 1990. Dublin, 1847.

OSBOURNE, S. GODOLPHIN. *Gleanings in the West of Ireland*. London, 1850.

SCROPE, G. P. *Some Notes of a Tour in England, Scotland and Ireland*. London, 1849.

SENIOR, NASSAU. *Journals, Conversations and Essays Relating to Ireland*, 2 vols. London, 1868.

SMITH, WILLIAM. *An Emigrant's Narrative, or A Voice From The Steerage*. New York, 1850.

THACKERAY, WILLIAM MAKEPEACE. *Irish Sketch Book*. London, 1844.

TOCQUEVILLE, ALEXIS DE. *Journeys in England and Ireland in 1835*. London, 1835.

TRENCH, F. F. Letter dealing with famine. Addressed to the Editor of *Saunder's News-Letter*. Ireland, 1847. Pamphlets on the famine. MS. 13397(4), NLI.

TREVELYAN, G. E. *The Irish Crisis*. London, 1848.

TUKE, JAMES H. *A Visit to Connaught in the Autumn of 1847.* London, 1848.

VALENTINE, DAVID T. *History of the City of New York.* New York, 1853.

WESTON, RICHARD. *A Visit to the United States & Canada in 1883.* New York, 1836.

WHYTE, ROBERT. *The Ocean Plague, or, A Voyage to Quebec in an Irish Emigrant Vessel, Embracing a Quarantine at Grosse Isle in 1847, with notes Illustrative of the Ship Pestilence of that Fatal Year.* Boston, 1848. Copy in Library of Congress.

WILDE, LADY. *Ancient Legends, Mystic Charms and Superstitions of Ireland.* London, 1889.

WILDE, WILLIAM R. *Irish Popular Superstitions.* Dublin, 1853.

NEWSPAPERS: 1845–1848

The Achill Missionary Herald
Advocate (Dublin)
American Celt (New York)
Boston Advertiser
Carrick's Morning Post (Dublin)
Commercial Advertiser (New York)
Cork Constitution
Cork Examiner
Cork Southern Reporter
Daily Tribune (New York)
Dublin Daily Express
Dublin Evening Mail
Dublin Evening Packet
Dublin Evening Post
Evening Freeman (Dublin)
Evening Post (New York)
Farmer's Gazette (Dublin)
Freeman's Journal (Dublin)
Galway Free Press
Galway Vindicator and Connaught Advertiser
Herald (New York)
Illustrated London News
Irish American (New York)

Irish Times (New York)
Irish Vindicator (New York)
Kerry Evening Post
Leinster Express (Maryborough)
Limerick Chronicle
Limerick Reporter
Londonderry Sentinel
Londonderry Standard
Mayo Telegraph
Mercantile Advertiser (Dublin)
Morning Chronicle (London)
Morning Herald (London)
Morning Telegraph (New York)
The Nation (Dublin)
Newry Telegraph
Northern Whig
The Packet (Dublin)
Pilot (Dublin)
Post (New York)
Quebec Mercury
Roscommon Journal and Western Reporter
Saunder's News-Letter and Daily Advertiser
Sligo Champion

Sligo Journal
Southern Reporter
Sun (New York)
Sunday Observer (London)
The Times (London)

Tipperary Vindicator
Tuam Herald (Galway)
Waterford Mail
Waterford Mirror
World (Dublin)

CONTEMPORARANEOUS PERIODICALS AND JOURNALS

Gardiner's Chronicle (Ireland)
Irish Farmer's Gazette (Ireland)
Irish Miscellany (New York)
The Lancet (London)
Post Office Directories
(New York)

Punch (London)
Quarterly Review (London)
Shamrock (New York)
Tablet (New York)
Thom's Directories (New York)
The Truth Teller (New York)

EMIGRANT GUIDES

A CITIZEN. *Thoughts on Emigration, Education, etc., in a Letter Addressed to the Right Honorable Lord John Russell, Prime Minister of England*. London, 1847.

COBBETT, WILLIAM. *The Emigrant's Guide—Containing Information Necessary to Persons about to Emigrate*. London, 1829.

FOSTER, VERE. *Work and Wages or The Penny Emigrant's Guide*. London, 1854.

O'HANLON, JOHN. *The Emigrants Guide to the United States*. Boston, 1851.

O'KELLY, PATRICK. *Advice and Guide to Emigrants Going to U.S.A.* Dublin, 1834.

PEYTON, ALEXANDER J. *The Emigrant's Friend, or Hints on Emigration to the United States of America, Addressed to the People of Ireland*. Cork, 1853.

SHAMROCK SOCIETY OF NEW YORK. *Hints to Irishmen*. Dublin, 1817.

SUTTON, THOMAS. The Emigrant's Guide by an Experienced Traveler. New York, 1848.

TRAILL, CATHERINE P. *The Female Emigrant's Guide*. London, 1854.

WILEY AND PUTNAM. *The Emigrant's True Guide to the United States, comprising advice and instruction in every state of the Voyage to America*. London, 1845.

ARTICLES

ADDAMS, JANE. "Why The Ward Boss Rules." *The Outlook*, April, 1898.

BOCOCK, JOHN PAUL. "The Irish Conquest of Our Cities." *The Forum*, April, 1894.

BRADY, JOHN. "Funeral Customs of the Past." *Irish Ecclesiastical Record*, 5th series, vol. LXXVIII (November 1952): 330–39.

BROWN, THOMAS N. "Nationalism And the Irish Peasant, 1800–48." *The Review of Politics*, October, 1953.

––––––. "The Origins And Character of Irish-American National-ism." *The Review of Politics*, July, 1956.

CHART, D. A. "Two Centuries of Irish Agriculture. A Statistical Ret-rospect, 1672–1905." *Journal of the Statistical and Social Inquiry Society of Ireland*, November, 1907–June 1908, pp. 162–174.

CONDON, PETER. "The Irish in Countries other than Ireland—1. In the United States." *Catholic Encyclopedia* 8 (1910):132–45.

CONNELL, K. H. "Land and Population in Ireland, 1780–1845." *Economic History Review*, 2nd series, vol. 11, no. 3 (1950): 278–89.

CROKER, RICHARD. "Tammany Hall And The Democracy." *The North American Review*, February, 1892.

DELERY, JOHN. "Native Americanism." *Brownson's Quarterly Review*, July 1854, pp. 328–54.

DOLAN, JAY P. "Immigrants In The City: New York's Irish and Ger-man Catholics." *Church History*, September, 1972.

DORSON, RICHARD M. "Collecting in County Kerry." *Journal of American Folklore* 66 (1953):19–42.

DOUGLAS, GEORGE M. "On Typhus or Ship Fever, Etc." *British American Journal of Medical and Physical Science*, March, 1848, pp. 281–88.

GEARY, R. C. "Irish Economic Development Since The Treaty." *Studies*, December, 1951, pp. 399–418.

––––––. "Some Reflections on Irish Population Questions." *Studies*, Summer, 1954, pp. 168–77.

GIBBONS, JAMES CARDINAL. "Irish Immigration to the United States." *Irish Ecclesiastical Record*, 4th series, vol. 1, February, 1897, pp. 97–109.

GRIMSHAW, T. W. "A Statistical Survey of Ireland, from 1840 to 1888." *Journal of the Statistical and Social Inquiry Society of Ireland*, December, 1888, pp. 321–61.

GWYNN, DENIS. "The Rising of 1848." *Studies*, March, 1948.

———. "Smith O'Brien And Young Ireland." *Studies*, March, 1947.

HANCOCK, W. NEILSON. "On the Remittances from North America by Irish Emigrants, considered as an indication of character of the Irish race, etc." *Journal of the Statistical and Social Inquiry Society of Ireland*, April–November, 1873, pp. 280–90.

IRELAND, JOHN. "The Catholic Church and The Saloon." *The North American Review*, October, 1894, pp. 498–505.

KEEP, G. R. C. "Official Opinion on Irish Emigration in the Later 19th Century." *Irish Ecclesiastical Record*, 5th series, vol. LXXXXI, no. 6, June, 1954, pp. 412–21.

KENNEDY, THOMAS. "Fifty Years of Irish Agriculture." *Journal of the Statistical and Social Inquiry Society of Ireland*, November 1898–June, 1899, pp. 398–404.

MACDONAGH, OLIVER. "The Irish Catholic Clergy and Emigration During the Great Famine." *Irish Historical Studies*, September, 1947, pp. 287–302.

MACAFFREY, LAWRENCE J. "Irish Nationalism and Irish Catholicism. A Study in Cultural Identity." *Church History*, December, 1973.

MACMANUS, SEUMUS. "A Revolution in Ireland." *Catholic World*, July, 1899, pp. 522–32.

MEEHAN, THOMAS E. "English Taxation In America." *The North American Review*, November, 1887, pp. 563–67.

O'BRIEN, GEORGE. "New Light on Irish Emigration." *Studies*, March, 1941, pp. 17–31.

O'GRADY, JOHN. "Irish Colonization in the United States." *Studies*, September, 1930, pp. 387–407.

OLDHAM, C. H. "The Incidence of Emigration on Town and Country Life in Ireland." *Journal of the Statistical and Social Inquiry Society of Ireland*, November, 1913–June, 1914, pp. 207–18.

O'SUILLEABHAIN, SEAD. "The Origin and Purpose of Irish Wakes and Their Amusements." *Irish Ecclesiastical Records*, 1967, pp. 166–75.

PURCELL, RICHARD J. "The New York Commissioners of Emigration and Irish Immigrants." *Studies* 37 (1948):29–42.

SCANLAN, MICHAEL. "The American Letter." *Shamrock*, April, 1874, p. 462.

SMITH, GOLDWIN. "Why Send More Irish to America?" *Nineteenth Century*, June, 1883, pp. 913–19.

SULLIVAN, A. M. "Why Send More Irish Out of Ireland?" *Nineteenth Century*, July, 1883, pp. 131–44.

WARD, ALAN J. "America and The Irish Problem." *Irish Historical Studies*, March, 1968.

SECONDARY SOURCES

ABBOTT, EDITH. *Historical Aspects of the Immigration Problem*. Chicago, 1926.

ADAMS, WILLIAM FORBES. *Ireland and Irish Emigration to the New World From 1815 to the Famine*. New Haven, 1932.

ALBION, R. C. *The Rise of the Port of New York*. New York, 1939.

ARENSBERG, CONRAD M. *The Irish Countryman*. New York, 1937.

ARENSBERG, CONRAD M., and KIMBALL, SOLON T. *Family and Community in Ireland*. Cambridge, Mass., 1940.

ASBURY, HERBERT. *The Gangs of New York*. New York, 1929.

BAGENAL, PHILIP H. *The American Irish and Their Influence on Irish Politics*. Boston, 1882.

———. *Crime In Ireland*. Boston, 1880.

BASSETT, A. TELNEY, ed. *Gladstone to His Wife*. London, 1936.

BELL, JOHN. *Report of the Importance and Economy of Sanitary Measures to Cities*. New York, 1860.

BILLINGTON, RAY ALLEN. *The Protestant Crusade 1800–1860*. New York, 1938.

BIRMINGHAM, GEORGE A. (Pseudonym for James Hannay). *The Lighter Side of Irish Life*. London, 1911.

———. *An Irishman Looks At His World*. New York, 1919.

BISHOP, ISABELLE LUCY BIRD. *The Englishwoman In America*. London, 1856.

BOLTON, G. C. *The Passing of the Irish Act of Union*. New York, 1961.

BOOTH, MARY L. *History of the City of New York*, 2 vols. New York, 1867.

BOTKIN, B. A. *New York City Folklore*. New York, 1956.

BOYER, PAUL. *Urban Masses and Moral Order in America, 1820–1920*. Cambridge, Mass., 1978.

BRADY, ALEXANDER. *Thomas D'Arcy McGee*. Toronto, 1925.

BRANN, HENRY. *A Most Reverend John Hughes.* New York, 1892.

BROWN, HENRY C., ed. *Brownstone Fronts and Saratoga Trunks.* New York, 1935.

————. *The Story of Old New York.* New York, 1934.

————. *Valentine's Manual of Old New York.* New York, 1920.

BROWN, JUNIUS HENRI. *The Great Metropolis: A Mirror of New York.* Hartford, Ct., 1868.

BROWN, STEPHEN J. *The Press in Ireland. A Survey and a Guide.* Dublin, 1937.

BURKE, EDMUND. *Letters, Speeches, and Tracts on Irish Affairs.* Edited by M. Arnold. Dublin, 1881.

BURN, JAMES D. *Three Years Among the Working Classes in the U.S. During the War.* London, 1865.

BYRNE, STEPHEN. *Irish Emigration to the United States: What It Has Been, and What It Is.* New York, 1879.

CAMPBELL, JOHN H. *History of the Friendly Sons of St. Patrick and of the Hibernian Society for the Relief of Emigrants from Ireland.* Philadelphia, 1892.

CHAPIN, ANNA A. *Greenwich Village.* New York, 1917.

CHART, D. A. *An Economic History of Ireland.* Dublin, 1920.

CLAGHORN, KATE HOLLADAY. *The Immigrant's Day In Court.* New York, 1923.

COBBETT, WILLIAM. *Rural Rides,* 2 vols. London, 1885.

COLLINS, FREDERICK L. *Money Town: The Story of Manhattan's Toe.* New York, 1946.

COLUM, PADRAIC. *The Road Round Ireland.* New York, 1926.

CONNELL, K. H. *The Population of Ireland, 1750–1845.* Dublin, 1950.

COSTELLO, A. E. *Our Firemen: A History of the New York Fire Department.* New York, 1887.

COSTIGAN, GIOVANNI. *A History of Modern Ireland.* New York, 1969.

CURTIN, JEREMIAH. *Irish Folktales.* New York, 1890.

CURTIS, EDMUND. *A History of Ireland.* London, 1937.

DANGERFIELD, GEORGE. *The Damnable Question.* Boston, 1976.

DARYL, PHILIPPE. *Ireland's Disease: Notes and Impressions.* London, 1888.

DAVENPORT, JOHN I. *The Election Frauds of New York City and Their Prevention,* 2 vols., New York, 1881.

DAVITT, MICHAEL. *The Fall of Feudalism in Ireland.* Dublin, 1904.

DE FOREST, ROBERT W., and VEILLER, LAWRENCE, eds. *The Tenement House Problem.* New York, 1903.

DELARGY, JAMES H. *The Gaelic Storyteller*. London, 1945.

DEVERE, AUBREY. *Recollections of Aubrey DeVere*. New York, 1897.

DEVOE, THOMAS F. *The Marke Book: Historical Account of Public Markets in New York, Boston, etc.* New York, 1862.

DICKENS, CHARLES. *American Notes for General Circulation*. New York, 1868.

DILLON, WILLIAM. *Life of John Mitchell*, 2 vols. London, 1888.

DODGE, WILLIAM E. *Old New York. A Lecture*. New York, 1880.

DUER, WILLIAM ALEXANDER. *Reminiscences of an Old New Yorker*. New York, 1867.

DUFFERIN, LORD. *Irish Emigration and the Tenure of Land in Ireland*. London, 1867.

DUFFY, CHARLES GAVIN. *Four Years of Irish History 1845–49*. London, 1883.

———. *My Life In Two Hemispheres*. London, 1898.

———. *Young Ireland*. London, 1896.

DUFFY, JOHN. *A History of Public Health in New York City: 1624–1866*. New York, 1968.

EDWARDS, DUDLEY R., and WILLIAMS, DESMOND T., Eds. *The Great Famine: Studies in Irish History*. Dublin, 1956.

ELLIS, EDWARD ROBB. *The Epic of New York*. New York, 1966.

ERNST, ROBERT. *Immigrant Life in New York City, 1825–1863*. New York, 1949.

EVANS, E. ESTYN. *Irish Folkways*. London, 1957.

———. *New York by Gaslight*. New York, 1850.

———. *New York in Slices*. New York, n.d.

———. *New York Naked*. New York, n.d.

FERENCZI, IMRE, ed. *International Migrations*, vol. 1. New York, 1929.

FITZPATRICK, W. J. *Correspondence of Daniel O'Connell*. Dublin, 1888.

FOSTER, G. G. *Fifteen Minutes Around New York*. New York, 1854.

FREEMAN, THOMAS WALTER. *Pre-Famine Ireland*. New York, 1957.

FROUDE, JAMES ANTHONY. *The English in Ireland in the 18th Century*. London, n.d.

GERARD, JAMES W. *The Impress of Nationalities Upon the City of New York*. New York, 1883.

GIBSON, FLORENCE E. *The Attitudes of the New York Irish Toward State and National Affairs*. New York, 1951.

GOLDSMITH, OLIVER. *The Deserted Village*. Dublin, 1770.

GOOD, JAMES W. *Irish Unionism*. Dublin, 1920.

GRACE, WILLIAM R. *The Irish in America*. Chicago, 1886.

GREELEY, ANDREW M. *That Most Distressful Nation*. Chicago, 1972.

GREGORY, LADY. *The Kiltartan History Book*. London, 1926.

———. *Laughter In Ireland*. New York, 1916.

———. *Visions and Beliefs in the West of Ireland*. London, n.d.

GRIFFITH, G. TALBOT. *Population Problems of the Age of Malthus*. London, 1926.

GUILLET, EDWIN C. *The Great Migration*. New York, 1937.

GWYNN, DENIS ROLLESTON. *Young Ireland and 1848*. Dublin, 1940.

GWYNN, STEPHEN. *Henry Grattan and His Times*. Dublin, 1949.

———. *Irish Book and Irish People*. Dublin, 1919.

———. *Thomas Moore*. Dublin, 1905.

HALE, EDWARD E. *Letters on Irish Emigration*. Boston, 1852.

HALL, ANNA MARIA (FIELDING). *Tales of Irish Life and Character*. London, 1913.

HALL, GLADYS MARY. *Prostitution in the Modern World: A Survey and a Challenge*. New York, 1936.

HAMMOND, J. L. *Gladstone and the Irish Nations*. London, 1938.

HANCOCK, WILLIAM. *An Emigrant's Five Years in the Free States of America*. New York, 1860.

HANDLIN, OSCAR. *Boston's Immigrants*. New York, 1972.

———. *The Uprooted*. Boston, 1951.

HANSEN, MARCUS LEE. *The Atlantic Migration 1607–1860*. Cambridge, 1940.

———. *The Immigrant in American History*. Cambridge, 1940.

HARDIE, JAMES. *Description of the City of New York*. New York, 1827.

HARLOW, ALVIN F. *Old Bowery Days*. New York, 1931.

HARRIGAN, JOHN J. *Political Change in the Metropolis*. Boston, 1976.

HARRISON, HENRY. *Parnell Vindicated: The Lifting of the Veil*. New York, 1931.

HARTMANN, HANS. *Der Totenkult In Ireland—Ein Beitrag zur Religion der Indogermanen*. Heidelberg, 1952.

HASSARD, JOHN R. G. *Life of the Most Reverend John Hughes, D.D.* New York, 1866.

HASWELL, CHARLES H. *Reminiscences of New York by an Octogenarian*. New York, 1896.

HEADLEY, JOEL T. *The Great Riots of New York, 1712–1873*. New York, 1873.

HEMSTREET, CHARLES. *Nooks and Corners of Old New York.* New York, 1899.

HERON, D. C. *Celtic Migrations.* Dublin, 1863.

HUESTON, ROBERT FRANCIS. *The Catholic Press and Nativism, 1840–1860.* New York, 1976.

HUSSEY, S. M. *Irish Reminiscences,* New York, 1898.

HYDE, DOUGLAS. *Beside the Fire: A Collection of Irish Gaelic Folk Stories.* New York, 1890.

The Irish Ironmonger. English and American periodicals and some newspapers, Columbia University Library.

JANVIER, T. A. *In Old New York.* New York, 1894.

JENKINS, STEPHEN. *The Old Boston Post Road.* New York, 1913.

JOHNSON, STANLEY C. *A History of Emigration from the United Kingdom to North America, 1763–1912.* New York, 1913.

JOYCE, WILLIAM LEONARD. *Editors and Ethnicity: A History of the Irish-American Press, 1848–1883.* New York, 1976.

JOYNESS, J. L. *The Adventures of a Tourist in Ireland.* London, 1882.

KAPP, FRIEDRICH. *Immigration and the Commissioners of Emigration of New York.* New York, 1870.

KENNEDY, PATRICK. *Legendary Fictions of the Irish Celts.* Dublin, 1866.

LAMB, MARTHE J. *History of the City of New York,* 2 vols. New York, 1880.

LARGE, E. C. *The Advance of the Fungi.* New York, 1940.

LEAMY, MARGARET. *Parnell's Faithful Few.* Dublin, 1936.

LECKY, WILLIAM E. H. *History of Ireland in the 18th Century,* 5 vols. New York, 1892.

———. *Leaders of Public Opinion In Ireland,* 2 vols. New York, 1903.

LOCK, JOHN, OF RATHMINES. *On Irish Emigration.* Dublin, 1854.

LOCKER-LAMPSON, GODFREY T. *A Consideration of the State of Ireland in the 19th Century.* London, 1907.

LYNCH, ARTHUR. *Ireland: Vital Hour.* London, 1912.

LYNCH, DENIS TILDEN. *"Boss" Tweed: The Story of a Grim Generation.* New York, 1927.

LYND, ROBERT. *Ireland: A Nation.* London, 1919.

MACAFFREY, LAWRENCE J. *The Irish Diaspora In America.* Bloomington, Ind., 1976.

MACDONAGH, MICHAEL. *The Home Rule Movement*. New York, 1920.

―――. *Irish Life and Character*. New York, 1898.

―――. *Life of William O'Brien*. New York, 1929.

MACMANUS, SEUMAS. *The Story of the Irish Race*. New York, 1921.

MAGINNIS, A. J. *The Atlantic Ferry: Its Ships, Men and Working*. New York, 1893.

MAGUIRE, JOHN FRANCIS. *America and Irish Emigration*. Cork, 1869.

―――. *Father Mathew: A Biography*, New York, 1864.

―――. *The Irish In America*. London, 1868.

MAHONEY, THOMAS A. D. *Edmund Burke and Ireland*. New York, 1959.

MANDAT-GRANCEY, BARON E. DE. *Paddy At Home ("Chez Paddy")*, 2nd ed., London, 1887.

MARJORIBANKS, ALEXANDER. *Travels in South and North America*. London, 1853.

MATHEW, FRANK J. *Father Mathew. His Life and Times*. London, 1890.

MAXWELL, CONSTANTIA. *The Stranger in Ireland, from the Reign of Elizabeth to the Great Famine*. New York, 1954.

MAYNARD, THEODORE. *The Story of American Catholicism*. New York, 1941.

MCCARTHY, JUSTIN. *Reminiscences*, 2 vols. New York, 1899.

MCDOWELL, ROBERT B. *Public Opinion and Government Policy in Ireland, 1801–1846*. London, 1952.

―――. *Social Life In Ireland (1800–45)*. New York, 1957.

MCGEE, THOMAS D'ARCY. *A History of the Irish Settlers in North America*. Boston, 1852.

MCKAY, RICHARD C. *South Street: A Maritime History of New York*. New York, 1934.

MCMANUS, M. J. *Irish Cavalcade, 1550–1850*. Columbia University Library, New York.

MILL, J. S. *England and Ireland*. London, 1868.

MILLIGEN, S. F., and MILLIGEN, A. *Glimpses of Erin*. London, 1888.

MITCHEL, JOHN. *Jail Journal, 1868*. Edited by Arthur Griffith. New York, 1913.

―――. *The Last Conquest of Ireland (Perhaps)*. Dublin, 1861.

MITCHELL, D. W. *Ten Years In the United States*. London, 1862.

MITCHELL, JOSEPH. *McSorley's Wonderful Saloon*. New York, 1943.

MOBERG, VILHELM. *The Emigrants*. New York, 1951.

MONAGHAN, FRANK, and LOWENTHAL, MARVIN. *This Was New York*. New York, 1943.

MOORE, THOMAS. *Irish Melodies*. Dublin, 1849.

MOSS, FRANK. *The American Metropolis*, 3 vols. New York, 1897.

MOTT, HOPPER STRIKER. *New York of Yesterday*. New York, n.d.

MYERS, GUSTAVUS. *History of Tammany Hall*. New York, 1917.

NOWLAN, KEVIN B. *The Politics of Repeal, 1841–50*. New York, 1964.

O'BRIEN, EDNA. *Mother Ireland*. New York, 1976.

O'BRIEN, GEORGE. *Economic History of Ireland from the Union to the Famine*. London, 1921.

O'BRIEN, WILLIAM. *Edmund Burke as an Irishman*. New York, 1926.

O'CONNOR, JAMES. *History of Ireland 1798–1924*, 2 vols. London, 1925.

O'CONNOR, RICHARD. *Hell's Kitchen*. New York, 1958.

O'CONNOR, THOMAS POWER. *The Parnell Movement*. London, 1886.

O'DONNELL, E. *The Irish Abroad*. N.d.

O'DONOVAN, JEREMIAH. *Irish Immigration in the United States: Immigrant Interviews, 1840–1860*. Pittsburgh, 1864.

O'FAOLAIN, SEAN. *The King of the Beggars: A Life of Daniel O'Connell*. Dublin, 1938.

OFFENBACH, JACQUES. *Offenback in America*. New York, 1877.

O'FLAHERTY, LIAM. *Famine*. New York, 1937.

O'HEGARTY, PATRICK SARSFIELD. *History of Ireland under the Union, 1800–1922*. New York, 1952.

O'ROURKE, JOHN. *The History of the Great Irish Famine of 1847*. Dublin, 1875.

ORTH, SAMUEL P. *Our Foreigners: A Chronicle of Americans in the Making*. New Haven, 1920.

OSGOOD, SAMUEL. *New York in the Nineteenth Century*. New York, 1867.

O'SUILLEABHAIN, SEAD, ed. *Folktales of Ireland*. London, 1966.

O'SUILLEABHAIN, SEAD. *Irish Folk Customs and Beliefs*. Unpublished manuscript, NLI.

O'SULLIVAN, T. F. *The Young Irelanders*. New York, 1944.

PAIRPOINT, ALFRED. *Uncle Sam and His Country*. London, 1857.

PASKO, W. W., ed. *Old New York: A Journal Relating to the History . . . of New York City*, 2 vols. New York, 1889–1891.

PELLEW, GEORGE. *In Castle and Cabin*. New York, 1888.

POLLARD, H. B. C. *The Secret Societies of Ireland.* London, 1922.

POMERANTZ, SIDNEY I. *New York: An American City.* New York, 1938.

POMFRET, JOHN E. *The Struggle for Land in Ireland, 1800–1923.* Princeton, 1930.

POTTER, GEORGE. *To the Golden Door.* Boston, 1960.

PRAEGER, ROBERT LLOYD. *The Way That I Went: An Irishman in Ireland.* London, 1937.

PRIM, J. G. A. *Royal Society of Antiquaries of Ireland.* Dublin, 1853.

REILLY, A. *Irish Landmarks in New York.* New York, 1939.

RIIS, JACOB A. *The Battle with The Slums.* New York, 1912.

———. *How the Other Half Lives.* New York, 1890.

ROBERTS, EDWARD F. *Ireland in America.* New York, 1931.

ROBINSON, SOLON. *Hot Corn—Life Scenes in New York Illustrated.* New York, 1854.

ROOSEVELT, THEODORE. *New York.* New York, 1901.

ROSENBERG, CHARLES. *The Cholera Years.* New York, 1962.

ROSSA, O'DONOVAN. *Rossa's Recollections, 1838 to 1898.* New York, 1898.

RUSH, THOMAS E. *The Port of New York.* New York, 1920.

SALAMAN, REDCLIFFE N. *The History and Social Influence of the Potato.* Cambridge, 1949.

SANGER, WILLIAM. *The History of Prostitution: Its Extent, Causes and Effects Throughout the World.* New York, 1913.

SCHRIER, ARNOLD. *Ireland and the American Emigration 1850–1900.* New York, 1958.

SELIGMAN, EDWIN R. A. *The Tenement House of New York City.* New York, 1891.

SHANNON, WILLIAM V. *The American Irish.* New York, 1963.

SHAUGHNESSY, GERALD. *Has the Immigrant Kept the Faith? A Study of Immigration and Catholic Growth in the U.S., 1790–1920.* New York, 1925.

SHEA, JOHN G. *History of the Catholic Church in the United States.* New York, 1892.

SHELDON, GEORGE W. *The Story of the Volunteer Firemen of New York.* New York, 1882.

SHRADY, JOHN. *Memorial History of New York.* Edited by J. G. Wilson, New York, 1892–93.

SKELTON, ISABEL. *The Life of Thomas D'Arcy McGee.* New York, 1925.

SMITH, GOLDWIN. *Irish Life and Character*. New York, 1861.

SMITH, MATTHEW H. *Sunshine and Shadow in New York*. Hartford, Ct., 1869.

SMITH, STEPHEN. *The City That Was New York*. New York, 1911.

SMITH, WILLIAM HENRY. *A Twelve-Month Residence in Ireland* . . . New York, 1850.

STILL, BAYARD. *Mirror for Gotham: New York as Seen by Contemporaries*. New York, 1956.

STOKES, ISAAC N. PHELPS, ed. *The Iconography of Manhattan Island*, 6 vols. New York, 1915–28.

———. *New York Past and Present: Its History and Landmarks, 1524–1939*. New York, 1939.

STONE, WILLIAM L. *History of New York City*. New York, 1868.

STRAUSS, EMIL. *Irish Nationalism and British Democracy*. New York, 1951.

STRODE, GEORGE K., ed. *Yellow Fever in New York*. New York, 1951.

STRONG, GEORGE TEMPLETON. *The Diary of George Templeton Strong*. Edited by Allan Nevins and Milton Halsey Thomas. New York, 1952.

SULLIVAN, A. M. *New Ireland*. London, 1877.

SULLIVAN, JAMES WILLIAM. *Tenement Tales of New York*. New York, n.d.

SULLIVAN, T. D. *Recollections of Troubled Times in Irish Politics*. New York, 1905.

SWIFT, JONATHAN. *The Drapier's Letter*. Dublin, 1724.

———. *A Modest Proposal*. Dublin, 1729.

———. *Short View of the State of Ireland*. Dublin, 1727.

THORNLEY, D. A. *Isaac Butt and Home Rule*. Dublin, 1964.

TODD, CHARLES B. *In Olde New York*. New York, 1907.

TONE, THEOBALD WOLFE. *Autobiography*. Edited by Sean O'Faolain. Dublin, 1937.

TREVELYAN, GEORGE MACAULAY. *British History in the Nineteenth Century and After (1782–1919)*, 2nd ed. London, 1937.

TREVELYAN, GEORGE OTTO. *The Life and Letters of Lord Macauley*. London, 1881.

VALENTINE, DAVID T. *Valentine's Manual of Old New York*. Edited by Henry Collins Brown. New York, 1926.

———. *History of the City of New York*. New York, 1853.

VEILLER, LAWRENCE. *The Tenement House Problem in New York (1830–1900)*. New York, 1903.

WALLACE, F. W. *In the Wake of the Wind Ships*. New York, 1927.

———. *Wooden Ships and Iron Men*. New York, 1924.

WALSH, LOUIS J. *John Mitchell*. Dublin, 1934.

WARD, ALAN J. *Ireland and Anglo-American Relations 1899–1921*. London, 1969.

WEGMANN, EDWARD. *The Water Supply of the City of New York, 1658–1895*. New York, 1896.

WERNER, M. R. *Tammany Hall*. New York, 1928.

WHALEN, RICHARD J. *The Founding Father: The Story of Joseph P. Kennedy*. New York, 1964.

WHITE, PHILIP L. *The Beekmans of New York in Politics and Commerce, 1647–1877*. New York, 1956.

WILSON, JAMES GRANT. *The Memorial History of the City of New York, 1658–1895*. New York, 1896.

WITTKE, CARL. *The Irish in America*. Baton Rouge, 1956.

———. *We Who Built America*. New York, 1939.

WOODHAM-SMITH, CECIL. *The Great Hunger*. New York, 1962.

YEATS, WILLIAM BUTLER. *Irish Folk Stories and Fairy Tales*. London, 1888.

YOUNG, ARTHUR. *A Tour of Ireland*, 2 vols. London, 1780.

ZEISLOFT, E. IDELL. *The New Metropolis, 1600–1900*. New York, 1899.

ZINNSER, HANS. *Rats, Lice and History*. New York, 1935.

Acknowledgments

Ten years ago in a London library, while researching material for a book on World War II, I made a fortuitous mistake. In requesting several issues of the London *Times* for the year 1946, I wrote on the call slip "1846." When the huge bound copies of the *Times* were placed on a slanted table before me, I realized what had happened, but just as I was about to carry them to the return counter, I decided first to flip through a few copies to see what life was like in Ireland during what I knew was a crucial period in its history. Unfortunately for my intended research that day, I spent the next six hours reading about the great famine in Ireland and what the *Times* editorial writers thought of the Irish.

Five years later I returned to England to do intensive research on the famine for this book. After several visits to the Colonial Office and the Public Records Office, in London, where I received the same generous consideration and attention as I had during my earlier research, I went to Ireland.

The National Library of Ireland in Kildare Street, Dublin, almost directly opposite the Power's Royal Hotel, my base of operations for the next three months, is stacked with its own copies of both the London *Times* and almost every Irish newspaper published during the years of the famine. All the pertinent English parliamentary papers are also available, along with the pamphlets and broadsides of the period, unpublished manuscripts, theses, letters, opinions, arguments, and the essential 1851 Census of Ireland, containing Sir William Wilde's Tables of Death.

This superbly equipped, efficient, and accommodating library reflects the leadership of its director and the grace, expertise, and dedication of its staff. Among the latter I gratefully mention Thomas Dempsey, who supplied me with items in the manuscript room and told me about material elsewhere in the library. At the main desk, where one requests general material, including old newspapers and English parliamentary reports, I became both a daily visitor and a friend of those who so kindly served me. James

Scully and Michael Keane were among them, as was Martin Ryan, who went far beyond the call of duty to see that I received some last-minute material before I rushed to the airport for my flight home. Catherine Fahy, Gerry Lyne, and Michael Whelan, in the office behind the main desk, were also kind and considerate no matter how often I bothered them for photostats of British government documents and papers.

I am deeply indebted to Linda Main at the main library of Trinity College in Dublin for helping me locate and collect much needed information. At Dublin Castle I was delighted by the conversations I had with Ms. Margaret Byrne, assistant to the director, who helped enormously in my quest for official government documents.

At the Society of Friends Meeting House I was greeted warmly and given copies of everything I found and needed in their historical collection. This Quaker organization, having done more than any other to save the lives of the starving Irish during the great famine, deserves and needs financial support for the humanitarian work it is still doing. Contributions, however large or small, can be sent to the Society of Friends, Eustace Street, Dublin, Ireland.

A visit to the Royal Irish Academy in Dublin uncovered fifty boxes of manuscripts relating to the Ordinance Survey of Ireland, compiled under the supervision of Jeremiah O'Donovan for the Irish government, as well as the Halliday Bequest, with its letters and documents. These were made available for my examination and use with the same warmth and friendliness that I found so frequently during my research in Ireland.

Several of this book's most important chapters were made possible through help given me by the Folklore Department of University College in Dublin. Seamus O'Cathain, who to my surprise and delight conversed with his students in Gaelic, was extremely gracious in seeing that I was given every manuscript I asked for and many others he thought would be important to my research. Professor Bo Almquist, a specialist in Irish folklore, was generous with the time he gave me in consultation and in allowing me to make a photostatic copy of Hugh Dorian's handwritten manuscript, "Donegal Sixty Years Ago." The Folklore Department at University College contains handwritten treasures, now bound, catalogued, and available to bona-fide scholars interested in Irish history. The first American-Irish millionaire who reads this would do well to donate a new photocopying machine to this trove at University College; it would be an important contribution toward the preservation and dissemination of the touching, human side of Irish history.

I would be remiss indeed if I did not mention Martha Reid, an Irish Protestant lady of great distinction, who drove me around Dublin in her runabout, introduced me to the Abbey Theatre, to Irish actors and writers, and to charming pubs I would never have found on my own. She was my sponsor at the National Library of Ireland. She is a warm friend and memorable human being, someone I would not have met had it not been for the good graces of Melvin and Joanna Hershkowitz here in America.

In New York, Dr. Lola Szladits, Curator of the Berg Collection at the New York Public Library, spoke to me at length about my project and introduced me to others who could help in my quest. Ms. Elizabeth E. Bentley, Acting Chief, Cooperative Services of the New York Public Library, located with admirable dispatch two very important, long-out-of-print volumes, one in the National Archives in Washington, D.C. and the other at Harvard University. The value of this expert guidance and aid is difficult to estimate and impossible to repay.

At the American-Irish Historical Society, of which I am a member, Thomas Bayne did everything possible to help in my research without being inquisitive as to my purpose. His knowledge of the Society's archives is exemplary; he found, way up in the attic, some old copies of *Punch* that I had been unable to locate in Europe. Dr. Kevin M. Cahill, President-General, and Mr. Gavin P. Murphy, Secretary-General, of this society are to be highly complimented for their splendid work in preserving and making more accessible this important collection.

At Columbia University, my alma mater, where I made frequent visits to the rare-book room and spent weeks in the stacks of the main library poring over books, I was, as always, helped enormously.

The assistance I received from the New York Historical Society was likewise essential to my research on early New York City.

Jonathan Beard and Walter B. Mahony, two old friends, followed the progress of this book and offered valuable suggestions, many of which I incorporated in the final version.

I owe a debt to Margot Mabie for her understanding and fastidious manuscript editing, and to Joan Judge for her effective and efficient handling of innumerable publishing details. Roberta Leighton has, as in the past, been a demanding, kindly guide.

I want to express particular appreciation to two friends, William Jovanovich, my publisher, and Julian Muller, my editor. Their constructive comment and steadfast belief were mainstays all the way.

Without the encouragement, patience, and enduring support of my wife, Josephine, this book could not have been undertaken and completed. To her, my constant love and unending gratitude.

Index